Reyna Inguanzo

WARFARE
BATTLECARDS

Copyright & Disclaimer

Copyright © 2025 Reyna Inguanzo
All Rights Reserved

Published by Winn Publications
Texas, United States • www.winnpublications.com

No part of Warfare BattleCards may be copied, reproduced, stored, or transmitted in any form—whether printed, digital, photocopied, recorded, or otherwise—without prior written permission from the author or publisher, except for brief quotations used in personal Bible study, church gatherings, or small group discussions, as permitted by copyright law.

This devotional has been prayerfully created to equip and encourage believers in their daily walk with God, offering biblical scriptures and focused prayers to help you stand firm in spiritual warfare. The author and publisher have made every effort to present scriptural content with accuracy, integrity, and reverence. However, the application of these devotions is the personal responsibility of the reader.

The prayers, scriptures, and reflections shared in this devotional are not intended to replace your own study of the Word of God, personal time in prayer, or the wisdom and covering of trusted spiritual leaders. Readers are encouraged to seek the guidance of the Holy Spirit and the counsel of mature believers when applying spiritual principles to their lives.

This devotional is offered in faith, with the heartfelt prayer that it will stir your spirit, strengthen your resolve, and remind you that you are equipped for the battle—through Christ who gives you victory.

All Scripture quotations, unless otherwise indicated, are taken from the ESV Global Study Bible®, ESV® Bible . Copyright © 2012 by Crossway.Used by permission. All rights reserved.

Book Title: Warfare Battlecards Author & Photography: Reyna Inguanzo

ISBNs: Paperback: 979-8-9926780-6-2 Hardcover: 979-8-9926780-5-5

Formatted and published by Winn Publications, Texas Cover Design and Interior Formatting: Arilia Winn

Printed in the United States of America

A Note From The Author

Thank you for taking the step to explore Scripture and discover its relevance in your everyday life. This book welcomes everyone—those strong in faith, just beginning to seek, or simply curious. As you read these reflections and speak God's Word aloud, expect to notice a meaningful shift in your life.

Consider this an open invitation to explore what it means to receive Jesus Christ as Lord and Savior—the Son of God who lived a perfect life, was crucified, and rose from the dead, now seated at the right hand of the Almighty Father. Whether ready to take that step or still searching for answers, you are welcome here. Feel free to explore, ask questions, and move at your own pace. Wherever you are on your spiritual journey, you are valued and loved.

Allow God to search your heart and bring healing and renewal to every part of your life—even those places kept hidden. Faith can become a steady and joyful part of daily living. Doubts and challenges are normal; what matters is to keep seeking, keep surrendering, and keep drawing closer to Him. May you experience seasons of real growth, learning to recognize God's voice and discovering His ways in a personal and meaningful way.

Welcome the Holy Spirit to renew and guide from within. As your heart opens, may a desire to know God, serve Him faithfully, and build a genuine friendship with Him grow stronger. Move from simply searching for God to truly walking with Him as a friend.

May a passion for Jesus ignite in every area of your life, inspiring you as it did the first followers of Christ. As you journey through this book—whether exploring, taking first steps, or running forward in faith—find space to ask questions and seek honest answers. Let the distractions of the world fade as you discover God's unique purpose for your life. As you learn about sharing His love with others (what Christians call the "Great Commission"), be encouraged to live out your faith in your own way. By God's grace and mercy, may you one day hear the words, "Well done, my good and faithful servant."

For HIS Glory,

Battle Sister

How to Use This

1. Reflect on Your Needs
Choose a focus word that resonates with you or someone you're praying for. Whether it's healing, peace, clarity, strength, or abundance—let that word become your intention and spiritual anchor.

2. Find Inspiration in Scripture
Read the selected Bible verses that speak to the meaning of the word. Let God's Word minister to your heart and renew your faith.

3. Pray Intentionally
Use the provided strategic prayer or personalize your own. Let the Holy Spirit guide your words as you pray with power and purpose.

4. Record Your Thoughts
Use the notes section to write down reflections, insights, or your own prayer. This becomes your personal record of faith, transformation, and growth.

Focus Word: Abundance
Part of Speech: noun
Pronunciation: ə-ˈbən-dən(t)s

Definition:
1. A large or ample quantity; overflowing amount
2. Wealth or affluence
3. A state of plentifulness

Scriptures to Meditate On
- **John 10:10**: "The thief comes only to steal and kill and destroy. I came that they may have life and have it abundantly."
- **Psalm 23:5**: You prepare a table before me in the presence of my enemies. You anoint my head with oil; my cup overflows.
- **Deuteronomy 28:11**: The Lord will make you abound in prosperity ...
- **Philippians 4:19**: And my God will supply every need of yours ...
- **2 Corinthians 9:8**: God is able to make all grace abound to you ...
- **Ephesians 3:20**: Now to him who is able to do far more abundantly than all we ask or think ...

Strategic Prayer

Heavenly Father,

I come before You in awe of Your abundance and generosity. Thank You, Jesus, for promising life more abundantly. You prepare a table before me, even in the presence of enemies, and You anoint me with oil—my cup truly overflows.

You are my source of prosperity and provision. You supply all my needs according to Your riches in glory. Let Your grace abound in my life so that I may abound in every good work and become a vessel of blessing to others.

You are able to do immeasurably more than I could ever ask, think, or imagine. Let Your abundance not only meet my needs but overflow into every area of my life.

In Jesus' name, Amen.

My Own Prayer / Notes
(Use this space to personalize your reflection)

_____

_____

_____

_____

_____

_____

_____

_____

_____

_____

_____

Foreword

The Lord said to Habakkuk, "Write the vision; make it plain on tablets, so he may run who reads it. For still the vision awaits its appointed time; it hastens to the end—it will not lie. If it seems slow, wait for it; it will surely come: it will not delay" (Habakkuk 2:2–3). These verses resounded in my spirit as this book was in the works.

As I prayed for this project to be fully directed by the Holy Spirit, there was a constant reminder of a message awaiting its appointed time. What you will soon read is a vision which has been written, it has been made clear, with the purpose that we who read it may run with it. "Run" meaning to take action, to move and believe in the message, to allow God's words to adjust our thinking and behavior. To allow the holy Word of God to change the way we operate in spiritual warfare.

How do we effectively combat spiritual strategies and demonic plans set up against us? How do we face cosmic conflicts that have eternal implications? How do we pull down spiritual fortresses and extinguish the lies of the enemy? God's Word! God's Word is a source of truth, authority, and power.

These warfare battle cards will train you, encourage you, and prepare your mind, soul, and spirit for an invisible war. Every time you reach for this book, may you be reminded that God's truth is active and alive, capable of not only cutting through deception, but capable of transforming our very being. May God use this book to awaken His children to the power of intercession. May the words, prayers, and scriptures found within these pages bring forth God's wisdom and revelation. For those who are lacking faith and hope, for those waiting on God, may this book remind you of the words spoken to Habakkuk, ". . . if it seems slow, wait for it; it will surely come."

Thank you Sister Reyna for your obedience to the Lord with this project. I've been a witness to your unwavering faith in God. You are a woman who walks clothed in the righteousness of Christ. Your ear is always attentive to His voice, and your life filled with visible fruit. This amazing project reflects your love for God and His kingdom. From all of us impacted, blessed, and transformed by this book, we are forever grateful.

Pastor Rocio Gonzalez

Table of Contents

A Note From The Author	v	Death	69
How to Use This	vii	Deception	73
Foreword	ix	Declare	77
		Deliverance	79
Abandonment	01	Demonic	83
Abundance	03	Dependence	85
Abuse	05	Destiny	87
Accuse	07	Destroy	89
Addiction	09	Discernment	93
Adultery	11	Divination	95
Affliction	13	Doorway	99
Ahab	15	Double-Minded	101
Alcoholism	17	Doubt	105
Angel of Light	19	Enemy	107
Anger	21	Evil	109
Anoint	23	Failure	111
Antichrist	25	Faith	113
Anxiety	27	False Prophets	115
Atonement	29	Familiar Spirits	119
Authority	31	Fasting	121
Battle	33	Father	123
Beauty	35	Favor	125
Blood	37	Favoritism	127
Bold[ness]	39	Fear	129
Bondage	41	Fire	131
Broken	43	Flesh	133
Capable	45	Forgiveness	135
Compassion	47	Fortitude	137
Confession	49	Freedom	139
Consecration	51	Friendship	141
Consume	53	Fruit of the Spirit	143
Contend	55	Generational Curse	145
Control	57	Gentle	147
Cope	59	GOD	149
Courage	61	Greed	151
Covenant	63	Grief	155
Curse	65	Guilt	157
Deaf and Dumb	67	Harmony	159

Harvest	161	Murder	245		
Haughty	163	Naive	247		
Health	165	Narcissism	249		
Heart	167	Neglect	251		
Help	169	Noble	253		
Hindrance	171	Occult	255		
Holy Spirit	173	Offense	259		
Honesty	175	Oppression	261		
Hope	177	Orphan	263		
Humility	179	Pain	265		
Hurt	181	Passion	269		
Immorality	183	Patience	271		
Infirmity	185	Peace	273		
Iniquity	187	Persecution	275		
Insecurity	189	Perseverance	277		
Isolation	191	Pornography	279		
Jealousy	193	Power	281		
Jesus	195	Praise	283		
Jezebel	197	Prayer	285		
Joy	199	Pride	289		
Justice	201	Profanity	291		
Kindness	203	Prosperity	293		
Kingdom	205	Protection	297		
Lazy	207	Provision	299		
Legion	209	Purification	301		
Leviathan	211	Quick Temper	303		
Life	213	Rebellion	305		
Lonely	215	Rebuild	307		
Loss	217	Redemption	309		
Love	219	Rejection	311		
Lukewarm	221	Religion	313		
Lust	223	Renounce	317		
Lying	225	Restore	319		
Malice	227	Revelation	321		
Manipulate	229	Revenge	323		
Marriage	231	Rude	325		
Medicine	233	Rumination	327		
Memory	235	Safety	329		
Mental Illness	237	Salt	331		
Mercy	239	Salvation	333		
Molech	241	Sanctification	335		
Mother	243	Satan	337		

Schizophrenia	339
Seducing	341
Self-Will	343
Sensation	345
Sensuality	347
Serpent	349
Shame	351
Sit	353
Slavery	355
Sober	357
Spirits	359
Squid	361
Stand	363
Steadfast	365
Stress	367
Stronghold	369
Suffering	371
Suicide	373
Surrender	375
Temptation	377
Thankful	379
Transform	381
Trauma	383
Treachery	385
Trial	387
Unbelief	389
Unclean	391
Understanding	393
Unforgiveness	395
Unity	397
Unworthy	399
Vanity	401
Vengeance	403
Victim	405
Victory	407
Waiting	409
Wall	411
Warfare	413
Watchman	415
Whoredom	419
Wicked	421
Wisdom	423
Word	425
Worry	427
Worship	429
Acknowledgements	432
About the Author	434

Abandonment

noun
ə-ˈban-dən-mənt

1. The act of abandoning (withdrawing protection, support, or help from) something or someone
2. The state of being abandoned

- **Psalm 27:10:** For my father and my mother have forsaken me, but the Lord will take me in.
- **Deuteronomy 31:6:** Be strong and courageous. Do not fear or be in dread of them, for it is the Lord your God who goes with you. He will not leave you or forsake you.
- **Matthew 28:20:** "Teaching them to observe all that I have commanded you. And behold, I am with you always, to the end of the age."
- **Lamentations 3:22–23:** The steadfast love of the Lord never ceases; his mercies never come to an end; they are new every morning; great is your faithfulness.

Reflections:

_____
_____
_____
_____
_____
_____
_____
_____
_____
_____
_____

Prayer:

Heavenly Father,

My refuge, I come before You with a heart that sometimes feels the weight of abandonment and loneliness. Yet, I am reminded of Your unfailing promises and eternal presence. Your Word assures me that even when my father and mother forsake me, You, Lord, will take me in. I find comfort in knowing that You are my refuge and strength.

Lord, You have commanded me to be strong and courageous, not to fear or dread, for You are with me. Help me to hold on to this truth, knowing that You will never leave me nor forsake me. In moments of doubt and fear, fill me with Your courage and peace. Jesus, You promised to be with us always, even to the end of the age. I cling to this assurance that Your presence is constant, guiding me through every season of life. May I always be aware of Your loving presence, teaching me and leading me in Your ways.

Father, I am grateful for Your steadfast love, which never ceases. And Your mercies, which are new every morning. Great is Your faithfulness, O Lord. May I rest in the knowledge of Your unchanging love and find hope in Your endless mercy.

Thank You, Lord, for being my ever-present help and my faithful companion. I trust in Your promises and place my life in Your hands.

In Jesus' name I pray, Amen.

My own prayer:

_____

_____

_____

_____

Abundance

noun

ə-ˈbən-dən(t)s

1. An ample quantity: an abundant amount
2. Affluence, wealth
3. Relative degree of plentifulness

- **John 10:10:** "The thief comes only to steal and kill and destroy. I came that they may have life and have it abundantly."
- **Psalm 23:5:** You prepare a table before me in the presence of my enemies; you anoint my head with oil; my cup overflows.
- **Deuteronomy 28:11:** And the Lord will make you abound in prosperity, in the fruit of your womb and in the fruit of your livestock and in the fruit of your ground, within the land that the Lord swore to your fathers to give you.
- **Philippians 4:19:** And my God will supply every need of yours according to his riches in glory in Christ Jesus.
- **2 Corinthians 9:8:** And God is able to make all grace abound to you, so that having all sufficiency in all things at all times, you may abound in every good work.
- **Ephesians 3:20:** Now to him who is able to do far more abundantly than all that we ask or think, according to the power at work within us.

Reflections:

_____
_____
_____
_____
_____
_____

Prayer:

Heavenly Father,

I come before You with reverence and honor, acknowledging Your infinite abundance and generosity. Lord Jesus, I thank You for coming that I may have life and have it abundantly. Your promise fills me with hope and gratitude. Father, I am humbled by how You prepare a table before me, even in the presence of my enemies. You anoint my head with oil, and my cup overflows with Your blessings. I stand in wonder at Your provision.

Lord, I trust in Your promise of abundant prosperity—in the fruit of my womb, the young of my livestock, and the crops of my ground. You are faithful to Your covenant, and I am grateful for Your bountiful blessings. I thank You that You supply every need of mine according to Your riches in glory in Christ Jesus. Your provision is beyond measure, and I am in awe of Your generosity.

Father, I acknowledge that You are able to make all grace abound to me, so that having all sufficiency in all things at all times, I may abound in every good work. Let Your abundance flow through me to bless others. I stand in wonder that You are able to do immeasurably more than all I ask or imagine, according to Your power that is at work within me. Your abundance surpasses my understanding, and I give You all the glory.

In Jesus' name I pray, Amen.

My own prayer:

_____

_____

_____

_____

_____

WARFARE BATTLECARDS

Abuse

noun
ə-ˈbyüs

1. A corrupt practice or custom
2. Improper or excessive use or treatment

- **Psalm 10:17–18:** O Lord, you hear the desire of the afflicted; you will strengthen their heart; you will incline your ear to do justice to the fatherless and the oppressed, so that man who is of the earth may strike terror no more.
- **Isaiah 1:17:** Learn to do good; seek justice, correct oppression; bring justice to the fatherless, plead the widow's cause.
- **Galatians 5:13:** For you were called to freedom, brothers. Only do not use your freedom as an opportunity for the flesh, but through love serve one another.
- **1 Peter 3:7:** Likewise, husbands, live with your wives in an understanding way, showing honor to the woman as the weaker vessel, since they are heirs with you of the grace of life, so that your prayers may not be hindered.
- **James 3:10:** From the same mouth come blessing and cursing. My brothers, these things ought not to be so.
- **Psalm 34:18:** The Lord is near to the brokenhearted and saves the crushed in spirit.

Reflections:

_____

_____

_____

_____

_____

_____

_____

Prayer:

Heavenly Father,

I come before You with a humble and broken heart, knowing that You hear the cries of the afflicted. Lord, incline Your ear to me and strengthen my heart. Bring justice to the fatherless and the oppressed, so that those who cause harm may strike terror no more.

Teach me, Lord, to do good, to seek justice, and to correct oppression. Help me to be an instrument of Your love, to plead the cause of the widow. Guide me to reflect Your heart for those in need. Thank You, Father, for calling me to freedom through Christ. Help me use this freedom not for selfish purposes, but to serve others in love. Let my life be a testimony of Your grace and compassion.

For husbands, I pray they may live with their wives in an understanding way, showing honor as equal heirs of the grace of life. May their actions reflect Your love and care. Guard my mouth, O Lord. Let it be a vessel of blessing and not cursing. May my words bring healing and not harm, reflecting Your truth and kindness.

Finally, Lord, I lift the brokenhearted to You. Be near to those crushed in spirit. Comfort the abused with Your love and bring them hope and healing. Let them know they are seen, valued, and loved by You.

In Your holy name I pray, Amen.

My own prayer:

_____
_____
_____
_____
_____
_____
_____

Accuse

verb
ə-ˈkyüz

1. To charge with a fault or offense: blame
2. To charge with an offense judicially or by a public process

- **Proverbs 11:9:** With his mouth the godless man would destroy his neighbor, but by knowledge the righteous are delivered.
- **Romans 8:1:** There is therefore now no condemnation for those who are in Christ Jesus.
- **Exodus 20:16:** You shall not bear false witness against your neighbor.
- **Exodus 23:1:** You shall not spread a false report. You shall not join hands with a wicked man to be a malicious witness.
- **Isaiah 53:5 (NKJV):** But He was wounded for our transgressions, He was bruised for our iniquities; the chastisement for our peace was upon Him, and by His stripes we are healed.

Reflections:

_____
_____
_____
_____
_____
_____
_____
_____
_____
_____
_____

Prayer:

Heavenly Father,

I come before You in humility and righteousness, seeking Your grace and mercy. Lord, I stand firmly on Your Word that I am a new creation in Christ Jesus.

Father, protect me from those who bear false witness and from the accuser who seeks to destroy. Your Word declares that there is no condemnation for those who are in Christ Jesus, and I claim this promise. Lord, deliver me by Your knowledge from the mouths of the godless who would seek to destroy their neighbor. Shield me from false reports and malicious witnesses.

I pray for those who accuse falsely, that they may turn from their ways and seek Your truth. Help me to respond with love and forgiveness, even in the face of unjust accusations.

Thank You, Lord, that by Your stripes I am healed, and by Your sacrifice, I am made new. Let Your light shine through me, dispelling all darkness and lies.

Amen.

My own prayer:

_____

_____

_____

_____

_____

_____

_____

_____

Addiction

noun
ə-ˈdik-shən

1. A compulsive, chronic, physiological or psychological need for a habit-forming substance, behavior, or activity having harmful physical, psychological, or social effects and typically causing well-defined symptoms upon withdrawal or abstinence
2. A strong inclination to do, use, or indulge in something repeatedly

- **Philippians 4:13:** I can do all things through him who strengthens me.
- **Luke 21:34–36:** "But watch yourselves lest your hearts be weighed down with dissipation and drunkenness and cares of this life, and that day come upon you suddenly like a trap. For it will come upon all who dwell on the face of the whole earth. But stay awake at all times, praying that you may have strength to escape all these things that are going to take place, and to stand before the Son of Man."
- **Psalm 51:10:** Create in me a clean heart, O God.
- **James 4:7:** Submit yourselves therefore to God. Resist the devil, and he will flee from you.
- **Proverbs 23:19–21:** Hear, my son, and be wise, and direct your heart in the way. Be not among drunkards or among gluttonous eaters of meat, for the drunkard and the glutton will come to poverty, and slumber will clothe them with rags.
- **Matthew 11:28-29:** "Come to me, all who labor and are heavy laden, and I will give you rest. Take my yoke upon you, and learn from me, for I am gentle and lowly in heart, and you will find rest for your souls."
- **Proverbs 31:4:** It is not for kings, O Lemuel, it is not for kings to drink wine, or for rulers to take strong drink.

Reflections:

_____
_____
_____
_____
_____
_____

WARFARE BATTLECARDS

Prayer:

Heavenly Father,

I come before You in humility, seeking Your strength and guidance. Lord, I acknowledge my weakness and my need for Your deliverance from addiction. Your Word proclaims that I can do all things through Christ who strengthens me. I cling to this promise, knowing that with Your power, I can overcome this affliction.

Forgive me, Lord, for serving my flesh before living a spirit-filled life. Create in me a clean heart, O God, and renew a right spirit within me. Grant me wisdom to direct my heart in Your way. Help me avoid the company of those who would lead me astray and give me the courage to separate myself from the temptations that have held me captive.

Lord Jesus, You invite all who are weary and burdened to come to You for rest. I come to You now, laying addiction at Your feet. I take Your yoke upon me; teach me, for You are gentle and humble in heart. Keep me watchful, Father, lest my heart be weighed down with dissipation and drunkenness. Give me strength to escape these traps and to stand firm in my faith.

Fill me with Your Spirit, Lord, and guide me to live a life that honors You, resisting the devil. May I find my satisfaction in You alone, not in the temporary pleasures of this world.

In Your holy name I pray, Amen.

My own prayer:

_____

_____

_____

_____

_____

Adultery

noun
ə-ˈdəl-t(ə-)rē

    1. Voluntary sexual intercourse between a married person and someone other than that person's current spouse or partner

- **Exodus 20:14:** You shall not commit adultery.
- **Matthew 5:29:** "If your right eye causes you to sin, tear it out and throw it away. For it is better that you lose one of your members than that your whole body be thrown into hell."
- **Psalm 23:1:** The Lord is my shepherd; I shall not want.
- **Matthew 19:6:** "So they are no longer two but one flesh. What therefore God has joined together, let not man separate."
- **Psalm 51:10:** Create in me a clean heart, O God, and renew a right spirit within me.
- **Matthew 3:8:** Bear fruit in keeping with repentance.
- **Psalm 51:2:** Wash me thoroughly from my iniquity, and cleanse me from my sin!
- **Psalm 51:11:** Cast me not away from your presence, and take not your Holy Spirit from me.
- **Luke 1:37:** For nothing will be impossible with God
- **1 Corinthians 10:13:** No temptation has overtaken you that is not common to man. God is faithful, and he will not let you be tempted beyond your ability, but with the temptation he will also provide a way of escape, that you may be able to endure it.

Reflections:

_____
_____
_____
_____
_____
_____
_____

Prayer:

Heavenly Father,

I come before you seeking strength and wisdom to guard my heart and remain pure. Help me to honor the commandment of sexual purity, give me the courage to turn away from impure desires.

For those times I have fallen short, I humbly repent. Wash me thoroughly from my iniquity and cleanse me from my sin! Help me bear fruit in keeping with repentance. Cast me not away from Your presence and take not Your Holy Spirit from me.

Grant me the wisdom to bind your teachings close to my heart and recognize that no temptation is stronger than Your power to provide a way of escape. Help me to flee from sexual immorality, to choose integrity and faithfulness. Reminding that my body is a temple of Your Holy Spirit. I am grateful that Your grace is sufficient, and Your strength is made perfect in my weakness. I firmly renounce all agreements made in partnership giving way to adultery. With You Jesus, nothing is impossible.

In Jesus' name, Amen.

My own prayer:

_____
_____
_____
_____
_____
_____
_____
_____

Affliction

noun
ə-ˈflik-shən
1. A cause of persistent pain or distress
2. A state of suffering or hardship

- **Psalm 34:19:** Many are the afflictions of the righteous, but the LORD delivers him out of them all.
- **2 Corinthians 4:17–18:** For this light momentary affliction is preparing for us an eternal weight of glory beyond all comparison, as we look not at the things that are seen but to the things that are unseen. For the things that are seen are transient, but the things that are unseen are eternal."
- **2 Corinthians 4:8–9:** We are afflicted in every way, but not crushed; perplexed, but not driven to despair; persecuted, but not forsaken; struck down, but not destroyed.
- **2 Corinthians 1:3–4:** Blessed be the God and Father of our Lord Jesus Christ, the Father of mercies and God of all comfort, who comforts us in all our affliction, so that we may be able to comfort those who are in any affliction, with the comfort with which we ourselves are comforted by God.
- **Romans 8:18:** For I consider that the sufferings of this present time are not worth comparing with the glory that is to be revealed to us.

Reflections:

_____
_____
_____
_____
_____
_____
_____
_____

Prayer:

Heavenly Father,

I come before You, acknowledging the afflictions in my life. Lord, I am reminded that the sufferings of this present time are not worth comparing with the glory that is to be revealed to us. In my moments of pain and struggle, help me to remember that You are the God of all comfort. Comfort me in my affliction, that I may in turn comfort others with the comfort I receive from You.

Though I may be afflicted in every way, remind me that I am not crushed; though perplexed, I am not driven to despair. You are my deliverer, and I trust that You will bring me through every trial. Grant me the strength to endure, knowing that this light and momentary affliction is preparing for me an eternal weight of glory beyond all comparison. Help me to fix my eyes not on what is seen, but on what is unseen and eternal.

Lord, restore, confirm, strengthen, and establish me through these trials. May they yield the peaceful fruit of righteousness in my life.

In Jesus' name I pray, Amen.

My own prayer:

_____
_____
_____
_____
_____
_____
_____
_____

Ahab

noun
ˈā-ˌhab

1. A king of Israel in the ninth century b.c. and husband of Jezebel

- **1 Kings 16:30**: Ahab son of Omri did evil in the sight of the Lord more than all who were before him.
- **1 Kings 21:17–18**: Then the word of the Lord came to Elijah the Tishbite, saying, "Arise, go down to meet Ahab king of Israel, who is in Samaria."
- **Ephesians 5:11**: Take no part in the unfruitful works of darkness, but instead expose them.
- **Ephesians 6:12**: For we do not wrestle against flesh and blood, but against the rulers, against the authorities, against the cosmic powers over this present darkness, against the spiritual forces of evil in the heavenly places.
- **Matthew 26:41**: "Watch and pray that you may not enter into temptation. The spirit indeed is willing, but the flesh is weak."

Reflections:

_____
_____
_____
_____
_____
_____
_____
_____
_____

Prayer:

Heavenly Father,

I come before You in humility, acknowledging Your sovereignty overall. Lord, in a world that often distorts Your design, help me resist the path of Ahab, who did more evil in Your eyes than those before him.

Grant me the strength to stand against influences that would lead me astray, as You warn us to have no fellowship with the unfruitful works of darkness. Holy Spirit, remind me that our struggle is not against flesh and blood, but against the spiritual forces of evil in the heavenly realms.

Teach me to watch and pray, Lord, that I may not fall into temptation. I recognize that my spirit is willing, but my flesh is weak. Strengthen my resolve to follow Your ways, even when faced with worldly pressures.

Father, I trust in Your faithfulness to protect and strengthen me against the evil one. Build me up to withstand the forces of Jezebel. May my life reflect Your truth, standing firm in the face of darkness, unadulterated in commitment to You Jesus.

In Jesus' name I pray, Amen.

My own prayer:

_____

_____

_____

_____

_____

_____

Alcoholism

noun
al-kə-ˌhȯ-ˌli-zəm

1. A chronic, progressive, potentially fatal ion

- **Ephesians 5:18:** And do not get drunk with wine, for that is debauchery, but be filled with the Spirit.
- **Luke 21:34–36:** "But watch yourselves lest your hearts be weighed down with dissipation and drunkenness and cares of this life, and that day come upon you suddenly like a trap. For it will come upon all who dwell on the face of the whole earth. But stay awake at all times, praying that you may have strength to escape all these things that are going to take place, and to stand before the Son of Man."
- **Proverbs 23:19–21:** Hear, my son, and be wise, and direct your heart in the way. Be not among drunkards or among gluttonous eaters of meat, for the drunkard and the glutton will come to poverty, and slumber will clothe them with rags.
- **Numbers 6:2–3**: Speak to the people of Israel and say to them, When either a man or a woman makes a special vow, the vow of a Nazirite, to separate himself to the Lord, he shall separate himself from wine and strong drink. He shall drink no vinegar made from wine or strong drink and shall not drink any juice of grapes or eat grapes, fresh or dried.

Reflections:

_____
_____
_____
_____
_____
_____
_____

Prayer:

Heavenly Father,

I come before You in surrender to Your mighty glory. Lord, I humbly ask You to free me from the yoke of alcoholism that has enslaved me.

As the world rationalizes a lifestyle of drunkenness, deliver me from such deception. Cleanse me, Lord, and teach me to resist the devil so that he flee. Holy Spirit, help me to remain sober-minded and watchful, lest my heart be weighed down with dissipation and drunkenness, and that day come upon me suddenly like a trap.

Forgive me for the times I have turned to alcohol to soothe or comfort my soul, rather than coming to You for rest. I renounce such drunkard practices and ask for Your strength to separate myself from strong drink.

Fill me with Your Spirit instead, Lord. Direct my heart in the way of wisdom and grant me the strength to escape the snares of this world. Help me to stand firm before the Son of Man.

In Jesus' name I pray, Amen.

My own prayer:

_____
_____
_____
_____
_____
_____

Angel of Light

noun
'ān-jəl əv 'līt

1. A spiritual being serving as a divine messenger and intermediary and often as a special protector of an individual or nation
2. The sensation aroused by stimulation of the visual receptors

- **2 Corinthians 11:13–15:** For such men are false apostles, deceitful workmen, disguising themselves as apostles of Christ. And no wonder, for even Satan disguises himself as an angel of light. So it is no surprise if his servants, also, disguise themselves as servants of righteousness. Their end will correspond to their deeds.
- **John 8:44:** "You are of your father the devil, and your will is to do your father's desires. He was a murderer from the beginning, and does not stand in the truth, because there is no truth in him. When he lies, he speaks out of his own character, for he is a liar and the father of lies."
- **Ephesians 1:17–18:** That the God of our Lord Jesus Christ, the Father of glory, may give you the Spirit of wisdom and of revelation in the knowledge of him, having the eyes of your hearts enlightened, that you may know what is the hope to which he has called you, what are the riches of his glorious inheritance in the saints.
- **Psalm 119:105**: Your word is a lamp to my feet and light to my path.

Reflections:

_____
_____
_____
_____
_____
_____
_____
_____

Prayer:

Heavenly Father,

I come before You with a surrendered heart, seeking Your divine wisdom and protection against the schemes of the enemy. Lord, I acknowledge that even Satan disguises himself as an angel of light, and his servants masquerade as servants of righteousness.

Grant me, O God, the spirit of wisdom and revelation in the knowledge of You. Enlighten the eyes of my heart, that I may know the hope to which You have called me and the riches of Your glorious inheritance.

Lord Jesus, remind me that the devil is the father of lies, with no truth in him. Help me to discern his falsehoods and cling to Your unchanging truth. May Your Word be a lamp to my feet and a light to my path.

In Jesus' name, Amen.

My own prayer:

_____
_____
_____
_____
_____
_____
_____
_____
_____

Anger

noun

ˈaŋ-gər

1. A strong feeling of displeasure and usually of antagonism
2. A threatening or violent appearance or state

- **Proverbs 15:1**: A soft answer turns away wrath, but a harsh word stirs up anger.
- **Psalm 37:8**: Refrain from anger, and forsake wrath! Fret not yourself; it tends only to evil.
- **Ecclesiastes 7:9**: Be not quick in your spirit to become angry, for anger lodges in the heart of fools.
- **James 1:19–20**: Know this, my beloved brothers: let every person be quick to hear, slow to speak, slow to anger; for the anger of man does not produce the righteousness of God.
- **Proverbs 19:11**: Good sense makes one slow to anger, and it is his glory to overlook an offense.
- **Ephesians 4:26–27**: Be angry and do not sin; do not let the sun go down on your anger, and give no opportunity to the devil.
- **Colossians 3:8**: But now you must put them all away: anger, wrath, malice, slander, and obscene talk from your mouth.

Reflections:

_____
_____
_____
_____
_____
_____
_____
_____

Prayer:

Heavenly Father,

Praise be Your name! Forgive me for acting out in anger, stirring up wrath, malice, slander, or obscene talk. Grant me wisdom to speak a soft answer, discipline to hear quickly, and self-control to speak slowly as a response. I surrender a reaction filled with anger to you.

Grant me the wisdom to respond with gentleness, for I know a soft answer turns away wrath. Help me to refrain from anger and forsake wrath, as these lead only to evil.

Lord, teach me to be slow in my spirit to become angry, for I do not wish to be counted among fools. Make me quick to hear, slow to speak, and slow to anger, knowing that human anger does not produce the righteousness You desire.

Give me good sense and grace to overlook offenses. When anger arises, help me not to sin, and to resolve conflicts before the day ends, giving no opportunity to the devil.

Finally, Father, help me to put away all anger, wrath, malice, and harmful speech. Fill me instead with Your peace and love.

In Jesus' name, Amen.

My own prayer:

_____
_____
_____
_____
_____
_____
_____

Anoint

verb
ə-ˈnȯint

1. To smear or rub with oil or an oily substance
2. To apply oil to as part of a religious ceremony

- **Psalm 23:5:** You prepare a table before me in the presence of my enemies; you anoint my head with oil; my cup overflows.
- **Exodus 28:41 (NIV):** After you put these clothes on your brother Aaron and his sons, anoint and ordain them. Consecrate them so they may serve me as priests.
- **Isaiah 61:1:** The Spirit of the Lord God is upon me because the Lord has anointed me to bring good news to the poor; he has sent me to bind up the brokenhearted, to proclaim liberty to the captives, and the opening of the prison to those who are bound.

Reflections:

_____
_____
_____
_____
_____
_____
_____
_____
_____
_____
_____

Prayer:

Heavenly Father,

I approach You with reverence, acknowledging Your supreme power and authority. As David wrote, "You prepare a table before me in the presence of my enemies; You anoint my head with oil; my cup overflows." Just as You anointed Aaron and his sons to serve as priests, I ask that You anoint me for Your purpose.

Lord, as You consecrated Your servants in times past, I dedicate myself to You now. Pour out Your oil upon me, not just as a symbol of honor, but as a healing balm for my wounds and a shield against life's turmoil.

Empower me, as You did the prophet, to "bind up the brokenhearted, to proclaim liberty to the captives, and the opening of the prison to those who are bound." Let Your anointing flow through me, that I may be an instrument of Your comfort and liberation to others.

In Jesus' name, Amen.

My own prayer:

_____
_____
_____
_____
_____
_____
_____
_____

Antichrist

noun
ˈanˌtīˌkrīst

1. One who denies or opposes Christ
2. Used in an exaggerated way to describe a person regarded as a powerful and malevolent adversary

- **1 John 4:1–6**: Beloved, do not believe every spirit, but test the spirits to see whether they are from God, for many false prophets have gone out into the world. By this you know the Spirit of God: every spirit that confesses that Jesus Christ has come in the flesh is from God, and every spirit that does not confess Jesus is not from God. This is the spirit of the antichrist, which you heard was coming and now is in the world already. Little children, you are from God and have overcome them, for he who is in you is greater than he who is in the world. They are from the world; therefore they speak from the world, and the world listens to them. We are from God. Whoever knows God listens to us; whoever is not from God does not listen to us. By this we know the Spirit of truth and the spirit of error.
- **1 John 2:18**: Children, it is the last hour, and as you have heard that antichrist is coming, so now many antichrists have come. Therefore we know that it is the last hour.
- **1 John 2:22**: Who is the liar but he who denies that Jesus is the Christ? This is the antichrist, he who denies the Father and the Son.
- **2 Thessalonians 2:3–4**: Let no one deceive you in any way. For that day will not come, unless the rebellion comes first, and the man if lawlessness is revealed, the son of destruction, who opposes and exalts himself against every so-called god or object of worship, so that he takes his seat in the temple of God, proclaiming himself to be God.
- **Matthew 24:24**: "For false christs and false prophets will arise and perform great signs and wonders, so as to lead astray, if possible, even the elect."

Reflections:

_____
_____
_____

Prayer:

Heavenly Father,

I come before You with a humble heart, seeking Your guidance and protection against the spirit of the antichrist. As Your Word warns us, many antichrists have come, and we must be vigilant.

Lord, help me to firmly hold to the truth that Jesus is the Christ, Your Son. Strengthen my faith so that I may never deny the Father or the Son, for this is the mark of the antichrist.

Father, keep me alert and sober-minded. Let me not be deceived by false Christs and false prophets who perform great signs and wonders. Sharpen my spiritual senses to distinguish truth from lies. Lord, anchor me in Your Word and Your love. When deception abounds, let me stand firm in the faith You have given me. May Your Holy Spirit guide me in all truth and righteousness. I proclaim that Jesus Christ has come in the flesh, crucified and rose again on the third day for all eternity and the savior of my soul.

In Jesus' name I pray, Amen.

My own prayer:

_____
_____
_____
_____
_____
_____
_____
_____
_____

Anxiety

noun
aŋ-ˈzī-ə-tē

1. Apprehensive uneasiness or nervousness usually over an impending or anticipated ill
2. Mentally distressing concern or interest
3. A strong desire sometimes mixed with doubt, fear, or uneasiness

- **Philippians 4:6–7:** Do not be anxious about anything, but in everything by prayer and supplication with thanksgiving let your requests be made known to God. And the peace of God, which surpasses all understanding, will guard your hearts and your minds in Christ Jesus.
- **1 Peter 5:6–7:** Humble yourselves, therefore, under the mighty hand of God so that at the proper time he may exalt you, casting all your anxieties on him, because he cares for you.
- **Matthew 6:25–27:** "Therefore I tell you, do not be anxious about your life, what you will eat or what you will drink, nor about your body, what you will put on. Is not life more than food, and the body more than clothing? Look at the birds of the air: they neither sow nor reap nor gather into barns, and yet your heavenly Father feeds them. Are you not of more value than they? And which of you by being anxious can add a single hour to his span of life?"

Reflections:

_____
_____
_____
_____
_____
_____
_____
_____

Prayer:

Heavenly Father,

I come before You, humbling myself under Your mighty hand. I acknowledge that You are sovereign over all things, including my concerns and worries. Lord, I choose not to be anxious about anything. Instead, in every situation, I present my requests to You through prayer and petition, with a heart of thanksgiving. I cast all my anxieties upon You, knowing that You care deeply for me.

Gracious God, I am reminded that worrying cannot add a single hour to my life. Just as You provide for the birds of the air, I trust that You will care for me, Your child, who is far more valuable in Your sight.

I surrender all my worries to You, King Jesus. I trust that in due time, You will lift me up according to Your perfect will. I pray for Your peace, which transcends all understanding, to guard my heart and mind in Jesus Christ.

In Jesus' name, Amen.

My own prayer:

_____
_____
_____
_____
_____
_____
_____
_____
_____

Atonement

noun
ə-ˈtōn-mənt

1. Reparation for an offense or injury
2. The reconciliation of God and humankind through the sacrificial death of Jesus Christ
3. The exemplifying of human oneness with God

- **Romans 3:23–24:** For all have sinned and fall short of the glory of God, and are justified by his grace as a gift, through the redemption that is in Christ Jesus.
- **John 11:35:** Jesus wept.
- **2 Corinthians 5:21:** For our sake he made him to be sin who knew no sin, so that in him we might become the righteousness of God.
- **1 Peter 2:24:** He himself bore our sins in his body on the tree, that we might die to sin and live to righteousness. By his wounds you have been healed.
- **Leviticus 17:11:** For the life of the flesh is in the blood, and I have given it for you on the altar to make atonement for your souls, for it is the blood that makes atonement by the life.

Reflections:

_____
_____
_____
_____
_____
_____
_____
_____

Prayer:

Heavenly Father,

I bow before You in humble gratitude for Your boundless mercy and grace. Thank You for the precious gift of Your Son, Jesus Christ, who became the ultimate sacrifice for our sins through His death on the cross. You have provided a way for us to be reconciled to You.

Lord, I am in awe of Your love that sent Jesus to bear our sins and take upon Himself the punishment we deserved. His blood, shed for us, has become the perfect atonement for our souls. I acknowledge that "the life of the flesh is in the blood," and through Christ's sacrifice, You have made atonement for us once and for all.

I thank You for the justification that comes through faith in Jesus Christ. By Your grace, we who were once sinners have been declared righteous. Help me to live in the freedom and joy of this truth, always remembering the great price paid for my redemption. May I never take for granted the magnitude of Christ's sacrifice. Let the reality of His atonement transform my daily life, drawing me closer to You and empowering me to live in a manner worthy of this great gift.

In the name of Jesus Christ, our Savior and Redeemer, I pray, Amen.

My own prayer:

_____
_____
_____
_____
_____
_____

Authority

noun
ə-ˈthȯr-ə-tē

1. Power to influence or command thought, opinion, or behavior
2. Freedom granted by one in authority
3. Persons in command

- **Matthew 28:18:** And Jesus came and said to them, "All authority in heaven and on earth has been given to me."
- **Luke 10:19:** "Behold, I have given you authority to tread on serpents and scorpions, and over all the power of the enemy, and nothing shall hurt you."
- **Mark 3:15:** And have authority to cast out demons.
- **Luke 4:32:** And they were astonished at his teaching, for his word possessed authority.
- **1 Peter 2:13–14:** Be subject for the Lord's sake to every human institution, whether it be to the emperor as supreme, or to governors as sent by him to punish those who do evil and to praise those who do good.

Reflections:

_____
_____
_____
_____
_____
_____
_____
_____
_____

Prayer:

Heavenly Father,

I come before You, acknowledging Your supreme authority over all creation. Lord Jesus, You said that all authority in heaven and on earth has been given to You, and I submit myself to Your lordship. Thank You for the authority You have granted me as Your follower. Help me to wisely use this power to tread on serpents and scorpions, and over all the power of the enemy. Strengthen me to stand firm against evil forces and deception.

Grant me the courage to speak Your truth with the same authority that astonished those who heard You teach. May Your words flow through me to bring light to darkness and hope to the lost. Guide me in being subject to human institutions for Your sake, recognizing that all authority ultimately comes from You. Give me discernment to know when to submit and when to stand firm in Your truth.

Lord, help me face problems and hard times with the confidence that comes from knowing I am under Your authority and protection. Nothing can truly harm me when I am in Your care.

In Jesus' name I pray, Amen.

My own prayer:

_____

_____

_____

_____

_____

_____

_____

Battle

noun
ˈba-tᵊl

1. A hostile encounter between opposing military forces
2. A usually lengthy contest, struggle, or controversy
3. A struggle to succeed or survive
4. A combat between two persons

-
- **Exodus 14:14:** The Lord will fight for you, and you have only to be silent.
- **2 Corinthians 10:3:** For though we walk in the flesh, we are not waging war according to the flesh.
- **Ephesians 6:11:** Put on the whole armor of God, that you may be able to stand against the schemes of the devil.
- **Ephesians 6:14:** Stand therefore, having fastened on the belt of truth, and having put on the breastplate of righteousness.
- **Psalm 20:7:** Some trust in chariots and some in horses, but we trust in the name of the Lord our God.

Reflections:

_____
_____
_____
_____
_____
_____
_____
_____

Prayer:

Heavenly Father,

I come before You, acknowledging the battles I face in this life. Lord, remind me that I need only be silent, for You will fight for me. In moments of struggle, help me to trust in Your strength rather than my own.

Thank You for providing me with the armor of God. As I face the challenges of each day, help me put on the whole armor—the belt of truth, the breastplate of righteousness, and all other pieces that I may need to stand firm against the schemes of the enemy. Guide me to walk by the Spirit, recognizing that though I walk in the flesh, I do not wage war according to the flesh. When confronted with spiritual battles, remind me that my weapons are not of this world, but have divine power to demolish strongholds.

Lord, while others may trust in chariots and horses, I choose to put my trust in Your name alone. In the face of adversity, let me not fret or worry, but instead rely on Your mighty power and unfailing love. With confidence in Your protection and guidance, I face each battle, knowing that the victory is already Yours.

In Your mighty name, Jesus, I pray, Amen.

My own prayer:

_____

_____

_____

_____

_____

_____

Beauty

noun
'byü-tē

1. The quality or group of qualities in a person or thing that gives pleasure to the senses or the mind
2. A person (especially a woman) who is beautiful

- **Song of Solomon 4:7:** You are altogether beautiful, my love; there is no flaw in you.
- **Proverbs 31:30:** Charm is deceitful, and beauty is vain, but a woman who fears the Lord is to be praised.
- **1 Timothy 2:9–10:** Likewise also that women should adorn themselves in respectable apparel, with modesty and self-control, not with braided hair and gold or pearls or costly attire, but with what is proper for women who profess godliness—with good works.
- **Psalm 139:14:** I praise you, for I am fearfully and wonderfully made. Wonderful are your works; my soul knows it very well.
- **Ecclesiastes 3:11:** He has made everything beautiful in its time. Also, he has put eternity into man's heart, yet so that he cannot find out what God has done from the beginning to the end.

Reflections:

_____
_____
_____
_____
_____
_____
_____
_____

Prayer:

Heavenly Father,

I come before You with a heart full of gratitude, acknowledging Your role as the Divine Creator of all beauty, as it is written "He has made everything beautiful in its time". I thank You for the splendor that surrounds us in Your creation.

Lord, help me maintain a posture of appreciation for the outer beauty in all things, while always remembering Your greater truth about inner beauty, as Proverbs 31:30 reminds us. Guide me to value and cultivate the unfading beauty of a gentle and quiet spirit. Creator God, I marvel at how You have fashioned each of us, for I am fearfully and wonderfully made. Wonderful are your works; my soul knows it very well. Help me see this divine craftsmanship in myself and others, always remembering that our purpose is to glorify You.

Father, teach me to adorn myself with good deeds and a godly character, rather than focusing excessively on outward appearance. Guard my heart against vanity, pride, and ego, which can distort the true beauty You've bestowed upon us.

Lord, like the beloved in Song of Solomon 4:7, let me see the flawless beauty in Your love for us, and help me reflect that love to others. May my life be a testament to Your beauty, inside and out.

In Jesus' name I pray, Amen.

My own prayer:

_____

_____

_____

_____

_____

Blood

noun
ˈbləd

1. The fluid that circulates in the heart, arteries, capillaries, and veins of a vertebrate animal, carrying nourishment and oxygen to and bringing away waste products from all parts of the body
2. Human stock or lineage
3. Relationship by descent from a common ancestor

- **Hebrews 12:24:** And to Jesus, the mediator of a new covenant, and to the sprinkled blood that speaks a better word than the blood of Abel.
- **Hebrews 9:18:** Therefore not even the first covenant was inaugurated without blood.
- **Hebrews 9:22:** Indeed, under the law almost everything is purified with blood, and without the shedding of blood there is no forgiveness of sins.
- **Ezekiel 16:6:** And when I passed by you and saw you wallowing in your blood, I said to you in your blood, 'Live!' I said to you in your blood, 'Live!'
- **1 John 1:7:** But if we walk in the light, as he is in the light, we have fellowship with one another, and the blood of Jesus his Son cleanses us from all sin.
- **Ephesians 2:13:** But now in Christ Jesus you who once were far off have been brought near by the blood of Christ.
- **1 Peter 1:2:** According to the foreknowledge of God the Father, in the sanctification of the Spirit, for obedience to Jesus Christ and for sprinkling with his blood: May grace and peace be multiplied to you.

Reflections:

_____
_____
_____
_____
_____
_____

WARFARE BATTLECARDS

Prayer:

Heavenly Father,

I approach Your throne with reverence, acknowledging the immeasurable value of Christ's precious blood, as it is written. Lord, I thank You for the new covenant established through Jesus' sacrifice. Help me grasp the profound significance of this inheritance, secured not by my own merit, but by the Lamb's ultimate sacrifice.

Father, remind me that my salvation rests solely on Your grace, received through faith. For it is by grace I have been saved, through faith—and this is not from myself, it is the gift of God—not by works, so that no one can boast.

Teach me, Lord, to fully comprehend the power of salvation through Christ's blood. Guide me away from empty religious rituals or legalistic practices, for I know that it is impossible for the blood of bulls and goats to take away sins. Instead, let me rest in the assurance that the blood of Jesus, his Son, purifies us from all sin. May my soul and spirit display a life covered by your blood.

In Jesus' name I pray, Amen.

My own prayer:

___

___

___

___

___

___

___

Bold[ness]

adjective
ˈbōld

1. Fearless before danger
2. Showing or requiring a fearless daring spirit
3. Impudent, presumptuous

- **Acts 4:29:** And now, Lord, look upon their threats and grant to your servants to continue to speak your word with all boldness.
- **Acts 28:31:** Proclaiming the kingdom of God and teaching about the Lord Jesus Christ with all boldness and without hindrance.
- **Ephesians 3:11–12:** This was according to the eternal purpose that he has realized in Christ Jesus our Lord, in whom we have boldness and access with confidence through our faith in him.
- **Proverbs 28:1:** The wicked flee when no one pursues, but the righteous are bold as a lion.
- **2 Corinthians 3:12:** Since we have such a hope, we are very bold.
- **Ephesians 6:19:** And also for me, that words may be given to me in opening my mouth boldly to proclaim the mystery of the gospel.

Reflections:

_____
_____
_____
_____
_____
_____
_____
_____

Prayer:

Heavenly Father,

I come before You with reverence, acknowledging Your sovereign power. Lord, I ask for Your strength as I face the challenges of this world.

Grant me, Your servant, the ability to speak Your Word with all boldness. Empower me to proclaim Your kingdom and teach about Jesus Christ fearlessly and without hindrance. Father, remind me that in Christ Jesus, I have boldness and access to You with confidence through my faith. Let this truth sink deep into my heart, transforming my actions and words.

I pray for courage to be as bold as a lion in righteousness, not fleeing when "no one" pursues. Fill me with Your Holy Spirit, so that I may continue to speak Your Word with unwavering boldness. Lord, give me the words to open my mouth boldly and proclaim the mystery of the gospel. May I approach You and others with freedom and confidence, knowing that You hear my prayers and guide my steps as I yield to You.

In Jesus' name I pray, Amen.

My own prayer:

_____
_____
_____
_____
_____
_____
_____

Bondage

noun
'bän-dij

1. A state of being bound usually by compulsion (as of law)
2. Slavery, serfdom
3. Servitude or subjugation to a controlling person or force

- **Romans 8:21:** That the creation itself will be set free from its bondage to corruption and obtain the freedom of the glory of the children of God.
- **Galatians 5:1:** For freedom Christ has set us free; stand firm therefore, and do not submit again to a yoke of slavery.
- **Romans 8:15:** For you did not receive the spirit of slavery to fall back into fear, but you have received the Spirit of adoption as sons, by whom we cry, "Abba! Father!"
- **2 Corinthians 3:17:** Now the Lord is the Spirit, and where the Spirit of the Lord is, there is freedom.
- **Hebrews 2:15–16:** And deliver all those who through fear of death were subject to lifelong slavery. For surely it is not angels that he helps, but he helps the offspring of Abraham.

Reflections:

_____
_____
_____
_____
_____
_____
_____
_____

Prayer:

Heavenly Father,

I come before You, seeking the freedom that Christ has secured for me. Lord, I thank You that for freedom, Christ has set me free. Grant me the strength to stand firm and not submit again to a yoke of slavery. Father, I am grateful that I did not receive a spirit of slavery to fall back into fear, but the Spirit of adoption as Your child. Help me to cry out to You, "Abba! Father!," with confidence and trust.

Holy Spirit, I invite Your presence into every area of my life, for where You are, there is freedom. Release me from any bondage to corruption and fear, especially the fear of death that can enslave.

Lord, I hold fast to the promise that creation itself will be set free from bondage and obtain the freedom of Your children's glory. Guide me into a life of true freedom, with You as my source and sustainer.

Help me break free from all deception and every yoke of slavery, walking in the liberty You have graciously provided. May I live as one truly free, serving You with joy and gratitude.

In Jesus' name, I pray, Amen.

My own prayer:

_____
_____
_____
_____
_____
_____
_____

Broken

adjective
ˈbrō-kən

1. Violently separated into parts
2. Damaged or altered by or as if by breaking

- **Psalm 34:18:** The Lord is near to the brokenhearted and saves the crushed in spirit.
- **Psalm 51:17:** The sacrifices of God are a broken spirit; a broken and contrite heart, O God, you will not despise.
- **Psalm 147:3:** He heals the brokenhearted and binds up their wounds.
- **Isaiah 65:14:** Behold, my servants shall sing for gladness of heart, but you shall cry out for pain of heart and shall wail for breaking of spirit.
- **John 16:33:** "I have said these things to you, that in me you may have peace. In the world you will have tribulation. But take heart; I have overcome the world."
- **Romans 8:28:** And we know that for those who love God all things work together for good, for those who are called according to his purpose.
- **1 John 1:9:** If we confess our sins, he is faithful and just to forgive us our sins and to cleanse us from all unrighteousness.
- **Proverbs 3:5–6:** Trust in the Lord with all your heart, and do not lean on your own understanding. In all your ways acknowledge him, and he will make straight your paths.
- **John 14:27:** Peace I leave with you; my peace I give to you. Not as the world gives do I give to you. Let not your hearts be troubled, neither let them be afraid.
- **Isaiah 41:10:** Fear not, for I am with you; be not dismayed, for I am your God; I will strengthen you, I will help you, I will uphold you with my righteous right hand.
- **Psalm 51:10:** Create in me a clean heart, O God, and renew a right spirit within me.

Reflections:

_____

_____

_____

_____

_____

Prayer:

Heavenly Father,

I come before You with a heart of surrender, broken and contrite. In my brokenness, I reach out to You, for I know You are near to the brokenhearted and save the crushed in spirit.

Lord, I offer You the sacrifice of a broken spirit, trusting that You will not despise it. Heal my wounded heart and bind up my wounds, as only You can do. Though I may have cried out in pain and wailed in the breaking of my spirit, I now choose to sing for gladness of heart as Your servant. I confess any rebellion or disobedience, seeking Your forgiveness and cleansing.

Grant me Your peace, Lord—not as the world gives, but the true peace that comes only from You. Help me to trust in You with all my heart and not lean on my own understanding. I take hold of Your promise that all things work together for good for those who love You. Strengthen me, help me, and uphold me with Your righteous right hand. Create in me a clean heart, O God, and renew a right spirit within me. May I find rest in You, knowing that You have overcome the world.

In Jesus' name I pray, Amen.

My own prayer:

_____
_____
_____
_____
_____
_____
_____

Capable

adjective
ˈkā-pə-bəl

1. Comprehensive
2. Having attributes (such as physical or mental power) required for performance or accomplishment
3. Having or showing general efficiency and ability

- **Philippians 4:13:** I can do all things through him who strengthens me.
- **Matthew 19:26:** But Jesus looked at them and said, "With man this is impossible, but with God all things are possible."
- **Ephesians 3:20:** Now to him who is able to do far more abundantly than all that we ask or think, according to the power at work within us.
- **2 Timothy 3:17:** That the man of God may be complete, equipped for every good work.
- **1 Peter 2:19:** For this is a gracious thing, when, mindful of God, one endures sorrows while suffering unjustly.
- **2 Corinthians 3:5:** Not that we are sufficient in ourselves to claim anything as coming from us, but our sufficiency is from God.

Reflections:

_____
_____
_____
_____
_____
_____
_____
_____

Prayer:

Heavenly Father,

I come before You in a posture of surrender, fully trusting in Your mighty power. Lord, Your Word assures me that I can do all things through Christ who strengthens me. I humbly ask for Your forgiveness for the times I've relied on my own strength or acted without seeking You first.

Grant me spiritual eyes, Father, to truly believe that what seems impossible with man is possible with You. Help me to remember that You are able to do far more abundantly than all I could ask or think.

Holy Spirit, equip me for every good work that You have prepared for me. Grow my faith, Lord, so that I may fully understand and embrace that my sufficiency comes from You alone, not from myself or anything within me. I surrender my capabilities, my strengths, and my weaknesses to You. Use them as You see fit, for Your glory. Even in times of unjust suffering, help me to endure with grace, mindful of Your presence and purpose.

Thank You for making me capable through Your power at work within me.

In Jesus' name I pray, Amen.

My own prayer:

_____
_____
_____
_____
_____
_____
_____

Compassion

noun
kəm-ˈpa-shən

1. Sympathetic consciousness of others' distress together with a desire to alleviate it

- **2 Corinthians 1:3–4:** Blessed be the God and Father of our Lord Jesus Christ, the Father of mercies and God of all comfort, who comforts us in all our affliction, so that we may be able to comfort those who are in any affliction, with the comfort with which we ourselves are comforted by God.
- **Psalm 103:13:** As a father shows compassion to his children, so the Lord shows compassion to those who fear him.
- **Matthew 9:13:** "Go and learn what this means: 'I desire mercy, and not sacrifice.' For I came not to call the righteous, but sinners."
- **Micah 7:19:** He will again have compassion on us; he will tread our iniquities underfoot. You will cast all our sins into the depths of the sea.
- **Lamentations 3:22–23:** The steadfast love of the Lord never ceases; his mercies never come to an end; they are new every morning; great is your faithfulness.

Reflections:

_____

_____

_____

_____

_____

_____

_____

_____

Prayer:

Heavenly Father,

I come before You in humility, seeking Your boundless compassion. You are the Father of mercies and the God of all comfort, and I am grateful for Your presence in my life. Lord, I thank You for comforting me in my afflictions. Help me to extend this same comfort to others who are suffering, using the very comfort You've given me.

As a loving Father, You show compassion to Your children. Teach me to fear You and walk in Your ways, that I may experience the fullness of Your compassion. I am grateful, Lord, that You desire mercy over sacrifice. Thank You for calling me, a sinner, into Your loving presence. Have compassion on me once again and cast my sins into the depths of the sea.

Father, I praise You for Your steadfast love that never ceases and Your mercies that are new every morning. Your faithfulness is great, and I am in awe of Your constant compassion. Help me to reflect Your compassion in my daily life, showing mercy and kindness to those around me. May Your love flow through me to touch others.

In Jesus' name I pray, Amen.

My own prayer:

_____
_____
_____
_____
_____
_____
_____

Confession

noun
kən-ˈfe-shən

1. An act of confessing
2. A written or oral acknowledgement of guilt by a party accused of an offense

- **James 5:16:** Therefore, confess your sins to one another and pray for one another, that you may be healed. The prayer of a righteous person has great power as it is working.
- **Proverbs 28:13:** Whoever conceals his transgressions will not prosper, but he who confesses and forsakes them will obtain mercy.
- **Ezra 10:11:** Now then make confession to the Lord, the God of your fathers, and do his will. Separate yourselves from the peoples of the land and from the foreign wives.
- **1 John 1:9:** If we confess our sins, he is faithful and just to forgive us our sins and to cleanse us from all unrighteousness.
- **Romans 10:9:** Because, if you confess with your mouth that Jesus is Lord and believe in your heart that God raised him from the dead, you will be saved.
- **Acts 3:19:** Repent therefore, and turn back, that your sins may be blotted out.
- **Numbers 5:7:** He shall confess his sin that he has committed. And he shall make full restitution for his wrong, adding a fifth to it and giving it to him to whom he did the wrong.

Reflections:

_____
_____
_____
_____
_____
_____
_____

Prayer:

Heavenly Father,

I come before You in humility and openness of heart. Lord, I confess my sins to You, knowing that in this confession, there is healing and righteousness.

Father, I will not conceal my transgressions, for I know that in confessing and forsaking them, I will obtain Your mercy. Grant me the courage to be vulnerable before You, freely bringing my faults and failures into Your throne room. I trust in Your faithfulness and justice, O God. As I confess, I believe You will forgive my sins and cleanse me from all unrighteousness. I declare with my mouth that Jesus is Lord, and I believe in my heart that You raised Him from the dead.

Lord, I repent and turn back from my sinful ways. I ask for Your guidance to make restitution where needed and to separate myself from things that lead me astray. Thank You for Your unfailing love and the power of confession.

In Jesus' name I pray, Amen.

My own prayer:

_____
_____
_____
_____
_____
_____
_____
_____

Consecration

noun

ˌkän(t)-sə-ˈkrā-shən

1. The act or ceremony of consecrating
2. The state of being consecrated (dedicated to a sacred purpose)

- **Romans 12:1–2:** I appeal to you therefore, brothers, by the mercies of God, to present your bodies as a living sacrifice, holy and acceptable to God, which is your spiritual worship. Do not be conformed to this world, but be transformed by the renewal of your mind, that by testing you may discern what is the will of God, what is good and acceptable and perfect.
- **2 Corinthians 7:1:** Since we have these promises, beloved, let us cleanse ourselves from every defilement of body and spirit, bringing holiness to completion in the fear of God.

Reflections:

_____
_____
_____
_____
_____
_____
_____
_____
_____
_____

Prayer:

Heavenly Father,

We come before You with grateful hearts, acknowledging the precious promises You have given us. As Your beloved children, we seek Your guidance in cleansing ourselves from every defilement of body and spirit. Lord, help us to bring holiness to completion in reverence for You.

We offer ourselves as living sacrifices, holy and acceptable in Your sight. May our lives be a spiritual act of worship, pleasing to You in every way. Transform us, O God, by the renewal of our minds. Grant us the strength to resist conforming to the patterns of this world.

Father, we ask for Your help in focusing our thoughts and actions on You. Give us the discernment to recognize Your will–what is good, acceptable, and perfect. May we be steadfast in our commitment to holiness, both in body and spirit. Lord, purify our hearts and minds. Remove any distractions that hinder our concentration on You and Your Word. Help us to fix our eyes on You, our Sovereign Lord, finding refuge in Your presence.

We pray for the strength to cleanse ourselves from all that opposes You, participating in the process of becoming more like Christ. May we live in the fear of the Lord, with great respect for Your power and righteousness.

In Jesus' name, I pray, Amen.

My own prayer:

_____

_____

_____

_____

Consume

verb
kən-ˈsüm

1. To do away with completely
2. To spend wastefully
3. To eat or drink, especially in great quantity

- **Deuteronomy 7:16:** And you shall consume all the peoples that the Lord your God will give over to you. Your eye shall not pity them, neither shall you serve their gods, for that would be a snare to you.
- **Psalm 37:20:** But the wicked will perish; the enemies of the Lord are like the glory of the pastures; they vanish—like smoke they vanish away.
- **Hebrews 12:28–29:** Therefore let us be grateful for receiving a kingdom that cannot be shaken, and thus let us offer to God acceptable worship, with reverence and awe, for our God is a consuming fire.

Reflections:

_____
_____
_____
_____
_____
_____
_____
_____

Prayer:

Heavenly Father,

I come before You with reverence and awe, acknowledging that You are a consuming fire. Your power and holiness are beyond measure, and I stand in awe of Your majesty. Help me to show no pity to the sins and idols that seek to ensnare me, for I know they are a snare to my soul.

Father, remind me that the wicked will perish, and Your enemies will vanish like smoke. Let this truth embolden me to stand firm in my faith, knowing that Your justice will prevail. Grant me the wisdom and the courage to discern and eliminate anything in my life that does not align with Your will. May I offer You acceptable worship, with reverence and awe, grateful for the unshakeable kingdom I have received through Christ.

Lord, consume all that is impure within me. Burn away my pride, selfishness, and worldly desires. Replace them with Your love, humility, and righteousness.

In Jesus' name I pray, Amen.

My own prayer:

_____

_____

_____

_____

_____

_____

_____

Contend

verb
kən-ˈtend

1. To strive or vie in a contest or rivalry or against difficulties
2. To strive in debate

- **Psalm 35:1:** Contend, O Lord, with those who contend with me; fight against those who fight against me!
- **Jeremiah 2:29:** Why do you contend with me? You have all transgressed against me, declares the Lord.
- **Proverbs 3:30:** Do not contend with a man for no reason, when he has done you no harm.
- **Isaiah 41:12:** You shall seek those who contend with you, but you shall not find them; those who war against you shall be as nothing at all.

Reflections:

_____
_____
_____
_____
_____
_____
_____
_____
_____
_____

Prayer:

Heavenly Father,

I come before You, acknowledging Your sovereignty and power. As I face contention in my life, I turn to Your Word for guidance and strength.

Lord, as the psalmist prayed, I ask that You contend with those who contend against me. Fight against those who fight against me, for this battle is ultimately Yours. I trust in Your righteous judgment and protection. Yet, Father, I humbly confess that I have often transgressed against You. Forgive me for the times I have contended with You, questioning Your ways and wisdom. Help me to submit to Your will and trust in Your perfect plan.

Grant me discernment, O God, to avoid unnecessary conflicts. May I heed the wisdom of Proverbs and not contend with others without cause. Let peace and understanding guide my interactions with those around me. I take comfort in Your promise, Lord, that those who war against I shall be as nothing. Strengthen my faith to seek You first in times of conflict, knowing that You are our ultimate defender and vindicator.

Give me a heart of reconciliation and mind of peace. When contention arises, may I respond with Your love, grace, and wisdom. Help me to be a peacemaker in a world full of strife. In all things, Lord, may I honor You and reflect Your character, even in the face of opposition. I trust in Your unfailing love and justice.

In Jesus' name we pray, Amen.

My own prayer:

_____

_____

_____

Control

noun
kən-ˈtrōl

1. The power to influence or direct people's behavior or the course of events
2. The ability to manage, direct, or command something

- **Ephesians 2:1–3:** And you were dead in the trespasses and sins in which you once walked, following the course of this world, following the prince of the power of the air, the spirit that is now at work in the sons of disobedience—among whom we all once lived in the passions of our flesh, carrying out the desires of the body and the mind, and were by nature children of wrath, like the rest of mankind.
- **1 Corinthians 4:6:** I have applied all these things to myself and Apollos for your benefit, brothers, that you may learn by us not to go beyond what is written, that none of you may be puffed up in favor of one against another.
- **Proverbs 19:2:** Desire without knowledge is not good, and whoever makes haste with his feet misses his way.
- **Matthew 20:25–26:** But Jesus called them to him and said, "You know that the rulers of the Gentiles lord it over them, and their great ones exercise authority over them. It shall not be so among you. But whoever would be great among you must be your servant."
- **Matthew 10:29–31:** "Are not two sparrows sold for a penny? And not one of them will fall to the ground apart from your Father. But even the hairs of your head are all numbered. Fear not, therefore; you are of more value than many sparrows."
- **Job 42:2:** I know that you can do all things, and that no purpose of yours can be thwarted.
- **Colossians 1:16–17:** For by him all things were created, in heaven and on earth, visible and invisible, whether thrones or dominions or rulers or authorities—all things were created through him and for him. And he is before all things, and in him all things hold together.

Reflections:

_____

_____

_____

_____

Prayer:

Heavenly Father,

I come before You in humility, acknowledging Your supreme control over all creation. Forgive me for the times I have tried to exert control over my life and others, forgetting that You are the ultimate authority. Lord, I confess that I have often walked according to the course of this world, following the desires of my flesh and mind. Forgive me for thinking beyond what is written and being puffed up.

Help me to remember, that while many plans are in my heart, it is Your purpose that prevails. Teach me to lead as a servant, not seeking to lord over others, as Jesus taught. I am in awe of Your attention to detail, knowing that even the sparrows are under Your care. Help me trust in Your perfect control.

Lord, I acknowledge, as Job did, that no purpose of Yours can be thwarted. All things were created through Christ and are held together by Him. Help me to rest in this truth. Guide me to surrender control to You, trusting in Your perfect will and timing for my life.

In Jesus' name I pray, Amen.

My own prayer:

_____
_____
_____
_____
_____
_____
_____
_____

Cope

verb
'kōp

1. To deal with and attempt to overcome problems and difficulties

- **Joshua 1:9:** Have I not commanded you? Be strong and courageous. Do not be frightened, and do not be dismayed, for the Lord your God is with you wherever you go.
- **John 14:27:** "Peace I leave with you; my peace I give to you. Not as the world gives do I give to you. Let not your hearts be troubled, neither let them be afraid."
- **1 John 1:9:** If we confess our sins, he is faithful and just to forgive us our sins and to cleanse us from all unrighteousness.
- **Philippians 4:13:** I can do all things through him who strengthens me.
- **Jeremiah 29:11:** For I know the plans I have for you, declares the Lord, plans for welfare and not for evil, to give you a future and a hope.
- **Psalm 23:** The Lord is my shepherd; I shall not want. He makes me lie down in green pastures. He leads me beside still waters. He restores my soul. He leads me in paths of righteousness for his name's sake. Even though I walk through the valley of the shadow of death, I will fear no evil, for you are with me; your rod and your staff, they comfort me. You prepare a table before me in the presence of my enemies; you anoint my head with oil; my cup overflows. Surely goodness and mercy shall follow me all the days of my life, and I shall dwell in the house of the Lord forever.

Reflections:

_____
_____
_____
_____
_____
_____

Prayer:

Heavenly Father,

I come before You, seeking Your strength and guidance to cope with life's challenges. As You commanded in Joshua, I will strive to be strong and courageous, knowing that You are with me wherever I go. Lord, I thank You for the peace You offer, which surpasses all understanding. I choose not to let my heart be troubled or afraid. Remind me to embrace the peace You freely give.

Father, I confess my sins and shortcomings to You, trusting in Your faithfulness and justice to forgive and cleanse me. When I feel weak, help me remember that through Your strength, I can face all things that come my way. God, I trust in Your plans for my life, help me to hold on to hope, even in difficult times, knowing that You have good intentions for my future.

Lord, I find comfort in You as You are my shepherd, guiding me through both peaceful meadows and dark valleys. I will not fear, for Your presence comforts me. May Your goodness and mercy follow me all the days of my life.

In Jesus' name I pray, Amen.

My own prayer:

_____

_____

_____

_____

_____

_____

Courage

noun
ˈkər-ij

1. Mental or moral strength to venture, persevere, and withstand danger, fear, or difficulty

- **Psalm 31:24:** Be strong, and let your heart take courage, all you who wait for the Lord!
- **Psalm 27:14:** Wait for the Lord; be strong, and let your heart take courage; wait for the Lord!
- **2 Chronicles 15:7:** But you, take courage! Do not let your hands be weak, for your work shall be rewarded.
- **2 Samuel 10:12:** Be of good courage, and let us be courageous for our people, and for the cities of our God, and may the Lord do what seems good to him.
- **Daniel 10:19**: And he said, "O man greatly loved, fear not, peace be with you; be strong and of good courage." And as he spoke to me, I was strengthened and said, "Let my lord speak, for you have strengthened me."
- **Joshua 1:9:** Have I not commanded you? Be strong and courageous. Do not be frightened, and do not be dismayed, for the Lord your God is with you wherever you go.

Reflections:

_____
_____
_____
_____
_____
_____
_____
_____

Prayer:

Heavenly Father,

I come before You with a humble heart, seeking Your strength and courage. In moments of uncertainty, help me wait upon You, trusting in Your perfect timing and divine plan.

When my hands grow weak and my spirit falters, remind me that my work in Your name is not in vain. Strengthen me for the tasks You've set before me. As I face challenges, both personal and communal, give me boldness to stand firm in my faith and to serve others courageously. Let me feel Your love deeply, dispelling my fears and filling me with Your peace that surpasses all understanding.

Help me remember that You are always with me, guiding and protecting me in every step I take and every challenge I face. Grant me the courage to be strong, not frightened or dismayed, knowing that You are with me wherever I go.

I thank You for Your unfailing love and the courage You instill within me.

In Jesus' name I pray, Amen.

My own prayer:

_____
_____
_____
_____
_____
_____
_____

Covenant

noun
ˈkəv-nənt
1. A usually formal, solemn, and binding agreement

- **Ephesians 2:11–13:** Therefore remember that at one time you Gentiles in the flesh, called "the uncircumcision" by what is called the circumcision, which is made in the flesh by hands—remember that you were at that time separated from Christ, alienated from the commonwealth of Israel and strangers to the covenants of promise, having no hope and without God in the world. But now in Christ Jesus you who once were far off have been brought near by the blood of Christ.
- **Exodus 23:32:** You shall make no covenant with them and their gods.
- **Jeremiah 31:31:** Behold, the days are coming, declares the Lord, when I will make a new covenant with the house of Israel and the house of Judah.
- **Proverbs 11:21:** Be assured, an evil person will not go unpunished, but the offspring of the righteous will be delivered.
- **Galatians 3:29:** And if you are Christ's, then you are Abraham's offspring, heirs according to promise.

Reflections:

_____
_____
_____
_____
_____
_____
_____
_____

Prayer:

Heavenly Father,

I come before You with a humble heart, recognizing the weight and significance of Your covenants. I am in awe of Your faithfulness throughout generations.

Lord, I repent for the times I have taken Your covenant lightly or forgotten the price paid to bring me near. Thank You for the blood of Christ that has bridged the gap between us. I am grateful that though I was once far off, a stranger to Your covenants of promise, You have brought me near. Through Jesus, I am now part of Your family, an heir according to Your promise.

Father, forgive me for the moments I've been tempted to make covenants with the world and its ways. Help me to remain faithful to You alone. I rejoice in the new covenant You have made, written not on tablets of stone but on my heart. Strengthen me to walk in Your ways and keep Your commandments.

Thank You for delivering me, as an offspring of the righteous through Christ. May my life honor the covenant relationship You have graciously extended to me.

In Jesus' name I pray, Amen.

My own prayer:

_____
_____
_____
_____
_____
_____
_____

Curse

verb

ˈkərs

1. To use profanely insolent language against
2. To call upon divine or supernatural power to send injury upon
3. To bring great evil upon

- **Luke 6:28:** "Bless those who curse you, pray for those who abuse you."
- **Romans 12:14:** Bless those who persecute you; bless and do not curse them.
- **Galatians 3:10–14:** For all who rely on works of the law are under a curse; for it is written, "Cursed be everyone who does not abide by all things written in the Book of the Law, and do them." Now it is evident that no one is justified before God by the law, for "The righteous shall live by faith." But the law is not of faith, rather "The one who does them shall live by them." Christ redeemed us from the curse of the law by becoming a curse for us—for it is written, "Cursed is everyone who is hanged on a tree"—so that in Christ Jesus the blessing of Abraham might come to the Gentiles, so that we might receive the promised Spirit through faith.

Reflections:

_____
_____
_____
_____
_____
_____
_____
_____
_____

Prayer:

Heavenly Father,

I come before You with a humble and repentant heart, seeking Your guidance and grace. Lord, I renounce any curses that may have been spoken over my life or that I have unknowingly embraced. I reject their power in the name of Jesus Christ.

Thank You, Father, for sending Your Son to redeem me from the curse of the law by becoming a curse for me. I gratefully receive the blessing of Abraham that comes through Christ Jesus.

Help me, Lord, to live by faith and not by works of the law. Strengthen me to bless those who curse me and to pray for those who mistreat me. Give me the grace to bless and not curse, even in the face of persecution. I choose to walk in the blessings You have prepared for me. Fill me with Your Holy Spirit, that I might live according to Your will and experience the fullness of Your promises.

In Jesus' name I pray, Amen.

My own prayer:

_____

_____

_____

_____

_____

_____

_____

_____

Deaf and Dumb

Adjectives

1. People who are spiritually "deaf" are those who do not listen to or heed God's Word or commands
2. "Dumb" indicates a lack of ability to proclaim or share God's truth

- **Mark 9:29:** And he said to them, "This kind cannot be driven out by anything but prayer."
- **Mark 9:25:** And when Jesus saw that a crowd came running together, he rebuked the unclean spirit, saying to it, "You mute and deaf spirit, I command you, come out of him and never enter him again."
- **Matthew 17:14–20:** And when they came to the crowd, a man came up to him and, kneeling before him, said, "Lord, have mercy on my son, for he has seizures and he suffers terribly. For often he falls into the fire, and often into the water. And I brought him to your disciples, and they could not heal him." And Jesus answered, "O faithless and twisted generation, how long am I to be with you? How long am I to bear with you? Bring him here to me." And Jesus rebuked the demon, and it came out of him, and the boy was healed instantly. Then the disciples came to Jesus privately and said, "Why could we not cast it out?" He said to them, "Because of your little faith. For truly, I say to you, if you have faith like a grain of mustard seed, you will say to this mountain, 'Move from here to there,' and it will move, and nothing will be impossible for you."
- **Mark 9:23:** And Jesus said to him, "'If you can'! All things are possible for one who believes."

Reflections:

_____
_____
_____
_____
_____
_____
_____

WARFARE BATTLECARDS

Prayer:

Almighty God,

I come before You in holy reverence, acknowledging Your supreme power over all creation. Lord, You who created the ears to hear and the mouth to speak, I stand in awe of Your authority over the deaf and dumb spirits.

Father, I confess my need for greater faith. Forgive my unbelief and increase my faith, even if it's as small as a mustard seed. Holy Spirit, awaken my soul and spirit, so that I may yield to the Son of God, calling Jesus my Lord and Savior.

Jesus, You demonstrated Your power by rebuking the unclean spirits and healing the afflicted. I believe that all things are possible for those who believe in You. Strengthen my faith, Lord, that I might trust fully in Your ability to overcome any obstacle.

I humbly recognize that some battles can only be won through prayer. Teach me to pray fervently and persistently, relying on Your power rather than my own understanding or abilities. May Your name be glorified through the miraculous works You perform.

I trust in Your mercy and compassion for those who suffer, just as You had mercy on the boy with seizures.

In the powerful name of Jesus Christ I pray, Amen.

My own prayer:

_____
_____
_____
_____

Death

noun
ˈdeth

1. A permanent cessation of all vital functions
2. The cause or occasion of loss of life

1. **Philippians 1:21:** For to me to live is Christ, and to die is gain.
2. **Hebrews 9:27–28:** And just as it is appointed for man to die once, and after that comes judgment, so Christ, having been offered once to bear the sins of many, will appear a second time, not to deal with sin but to save those who are eagerly waiting for him.
3. **1 Thessalonians 4:16:** For the Lord himself will descend from heaven with a cry of command, with the voice of an archangel, and with the sound of the trumpet of God. And the dead in Christ will rise first.
4. **Proverbs 18:21:** Death and life are in the power of the tongue, and those who love it will eat its fruits.
5. **John 14:6:** Jesus said to him, "I am the way, and the truth, and the life. No one comes to the Father except through me."
6. **Acts 3:14–16:** But you denied the Holy and Righteous One, and asked for a murderer to be granted to you, and you killed the Author of life, whom God raised from the dead. To this we are witnesses. And his name—by faith in his name—has made this man strong whom you see and know, and the faith that is through Jesus has given the man this perfect health in the presence of you all.
7. **Romans 6:4:** We were buried therefore with him by baptism into death, in order that, just as Christ was raised from the dead by the glory of the Father, we too might walk in the newness of life.
8. **2 Corinthians 1:8–9:** For we do not want you to be unaware, brothers, of the affliction we experienced in Asia. For we were so utterly burdened beyond our strength that we despaired of life itself. Indeed, we felt that we had received the sentence of death. But that was to make us rely not on ourselves but on God who raises the dead.

Reflections:

Prayer:

Heavenly Father,

I come before You, acknowledging that You are the author of life. In Your wisdom, You have appointed a time for all to die, and I trust in Your perfect plan. Lord, I am grateful that for me, to live is Christ and to die is gain. Though I may face the shadow of death, I find hope in Your promise of eternal life through Jesus Christ. I am comforted knowing that Christ has borne my sins and will return to save those who eagerly await Him. I look forward to the day when the dead in Christ will rise at the sound of Your trumpet.

Father, help me to use the power of my tongue to speak life, not death. May my words bring hope and encouragement to those around me. I am thankful that Jesus is the Way, the Truth, and the Life. Through Him, I have access to You and the assurance of everlasting life. Lord, just as Christ was raised from the dead, I pray for the strength to walk in newness of life. In times of affliction and despair, teach me to rely not on myself, but on You, the God who raises the dead.

In Jesus' name I pray, Amen.

My own prayer:

_____

_____

_____

_____

_____

_____

_____

_____

Look to the LORD and his strength; seek his face always. - 1 Chronicles 16:11

Deception

noun
di-'sep-shən

1. The act of causing someone to accept as true or valid what is false or invalid

- **Galatians 6:7–8:** Do not be deceived: God is not mocked, for whatever one sows, that will he also reap. For the one who sows to his own flesh will from the flesh reap corruption, but the one who sows to the Spirit will from the Spirit reap eternal life.
- **Proverbs 10:9:** Whoever walks in integrity walks securely, but he who makes his ways crooked will be found out.
- **Proverbs 12:22:** Lying lips are an abomination to the Lord, but those who act faithfully are his delight.
- **1 Corinthians 15:33:** Do not be deceived: "Bad company ruins good morals."
- **1 John 2:15:** Do not love the world or the things in the world. If anyone loves the world, the love of the Father is not in him.
- **Proverbs 19:9:** A false witness will not go unpunished, and he who breathes out lies will perish.
- **2 Corinthians 11:13–15:** For such men are false apostles, deceitful workmen, disguising themselves as apostles of Christ. And no wonder, for even Satan disguises himself as an angel of light. So it is no surprise if his servants, also, disguise themselves as servants of righteousness. Their end will correspond to their deeds.
- **Romans 12:2:** Do not be conformed to this world, but be transformed by the renewal of your mind, that by testing you may discern what is the will of God, what is good and acceptable and perfect.
- **Proverbs 11:3:** The integrity of the upright guides them, but the crookedness of the treacherous destroys them.
- **James 1:22:** But be doers of the word, and not hearers only, deceiving yourselves.
- **1 John 4:1:** Beloved, do not believe every spirit, but test the spirits to see whether they are from God, for many false prophets have gone out into the world.
- **2 Peter 2:1:** But false prophets also arose among the people, just as there will be false teachers among you, how will secretly bring destructive heresies.
- **James 1:26:** If anyone thinks he is religious and does not bridle his tongue but deceives his heart, this person's religion is worthless.
- **James 4:11:** Do not speak evil against one another, brothers. The one who speaks against a

brother or judges his brother, speaks evil against the law and judges the law. But if you judge the law, you are not a doer of the law but a judge.
- **2 Timothy 3:13:** While evil people and impostors will go on from bad to worse, deceiving and being deceived.
- **1 Timothy 4:1:** Now the Spirit expressly says that in later times some will depart from the faith by devoting themselves to deceitful spirits and teachings of demons.

Reflections:

___

Prayer:

Heavenly Father,

I come before You in humility and reverence, acknowledging Your supreme wisdom and truth. Lord, I trust You above all else. Father, Your Word repeatedly warns us not to be deceived. Grant me discernment to distinguish Your truth from deceit.

Holy Spirit, help me control my emotions so I remain focused on the foundational truths of my God, not swayed by cultural trends or new age deceptions.

Lord, instill in me a deep love for Your truth. Guide me to walk in integrity, that I may not fall prey to false teachers. Sharpen my words to align with Your godly truth. Give me courage to distance myself from bad company, remembering Your warning that it corrupts good character. Holy Spirit, bridle my tongue; let no evil or deceit come from my lips.

Forgive me, Lord, for times I've spread deception or unknowingly participated in evil schemes. Teach me to test every spirit, as instructed in James. Transform me by the renewal of my mind, that I may discern Your will—what is good, acceptable, and perfect. Let me be a doer of Your Word, not merely a hearer, deceiving myself.

In Jesus' name I pray, Amen

My own prayer:

_____

_____

_____

_____

_____

You rule over the surging sea; when its waves mount up, you still them. - Psalm 89:9

Declare

verb
di-ˈkler

1. To make known formally, officially, or explicitly
2. To make known as a determination

- **Philippians 4:13:** I can do all things through [Christ] who strengthens me.
- **2 Corinthians 5:17:** Therefore, if anyone is in Christ, he is a new creation. The old has passed away; behold, the new has come.
- **1 John 4:4:** Little children, you are from God and have overcome them, for he who is in you is greater than he who is in the world.
- **Isaiah 54:17:** No weapon that is fashioned against you shall succeed.
- **Deuteronomy 28:6:** Blessed shall you be when you come in, and blessed shall you be when you go out.
- **Nehemiah 8:10:** . . . for the joy of the Lord is your strength.
- **Matthew 5:14:** "You are the light of the world. A city on a hill cannot be hidden."
- **Romans 8:37:** No, in all these things we are more than conquerors through him who loved us.
- **Romans 8:1:** There is therefore now no condemnation for those who are in Christ Jesus.
- **Psalm 23:1:** The Lord is my shepherd; I shall not want.

Reflections:

_____
_____
_____
_____
_____
_____
_____

Prayer:

Heavenly Father,

I come before You, acknowledging Your sovereignty and the power of Your Word. Lord, I declare: I am strengthened through Christ to accomplish all things. In Jesus, I am made new. Your presence within me is greater than any worldly force. No weapon formed against me shall succeed. I am blessed in all my comings and goings. Your joy, Lord, is the source of my strength. As Your child, I am called to be a light in this world.

Through Your love, I am more than a conqueror. In Christ, I stand free from condemnation. You are my shepherd, providing for all my needs. Holy Spirit, guide me to speak these truths in faith, aligning my words with Your will. Forgive me for the times I've spoken contrary to Your truth. Help me to declare Your Word boldly, not as a formula, but as an expression of my trust in You.

In Jesus' name I pray, Amen.

My own prayer:

_____
_____
_____
_____
_____
_____
_____

Deliverance

noun

di-'li-v(ə-)rən(t)s

1. The act of delivering someone or something; the state of being delivered (set free)

- **Psalm 18:2:** The Lord is my rock and my fortress and my deliverer, my God, my rock, in whom I take refuge, my shield, and the horn of my salvation, my stronghold.
- **Ephesians 6:10–20:** Finally, be strong in the Lord and in the strength of his might. Put on the whole armor of God, that you may be able to stand against the schemes of the devil. For we do not wrestle against flesh and blood, but against the rulers, against the authorities, against the cosmic powers over this present darkness, against the spiritual forces of evil in the heavenly places. Therefore take up the whole armor of God, that you may be able to withstand in the evil day, and having done all, to stand firm. Stand therefore, having fastened on the belt of truth, and having put on the breastplate of righteousness, and, as shoes for your feet, having put on the readiness given by the gospel of peace. In all circumstances take up the shield of faith, with which you can extinguish all the flaming darts of the evil one; and take the helmet of salvation, and the sword of the Spirit, which is the word of God, praying at all times in the Spirit, with all prayer and supplication. To that end, keep alert with all perseverance, making supplication for all the saints, and also for me, that words may be given to me in opening my mouth boldly to proclaim the mystery of the gospel, for which I am an ambassador in chains, that I may declare it boldly, as I ought to speak.
- **James 5:16:** Therefore, confess your sins to one another and pray for one another, that you may be healed. The prayer of a righteous person has great power as it is working.
- **John 8:32:** "And you will know the truth, and the truth will set you free."
- **Psalm 34:4:** I sought the Lord, and he answered me and delivered me from all my fears.
- **Psalm 107:6:** Then they cried to the Lord in their trouble, and he delivered them from their distress.
- **Psalm 50:15:** And call upon me in the day of trouble; I will deliver you, and you shall glorify me.
- **Matthew 10:8:** "Heal the sick, raise the dead, cleanse lepers, cast out demons. You received without paying; give without pay."
- **Luke 1:71:** That we should be saved from our enemies and from the hand of all who hate us.
- **Acts 16:31:** And they said, "Believe in the Lord Jesus, and you will be saved, you and your household."

- **James 1:21:** Therefore put away all filthiness and rampant wickedness and receive with meekness the implanted word, which is able to save your souls.
- **Galatians 5:1:** For freedom Christ has set us free; stand firm therefore, and do not submit again to a yoke of slavery.
- **Romans 1:16:** For I am not ashamed of the gospel, for it is the power of God for salvation to everyone who believes, to the Jew first and also to the Greek.
- **Isaiah 45:22:** Turn to me and be saved, all the ends of the earth! For I am God, and there is no other.
- **Exodus 15:2:** The Lord is my strength and my song, and he has become my salvation; this is my God, and I will praise him, my father's God, and I will exalt him.
- **Ephesians 2:8:** For by grace you have been saved through faith. And this is not your own doing; it is the gift of God.
- **Psalm 18:17:** He rescued me from my strong enemy and from those who hated me, for they were too mighty for me.

Reflections:

_____

_____

_____

_____

_____

_____

_____

_____

_____

_____

_____

Prayer:

Heavenly Father,

I come before You in desperation and humility, acknowledging You as my rock, my fortress, and my deliverer. Lord, I am in dire need of Your salvation and deliverance. I confess my sins to You, O God. I repent of my filthiness and rampant wickedness. Create in me a clean heart and renew a right spirit within me. I receive with meekness Your implanted word, which is able to save my soul.

Lord, I recognize that my struggle is not against flesh and blood, but against the rulers, authorities, powers of this dark world, and spiritual forces of evil in the heavenly realms. Strengthen me in You and in Your mighty power. I put on the full armor of God. I fasten the belt of truth around my waist and put on the breastplate of righteousness. I fit my feet with the readiness that comes from the gospel of peace. I take up the shield of faith to extinguish all the flaming arrows of the evil one. I put on the helmet of salvation and take the sword of the Spirit, which is Your Word.

Lord, deliver me from all my fears and from the hands of my enemies who are too mighty for me. In my distress, I cry out to You. Save me from those who hate me and from all who seek to harm me. As You deliver me, I pray for Your Holy Spirit to fill every place in me that has been liberated. Where darkness once dwelt, let Your light shine. Where bondage held sway, let Your freedom reign. Fill me with Your presence, Your power, and Your love. I believe in the Lord Jesus Christ. I am not ashamed of the gospel, for it is the power of God for salvation. I turn to You, Lord, to be saved. You alone are God, and there is no other.

Set me free, O Christ, and help me stand firm in the freedom You have given. Let me not submit again to any yoke of slavery. May Your truth liberate me from all bondage. Be my strength and my song, O God. Become my salvation anew. I will praise and exalt You, for You are my God and my deliverer.

In Jesus' name I pray, Amen.

My own prayer:

Demonic

adjective
di-'mä-nik

1. Of, relating to, or suggestive of a demon

- **James 4:7:** Submit yourselves therefore to God. Resist the devil, and he will flee from you.
- **James 2:19:** You believe that God is one; you do well. Even the demons believe—and shudder!
- **1 Peter 5:8:** Be sober-minded; be watchful. Your adversary the devil prowls around like a roaring lion, seeking someone to devour.
- **Ephesians 6:12:** For we do not wrestle against flesh and blood, but against the rulers, against the authorities, against the cosmic powers over this present darkness, against the spiritual forces of evil in the heavenly places.
- **1 John 4:1:** Beloved, do not believe every spirit, but test the spirits to see whether they are from God, for many false prophets have gone out into the world.
- **1 Corinthians 10:20:** No, I imply that what pagans sacrifice they offer to demons and not to God. I do not want you to be participants with demons.
- **Mark 3:11:** And whenever the unclean spirits saw him, they fell down before him and cried out, "You are the Son of God."

Reflections:

_____
_____
_____
_____
_____
_____
_____

Prayer:

Heavenly Father,

I come before You in complete surrender, acknowledging Your supreme authority over all creation, including the demonic realm. Lord, I submit myself entirely to You. In Your strength, I resist the devil, trusting in Your promise that he will flee from me. I recognize that even demons believe in Your existence and tremble before You.

Father, grant me a sober and watchful mind. I know that my adversary, the devil, prowls around like a roaring lion, seeking someone to devour. Keep me vigilant and protected under Your mighty wings. I acknowledge, O God, that my struggle is not against flesh and blood, but against the rulers, authorities, cosmic powers over this present darkness, and the spiritual forces of evil in the heavenly places. Equip me with Your full armor to stand firm against these forces.

Holy Spirit, grant me discernment to test every spirit, knowing that many false prophets have gone out into the world. Keep me from being deceived by demonic influences disguised as light.

Lord Jesus, I recognize You as the Son of God, before whom even unclean spirits fall and cry out. In Your name, I renounce any participation with demons or pagan practices. I surrender all areas of my life to You, Lord. Where there is darkness, bring Your light. Where there is bondage, bring Your freedom. I trust in Your power to overcome all evil.

In the mighty name of Jesus Christ I pray, Amen.

My own prayer:

_____

_____

_____

_____

Dependence

noun

di-ˈpen-dən(t)s

1. The quality or state of being influenced or determined by or subject to another
2. Reliance

- **John 5:15:** The man went away and told the Jews that it was Jesus who had healed him.
- **John 6:47–50:** "Truly, truly, I say to you, whoever believes has eternal life. I am the bread of life. Your fathers ate the manna in the wilderness, and they died. This is the bread that comes down from heaven, so that one may eat of it and not die."
- **Isaiah 41:13:** For I, the Lord your God, hold your right hand; it is I who say to you, "Fear not, I am the one who helps you."
- **Psalm 73:26:** My flesh and my heart may fail, but God is the strength of my heart and my portion forever.
- **Psalm 94:18:** When I thought, "My foot slips," your steadfast love, O Lord, held me up.
- **Proverbs 3:5–6:** Trust in the Lord with all your heart, and do not lean on your own understanding. In all your ways acknowledge him, and he will make straight your paths.
- **Psalm 121:1–2:** I lift up my eyes to the hills. From where does my help come? My help comes from the Lord, who made heaven and earth.
- **John 5:19:** So Jesus said to them, "Truly, truly, I say to you, the Son can do nothing of his own accord, but only what he sees the Father doing. For whatever the Father does, that the Son does likewise."

Reflections:

_____
_____
_____
_____
_____
_____

Prayer:

Heavenly Father,

I come before You in humility, acknowledging my complete dependence on You. Lord, You are the bread of life, the source of my eternal sustenance. Just as You provided manna in the wilderness, I trust You to nourish my soul daily. Father, I confess my tendency to rely on my own understanding. Forgive me for the times I've leaned on my own strength instead of Yours. I lift my eyes to You, for my help comes from You alone, the Maker of heaven and earth.

Lord, hold my right hand and calm my fears. When my foot slips, let Your steadfast love hold me up. Though my flesh and heart may fail, I declare that You are the strength of my heart and my portion forever.

Jesus, teach me to follow Your example, doing nothing of my own accord but only what I see the Father doing. May I trust in You with all my heart, acknowledging You in all my ways. Guide my paths, O Lord. May I always recognize and proclaim that it is You who heals, sustains, and gives life. In my weakness, be my strength. In my uncertainty, be my wisdom.

In Jesus' name I pray, Amen.

My own prayer:

_____
_____
_____
_____
_____
_____
_____

Destiny

noun
'de-stə-nē

1. Something to which a person or thing is destined
2. A predetermined course of events

- **Philippians 3:12 (NKJV):** Not that I have already attained, or am already perfected; but I press on, that I may lay hold of that for which Christ Jesus has also laid hold of me.
- **Jeremiah 29:11:** For I know the plans I have for you, declares the Lord, plans for welfare and not for evil, to give you a future and a hope.
- **Job 23:14:** For he will complete what he appoints for me, and many such things are in his mind.
- **Psalm 73:24:** You guide me with your counsel, and afterward you will receive me to glory.
- **Daniel 12:13:** But go your way till the end. And you shall rest and shall stand in your allotted place at the end of the days.
- **Revelation 1:8:** "I am the Alpha and the Omega," says the Lord God, "who is and who was and who is to come, the Almighty."

Reflections:

___

___

___

___

___

___

___

___

___

Prayer:

Heavenly Father,

I come before You in humility, acknowledging Your almighty power and sovereignty over my life. I trust You with full faith regarding my destiny. Lord, I surrender my will to align with Yours. Guide my future, my purpose, my plans, and desires. Purge anything in me that is contrary to the destiny You have prepared for me.

Abba, help me to press on, that I may lay hold of that for which Christ Jesus has laid hold of me. I trust in Your word spoken through Jeremiah, that You know the plans You have for me–plans for good not evil, to give me a future and a hope.

Holy Spirit, strengthen my faith to believe that You will complete what You have appointed for me. Guide me with Your counsel, and I trust that afterward, You will receive me to glory.

Lord, grant me the perseverance to continue in Your service, even when I don't fully understand Your plans. Help me to trust in Your wisdom and timing, knowing that You have appointed my days. I thank You for the promise of rest that awaits me. When my earthly journey is complete, I look forward to the peace and comfort of resting in Your presence.

I rest in the assurance that You are the Alpha and the Omega, who is and who was and who is to come. My destiny is secure in Your hands.

In Jesus' name I pray, Amen.

My own prayer:

_____

_____

_____

_____

Destroy

verb
di-ˈstrȯi

1. To ruin the structure, organic existence, or condition of

- **Psalm 18:10–12 (KJV):** And he rode upon a cherub, and did fly: yea, he did fly upon the wings of the wind. He made darkness his secret place; his pavilion round about him were dark waters and thick clouds of the skies. At the brightness that was before him his thick clouds passed, hail stones and coals of fire.
- **Psalm 144:5–6:** Bow your heavens, O Lord, and come down! Touch the mountains so that they smoke! Flash forth the lightning and scatter them; send out your arrows and rout them!
- **Psalm 145:20:** The Lord preserves all who love him, but all the wicked he will destroy.
- **Ecclesiastes 7:16:** Be not overly righteous, and do not make yourself too wise. Why should you destroy yourself?
- **Isaiah 42:14 (KJV):** I have long time holden my peace; I have been still, and refrained myself: now will I cry like a travailing woman; I will destroy and devour at once.
- **Jeremiah 17:18:** Let those be put to shame who persecute me, but let me not be put to shame; let them be dismayed, but let me not be dismayed; bring upon them the day of disaster; destroy them with double destruction!
- **Jeremiah 49:38:** And I will set my throne in Elam and destroy their king and officials, declares the Lord.
- **Mark 1:24–25:** "What have you to do with us, Jesus of Nazareth? Have you come to destroy us? I know who you are—the Holy One of God." But Jesus rebuked him, saying, "Be silent, and come out of him!"
- **Mark 9:21–23:** And Jesus asked his father, "How long has this been happening to him?" And he said, "From childhood. And it has often cast him into fire and into water, to destroy him. But if you can do anything, have compassion on us and help us." And Jesus said to him, "'If you can'! All things are possible for one who believes."
- **John 10:10:** "The thief comes only to steal and kill and destroy. I came that they may have life and have it abundantly."

Reflections:

Prayer:

Heavenly Father,

I come before You in reverence, surrendering to Your mighty power and seeking Your wisdom and protection.

Lord, keep me close to You. Your Word warns that in later times, some will depart from the faith, devoting themselves to deceitful spirits and teachings of demons. I proclaim my unwavering faith in You, and ask that You remove any doubt from my soul. Abba, You are the God who builds and breaks, who gives and takes away. As Your Word says, "Bow your heavens, O Lord, and come down! Touch the mountains so that they smoke!" I turn my whole heart to You, knowing that while the wicked will be destroyed, You preserve all who love You.

Holy Spirit, help me remain humble. Keep me from being overly righteous or too wise, lest I destroy myself. Grant me alertness to recognize the thief who comes to steal, kill, and destroy. Instead, let me turn to You, the one who gives life abundantly.

Lord, as You have promised to set Your throne in Elam and destroy their king and officials, I trust in Your sovereignty over all powers and authorities. When faced with spiritual opposition, let me remember Jesus' authority to silence and cast out evil. Father, I believe that all things are possible for one who believes. Strengthen my faith, that I may stand firm against any force that seeks to destroy. Let me not be put to shame or dismayed, but rather, let Your light shine through me.

In Jesus' name I pray, Amen.

My own prayer:

_____

_____

_____

_____

**For in him all things were created: things in heaven and on earth, visible and invisible, whether thrones or powers or rulers or authorities; all things have been created through him and for him.
- Colossians 1:16**

Discernment

noun

di-ˈsərn-mənt

1. The quality of being able to comprehend what is obscure

- **Hebrews 5:14:** But solid food is for the mature, for those who have their powers of discernment trained by constant practice to distinguish good from evil.
- **Philippians 1:9–10:** And it is my prayer that your love may abound more and more, with knowledge and all discernment, so that you may approve what is excellent, and so be pure and blameless for the day of Christ.
- **1 Kings 3:9:** Give your servant therefore an understanding mind to govern your people, that I may discern between good and evil, for who is able to govern this your great people?
- **1 Corinthians 2:14:** The natural person does not accept the things of the Spirit of God, for they are folly to him, and he is not able to understand them because they are spiritually discerned.
- **1 Thessalonians 5:21:** But test everything; hold fast to what is good.
- **Hosea 14:9:** Whoever is wise, let him understand these things; whoever is discerning, let him know them; for the ways of the Lord are right, and the upright walk in them, but transgressors stumble in them.
- **Proverbs 15:14:** The heart of him who has understanding seeks knowledge, but the mouths of fools feed on folly.
- **John 7:24:** "Do not judge by appearances, but judge with right judgment."

Reflections:

_____

_____

_____

_____

_____

_____

Prayer:

Heavenly Father,

I come before You in awe of Your grace and mercy. Lord, I humbly seek Your wisdom and discernment. Grant me the discipline to consume the solid food of Your Word, training my powers of discernment through constant practice to distinguish good from evil. Father, I echo Paul's prayer for the Philippians: may my love abound more and more, with knowledge and all discernment, so that I may approve what is excellent and be pure and blameless for the day of Christ.

Holy Spirit, give me an understanding mind to discern between good and evil. Help me to accept and understand the things of the Spirit, which are spiritually discerned.

Lord, teach me to test everything and hold fast to what is good. May I seek knowledge with a pure heart, growing in wisdom and understanding of Your ways. Almighty God, keep me from judging by appearances. Instead, guide me to judge with right judgment, always seeking Your perspective.

In Jesus' name I pray, Amen.

My own prayer:

_____

_____

_____

_____

_____

_____

_____

_____

Divination

noun

di-və-ˈnā-shən

1. That art or practice that seeks to foresee future events or discover hidden knowledge, usually by the interpretations of omens or by the aid of supernatural powers

- **Leviticus 19:31:** Do not turn to mediums or necromancers; do not seek them out, and so make yourselves unclean by them: I am the Lord your God.
- **Leviticus 19:26:** You shall not eat any flesh with the blood in it. You shall not interpret omens or tell fortunes.
- **Leviticus 20:27:** A man or a woman who is a medium or a necromancer shall surely be put to death. They shall be stoned with stones; their blood shall be upon them.
- **Leviticus 20:6:** If a person turns to mediums and necromancers, whoring after them, I will set my face against that person and will cut him off from among his people.
- **1 Samuel 15:23:** For rebellion is as the sin of divination, and presumption is as inquiry and idolatry. Because you have rejected the word of the Lord, he has also rejected you from being king.
- **Isaiah 8:19:** And when they say to you, "Inquire of the mediums and the necromancers who chirp and mutter," should not a people inquire of their God? Should they inquire of the dead on behalf of the living?
- **Galatians 5:19–24:** Now the works of the flesh are evident: sexual immorality, impurity, sensuality, idolatry, sorcery, enmity, strife, jealousy, fits of anger, rivalries, dissensions, divisions, envy, drunkenness, orgies, and things like these. I warn you, as I warned you before, that those who do such things will not inherit the kingdom of God. But the fruit of the Spirit is love, joy, peace, patience, kindness, goodness, faithfulness, gentleness, self-control; against such things there is no law. And those who belong to Christ Jesus have crucified the flesh with its passions and desires.
- **Deuteronomy 18:10:** There shall not be found among you anyone who burns his son or his daughter as an offering, anyone who practices divination or tells fortunes or interprets omens, or a sorcerer.
- **Hosea 4:12:** My people inquire of a piece of wood, and their walking staff gives them oracles. For a spirit of whoredom has led them astray, and they have left their God to play the whore.

- **Zechariah 10:2 (NKJV)**: For the idols speak delusion; the diviners envision lies; and they tell false dreams; they comfort in vain. Therefore the people wend their way like sheep; they are in trouble because there is no shepherd.
- **2 Kings 21:6**: And he burned his son as an offering, and used fortune-telling and omens, and dealt with mediums and with necromancers. He did much evil in the sight of the Lord, provoking him to anger.
- **Jeremiah 14:14**: And the Lord said to me, "The prophets are prophesying lies in my name. I did not send them, nor did I command them or speak to them. They are prophesying to you a lying vision, worthless divination, and the deceit of their own minds."
- **Isaiah 44:25**: who frustrates the signs of liars and makes fools of diviners, who turns wise men back and makes their knowledge foolish.
- **Hosea 4:13**: They sacrifice on the tops of mountains and burn offerings on the hills, under oak, poplar, and terebinth, because their shade is good. Therefore your daughters play the whore, and your brides commit adultery.
- **Isaiah 47:13**: You are wearied with your many counsels; let them stand forth and save you, those who divide the heavens, who gaze at the stars, who at the new moons make known what shall come upon you.
- **1 John 4:2**: By this you know the Spirit of God: every spirit that confesses that Jesus Christ has come in the flesh is from God.
- **Matthew 28:18**: And Jesus came and said to them, "All authority in heaven and on earth has been given to me."
- **Acts 19:18–19**: Also many of those who were now believers came, confessing and divulging their practices. And a number of those who had practiced magical arts brought their books together and burned them in the sight of all. And they counted the value of them and found it came to fifty thousand pieces of silver.
- **Acts 1:8**: But you will receive power when the Holy Spirit has come upon you, and you will be my witnesses in Jerusalem and in all Judea and Samaria, and to the end of the earth.
- **1 John 4:1**: Beloved, do not believe every spirit, but test the spirits to see whether they are from God, for many false prophets have gone out into the world.

Reflections:

_____

_____

_____

_____

Prayer:

Heavenly Father,

Almighty Creator of heaven and earth, the one true God of Abraham, Isaac, and Jacob. I come before You with reverence and repentance. Your Word is mighty and powerful, filled with instructions on how to communicate with You and obey Your will.

Lord, forgive me and my bloodline for any and all practices of divination. Your Word clearly states, "Do not turn to mediums or necromancers; do not seek them out and so make yourselves unclean by them: I am the Lord your God."

Holy Spirit, convict me and rid my soul of any form of rebellion, for Your Word declares that rebellion is as the sin of divination. Grant me awareness and strength to resist the carnal nature described in Galatians. As the world presents counterfeits to Your truth, give me spiritual eyes to discern such trickery. Put a pure desire in my heart to seek You and Your Word above man, culture, and the snares of the enemy.

Give me boldness and courage to speak Your truth with grace and love should I encounter divination. Help me to remember that we should inquire of You, our living God, not of the dead or false prophets. Lord, I pray for the fruit of Your Spirit to be evident in my life: love, joy, peace, patience, kindness, goodness, faithfulness, gentleness, and self-control. May these qualities guard me against the temptations of divination and sorcery.

In Jesus' name I pray, Amen.

My own prayer:

_____

_____

_____

_____

Fear not, for I am with you; be not dismayed, for I am your God; I will strengthen you, I will help you, I will uphold you with my righteous right hand. - Isaiah 41:10

Doorway

noun
ˈdȯr-ˌwā

1. The opening that a door closes

- **Ecclesiastes 10:8:** He who digs a pit will fall into it, and a serpent will bite him who breaks through a wall.
- **Hosea 4:6:** Many people are destroyed for lack of knowledge; because you have rejected knowledge, I reject you from being a priest to me. And since you have forgotten the law of your God, I will also forget your children.
- **2 Corinthians 4:3–4 (AMP):** But even if our gospel is [in some ways] hidden [behind a veil], it is hidden [only] to those who are perishing; among them the god of this world [Satan] has blinded the minds of the unbelieving, to prevent them from seeing the illuminating light of the gospel of the glory of Christ, who is the image of God.
- **Psalm 119:9–11:** How can a young man keep his way pure? By guarding it according to your word. With my whole heart I seek you; Let me not wander from your commandments! I have stored up your word in my heart, that I might not sin against you.
- **Isaiah 26:3:** You keep him in perfect peace whose mind is stayed on you, because he trusts in you.

Reflections:

_____
_____
_____
_____
_____
_____
_____

Prayer:

Heavenly Father,

I come before You in surrender to Your mighty power, love, and grace. Lord, make me aware of any pits I have dug that allow serpents to bite. By Your undeserved mercy, reveal to me any doorways I may have opened, causing my own demise and hindering my destiny and purpose.

When such doorways are revealed, grant me boldness and humility to follow Your commandments. Help me close these doorways permanently so that destruction ends with me. Create a pure and righteous heart within me, carrying over to generations to come.

Teach me, Lord, not the teachings of this world or false tongues, but how to avoid such doorways of destruction. Holy Spirit, wash me clean so that the gospel may shine, ushering in Your presence and displaying Your grand glory.

I seek Your Word as truth, renouncing any pledges or oaths made elsewhere. Keep my mind focused on You and You alone, O God. May I hide Your Word in my heart, that I might not sin against You.

In Jesus' name I pray, Amen

My own prayer:

_____
_____
_____
_____
_____
_____
_____

Double-Minded

adjective

1. Wavering in mind
2. Marked by hypocrisy

- **James 4:8:** Draw near to God, and he will draw near to you. Cleanse your hands, you sinners, and purify your hearts, you double-minded.
- **James 1:5–8:** If any of you lacks wisdom, let him ask God, who gives generously to all without reproach, and it will be given him. But let him ask in faith, with no doubting, for the one who doubts is like a wave of the sea that is driven and tossed by the wind. For that person must not suppose that he will receive anything from the Lord; he is a double-minded man, unstable in all his ways.
- **1 Peter 5:8:** Be sober-minded; be watchful. Your adversary the devil prowls around like a roaring lion, seeking someone to devour.
- **Matthew 6:22–24:** "The eye is the lamp of the body. So, if your eye is healthy, your whole body will be full of light, but if your eye is bad, your whole body will be full of darkness. If then the light in you is darkness, how great is the darkness! No one can serve two masters, for either he will hate the one and love the other, or he will be devoted to the one and despise the other. You cannot serve God and money."
- **James 4:7:** Submit yourselves therefore to God. Resist the devil, and he will flee from you.
- **1 Peter 4:12–13:** Beloved, do not be surprised at the fiery trial when it comes upon you to test you, as though something strange were happening to you. But rejoice insofar as you share Christ's sufferings, that you may also rejoice and be glad when his glory is revealed.
- **2 Corinthians 7:1:** Since we have these promises, beloved, let us cleanse ourselves from every defilement of body and spirit, bringing holiness to completion in the fear of God.
- **Galatians 5:16:** But I say, walk by the Spirit, and you will not gratify the desires of the flesh.
- **Acts 2:38:** And Peter said to them, "Repent and be baptized every one of you in the name of Jesus Christ for the forgiveness of your sins, and you will receive the gift of the Holy Spirit."
- **Isaiah 11:2:** And the Spirit of the Lord shall rest upon him, the Spirit of wisdom and understanding, the Spirit of counsel and might, the Spirit of knowledge and fear of the Lord.
- **John 14:26:** "But the Helper, the Holy Spirit, whom the Father will send in my name, he will teach you all things and bring to your remembrance all that I have said to you."
- **Deuteronomy 6:4–9:** Hear, O Israel: The Lord our God, the Lord is one. You shall love the Lord your God with all your heart and with all your soul and with all your might. And these

words that I command you today shall be on your heart. You shall teach them diligently to your children, and shall talk of them when you sit in your house, and when you walk by the way, and when you lie down, and when you rise. You shall bind them as a sign on your hand, and they shall be as frontlets between your eyes. You shall write them on the doorposts of your house and on your gates.

- **Psalm 91:** He who dwells in the shelter of the Most High will abide in the shadow of the Almighty. I will say to the Lord, "My refuge and my fortress, my God, in whom I trust." For he will deliver you from the snare of the fowler and from the deadly pestilence. He will cover you with his pinions, and under his wings you will find refuge; his faithfulness is a shield and buckler. You will not fear the terror of the night, nor the arrow that flies by day, nor the pestilence that stalks in darkness, nor the destruction that wastes at noonday. A thousand may fall at your side, ten thousand at your right hand, but it will not come near you. You will only look with your eyes and see the recompense of the wicked. Because you have made the Lord your dwelling place the Most High, who is my refuge—no evil shall be allowed to befall you, no plague come near your tent. For he will command his angels concerning you to guard you in all your ways. On their hands they will bear you up, lest you strike your foot against a stone. You will tread on the lion and the adder; the young lion and the serpent you will trample underfoot. "Because he holds fast to me in love, I will deliver him; I will protect him, because he knows my name. When he calls to me, I will answer him; I will be with him in trouble; I will rescue him and honor him. With long life I will satisfy him and show him my salvation."
- **James 1:2:** Count it all joy, my brothers, when you meet trials of various kinds.

Reflections:

_____
_____
_____
_____
_____
_____
_____
_____

Prayer:

Heavenly Father,

I come before You, seeking refuge, clarity, and understanding. I am drawing near to You, O God, trusting that You will cleanse my hands and purify my heart. I am seeking Your wisdom, Lord, in full faith that You give it generously. Help me to be of a sober mind, submitting myself to You and Your Word, resisting the schemes of the enemy.

I declare that I cannot serve two masters. My eyes are fixed on You, Lord, that my whole body may be full of light. I choose to serve You alone, not money or worldly desires. I submit myself to You, God. I resist the devil, knowing he will flee from me. In trials, I choose to rejoice, sharing in Christ's sufferings, looking forward to the revelation of His glory.

I am cleansing myself from every defilement of body and spirit, bringing holiness to completion in the fear of You, Lord. I choose to walk by the Spirit, not gratifying the desires of the flesh. I repent and receive the gift of Your Holy Spirit. May Your Spirit of wisdom, understanding, counsel, might, knowledge, and fear of the Lord rest upon me.

I love You, Lord my God, with all my heart, soul, and might. Your words are on my heart, guiding my every step. I dwell in Your shelter, Most High, abiding in Your shadow. You are my refuge and fortress, my God in whom I trust. I hold fast to You in love, knowing You will deliver, protect, and answer me. In all trials, I count it joy, for I know You are working in me. I am no longer double-minded, but stable and grounded in You.

In Jesus' name I pray, Amen.

My own prayer:

_____

_____

_____

Cast me not away from your presence, and take not your Holy Spirit from me. - Psalm 51:11

Doubt

verb
'daut

1. To call into question the truth of
2. To lack confidence in

- **James 1:6:** But let him ask in faith, with no doubting, for the one who doubts is like a wave of the sea that is driven and tossed by the wind.
- **Jude 1:22:** And have mercy for those who doubt.
- **Hebrews 11:1:** Now faith is the assurance of things hoped for, the conviction of things not seen.
- **Proverbs 3:5:** Trust in the Lord with all your heart and do not lean on your own understanding.
- **Mark 11:23:** "Truly, I say to you, whoever says to this mountain, 'Be taken up and thrown into the sea,' and does not doubt in his heart, but believes that what he says will come to pass, it will be done for him."
- **Mark 9:24:** Immediately the father of the child cried out and said, "I believe; help my unbelief!"
- **Isaiah 41:10:** Fear not, for I am with you; be not dismayed, for I am your God; I will strengthen you, I will help you, I will uphold you with my righteous right hand.
- **Proverbs 14:23:** In all toil there is profit, but mere talk tends only to poverty.
- **John 20:27:** Then he said to Thomas, "Put your finger here, and see my hands; and put out your hand, and place it in my side. Do not disbelieve, but believe."

Reflections:

_____
_____
_____
_____
_____
_____
_____

Prayer:

Heavenly Father,

I come before You in need of Your refreshment and mercy, as doubt has found a perch upon my head. With the small mustard seed of faith I possess, I come to You, not wanting to be like the waves getting tossed about by the wind.

Grant me the assurance of things hoped for and the conviction of things not seen. Let my life display the very words, "I trust in the Lord with all my heart and lean not on my own understanding." Lord, allow me the courage to grow my faith so that I can live Your Word, telling a mountain to move, glorifying You and You alone. I believe, help my unbelief!

I choose not to fear, for You are with me. I will not be dismayed, for You are my God. You will strengthen me, help me, and uphold me with Your righteous right hand. In all my toil, I trust there is profit. I will not merely talk, but act on my faith. Like Thomas, I reach out to touch Your wounds, choosing to believe and not disbelieve. Have mercy on me in my moments of doubt. Strengthen my faith, that I may stand firm and unwavering in my trust in You.

In Jesus' name I pray, Amen.

My own prayer:

_____
_____
_____
_____
_____
_____

Enemy

noun

'e-nə-mē

1. One that is antagonistic to another
2. Something harmful or deadly

- **Romans 12:14–21:** Bless those who persecute you; bless and do not curse them. Rejoice with those who rejoice, weep with those who weep. Live in harmony with one another. Do not be haughty, but associate with the lowly. Never be wise in your own sight. Repay no one evil for evil, but give thought to do what is honorable in the sight of all. If possible, so far as it depends on you, live peaceably with all. Beloved, never avenge yourselves, but leave it to the wrath of God, for it is written, "Vengeance is mine, I will repay, says the Lord." To the contrary, "if your enemy is hungry, feed him; if he is thirsty, give him something to drink; for by so doing you will heap burning coals on his head." Do not be overcome by evil, but overcome evil with good.
- **Luke 6:27–29:** "But I say to you who hear, Love your enemies, do good to those who hate you, bless those who curse you, pray for those who abuse you. To one who strikes you on the cheek, offer the other also, and from one who takes away your cloak do not withhold your tunic either."
- **Deuteronomy 31:6:** Be strong and courageous. Do not fear or be in dread of them, for it is the Lord your God who goes with you. He will not leave you or forsake you.
- **Psalm 23:4:** Even though I walk through the valley of the shadow of death, I will fear no evil, for you are with me; your rod and your staff, they comfort me.
- **Proverbs 25:21:** If your enemy is hungry, give him bread to eat, and if he is thirsty, give him water to drink.
- **Ephesians 2:8–9:** For by grace you have been saved through faith. And this is not your own doing; it is the gift of God, not a result of works, so that no one may boast.

Reflections:

_____

_____

_____

Prayer:

Heavenly Father,

I come before You in humility, seeking Your wisdom and strength. Lord, You are the almighty Creator of heaven and earth, the God who parted the Red Sea and brought down the walls of Jericho with shouts of praise. Nothing compares to Your power and love. Grant me, O Lord, the ability to bless those who persecute me, not to curse as the world would. When I am tempted to repay evil for evil, help me choose peace instead. Make me a peacemaker, overcoming evil with good.

Create in me a clean heart, Father, that I may love my enemies and do good to those who hate me. Give me the strength to bless those who curse me and to pray for those who abuse me. When my enemy is hungry, help me feed them; when they are thirsty, to give them something to drink. I trust in Your promise, Lord, that You will never leave nor forsake me. Even as I walk through the valley of the shadow of death, I will fear no evil, for You are with me. Your rod and Your staff comfort me.

Thank You, Abba, for Your grace which has saved me through faith. I acknowledge this is not my own doing, but Your gift, so that I cannot boast. Help me to be strong and courageous, not fearing or dreading my enemies, for I know that You, Lord my God, go with me. May my actions reflect Your love and bring glory to Your name.

In Jesus' name I pray, Amen.

My own prayer:

_____
_____
_____
_____
_____
_____

Evil

adjective
'ē-vəl

1. Morally reprehensible
2. Arising from actual or imputed bad character or conduct

- **Romans 12:21:** Do not be overcome by evil, but overcome evil with good.
- **Proverbs 8:13:** The fear of the Lord is hatred of evil. Pride and arrogance and the way of evil and perverted speech I hate.
- **Isaiah 5:20:** Woe to those who call evil good and good evil, who put darkness for light and light for darkness, who put bitter for sweet and sweet for bitter!
- **Genesis 50:20:** As for you, you meant evil against me, but God meant it for good, to bring it about that many people should be kept alive, as they are today.
- **Psalm 34:14:** Turn away from evil and do good; seek peace and pursue it.
- **Romans 12:9:** Let love be genuine. Abhor what is evil; hold fast to what is good.
- **Matthew 6:13:** "And lead us not into temptation, but deliver us from evil."
- **Proverbs 3:7:** Be not wise in your own eyes; fear the Lord, and turn away from evil.
- **1 John 1:9:** If we confess our sins, he is faithful and just to forgive us our sins and to cleanse us from all unrighteousness.

Reflections:

_____
_____
_____
_____
_____
_____
_____
_____

Prayer:

Heavenly Father,

I come before You in humility, seeking Your wisdom and salvation. As Your precious prayer declares, deliver me from evil.

Lord, I confess my sins to You, trusting in Your faithfulness and justice to forgive me and cleanse me from all unrighteousness. Uproot all forms of evil from my heart, mind, and soul.

Keep me teachable, O God, that I may run away from evil, fearing You and You alone. Holy Spirit, guide me to pursue peace, cultivating a genuine heart of love that turns away from evil and its temptations all the days of my life.

Grant me the strength to overcome evil with good, and the discernment to recognize and abhor what is evil, while holding fast to what is good. Let me not be wise in my own eyes but help me to fear You and turn away from evil.

When faced with those who call evil good and good evil, grant me the courage to speak truth with love and grace. Help me to see as You see, recognizing that even what others may intend for evil, You can use for good. May the fear of the Lord guide me to hate evil, pride, arrogance, and perverted speech. Let my life be a testament to Your goodness, overcoming darkness with Your light.

In Jesus' name I pray, Amen.

My own prayer:

_____

_____

_____

_____

Failure

noun
ˈfāl-yər

1. A failing to perform a duty or expected action
2. A state of inability to perform a normal function

- **Psalm 73:26:** My flesh and my heart may fail, but God is the strength of my heart and my portion forever.
- **Romans 3:23:** For all have sinned and fall short of the glory of God.
- **James 3:2:** For we all stumble in many ways. And if anyone does not stumble in what he says, he is a perfect man, able also to bridle his whole body.
- **Philippians 4:13:** I can do all things through him who strengthens me.
- **1 John 1:9:** If we confess our sins, he is faithful and just to forgive us our sins and to cleanse us from all unrighteousness.
- **Proverbs 24:16:** For the righteous falls seven times and rises again, but the wicked stumble in times of calamity.
- **Psalm 145:14:** The Lord upholds all who are falling and raises up all who are bowed down.

Reflections:

_____
_____
_____
_____
_____
_____
_____
_____
_____

Prayer:

Heavenly Father,

I come before You in humility, acknowledging my weaknesses and failures. Lord, my flesh and heart may fail, but You are the strength of my heart and my portion forever. Father, I confess that I have sinned and fallen short of Your glory. Like all others, I stumble in many ways. Yet, I take comfort in knowing that, when I confess, You are faithful and just to forgive my sins and cleanse me from all unrighteousness.

Holy Spirit, renew my spirit and remind me that I can do all things through Christ who strengthens me. When I fall, help me to rise again, for I know that the righteous may fall seven times but still get up.

Lord, I am grateful that You uphold all who are falling and raise up those who are bowed down. Grant me the humility to seek Your guidance first, and the strength to persevere through my failures.

In Jesus' name I pray, Amen.

My own prayer:

_____
_____
_____
_____
_____
_____
_____
_____
_____

Faith

noun
ˈfāths

1. Allegiance to duty or a person
2. Fidelity to one's promises

- **Matthew 21:22:** "And whatever you ask in prayer, you will receive, if you have faith."
- **Galatians 2:16:** Yet we know that a person is not justified by works of the law but through faith in Jesus Christ, so we also have believed in Christ Jesus, in order to be justified by faith in Christ and not by works of the law, because by works of the law no one will be justified.
- **Hebrews 11:6:** And without faith it is impossible to please him, for whoever would draw near to God must believe that he exists and that he rewards those who seek him.
- **Hebrews 11:1:** Now faith is the assurance of things hoped for, the conviction of things not seen.
- **Ephesians 2:8–9:** For by grace you have been saved through faith. And this is not your own doing; it is the gift of God, not a result of works, so that no one may boast.
- **James 2:17:** So also faith by itself, if it does not have works, is dead.
- **John 3:16:** "For God so loved the world, that he gave his only Son, that whoever believes in him should not perish but have eternal life."
- **Mark 9:23:** And Jesus said to him, "If you can'! All things are possible for one who believes."

Reflections:

_____
_____
_____
_____
_____
_____
_____
_____

Prayer:

Heavenly Father,

I come before You in complete surrender and unwavering faith. Your Word declares that whatever I ask in prayer, I shall receive if I have faith. I cling to this promise, trusting in Your faithfulness.

Lord, I thank You for the everlasting covenant through Jesus Christ. I acknowledge that I am not justified by the law or works, but through faith in Your Son. I understand that without faith, it is impossible to please You.

Father, I seek You earnestly, pressing into Your throne room to sit at Your feet. I choose faith over busyness, knowing that faith without works is dead. Yet, I also recognize that my salvation is by Your grace through faith, not of my own doing, so that I cannot boast.

I declare my belief that all things are possible through You. Strengthen my faith, Lord, that it may be the assurance of things hoped for and the conviction of things not seen.

Thank You for loving the world so much that You gave Your only Son. I place my trust in Him for eternal life.

Hear my prayer, O God, as I declare my faith in You and You alone. May my faith be alive and active, pleasing to You in every way.

In Jesus' name I pray, Amen.

My own prayer:

_____

_____

_____

_____

False Prophets

noun (plural)
ˈfȯls ˈprä-fət

1. Individuals who falsely claim to speak for God, often leading others astray with deceitful teachings
2. People who proclaim teachings contrary to sound doctrine, misleading followers for personal gain

- **Matthew 7:15:** "Beware of false prophets, who come to you in sheep's clothing but inwardly are ravenous wolves."
- **1 John 4:1:** Beloved, do not believe every spirit, but test the spirits to see whether they are from God, for many false prophets have gone out into the world.
- **Matthew 24:24:** "For false christs and false prophets will arise and perform great signs and wonders, so as to lead astray, if possible, even the elect."
- **2 Peter 2:1:** But false prophets also arose among the people, just as there will be false teachers among you, who will secretly bring in destructive heresies, even denying the Master who bought them, bringing upon themselves swift destruction.
- **2 Corinthians 13:5–8:** Examine yourselves, to see whether you are in the faith. Test yourselves. Or do you not realize this about yourselves, that Jesus Christ is in you?—unless indeed you fail to meet the test! I hope you will find out that we have not failed the test. But we pray to God that you may not do wrong—not that we may appear to have met the test, but that you may do what is right, though we may seem to have failed. For we cannot do anything against the truth, but only for the truth.
- **2 Timothy 4:3–4:** For the time is coming when people will not endure sound teaching, but having itching ears they will accumulate for themselves teachers to suit their own passions, and will turn away from listening to the truth and wander off into myths.
- **Jude 1:4:** For certain people have crept in unnoticed who long ago were designated for this condemnation, ungodly people, who pervert the grace of our God into sensuality and deny our only Master and Lord, Jesus Christ.
- **Romans 16:17–18:** I appeal to you, brothers, to watch out for those who cause divisions and create obstacles contrary to the doctrine that you have been taught; avoid them. For such persons do not serve our Lord Christ, but their own appetites, and by smooth talk and flattery they deceive the hearts of the naive.

Reflections:

Prayer:

Heavenly Father,

I come before You in humility, seeking Your wisdom and discernment. Lord, sharpen my spiritual senses to recognize false prophets who come in sheep's clothing but inwardly are ravenous wolves.

Grant me the discipline and courage to test every spirit, knowing that many false prophets have gone out into the world. Keep me grounded in Your Word, that I may not be led astray by signs and wonders.

Holy Spirit, guide me to discern truth from heresy. Help me examine my own faith, testing myself to ensure that Christ is truly in me.

Father, instill in me a love for sound teaching. May I hunger for Your truth that pierces through joint and marrow, rather than seeking words that merely tickle my ears.

Give me wisdom to recognize those who pervert Your grace and deny our Lord Jesus Christ. Help me watch for those who cause division and create obstacles contrary to Your doctrine. Lord, keep me vigilant against smooth talk and flattery that deceive the hearts of the naive. May I serve You alone, not my own appetites.

In Jesus' name I pray, Amen.

My own prayer

_____

_____

_____

_____

_____

Beloved, do not believe every spirit, but test the spirits to see whether they are from God, for many false prophets have gone out into the world. - John 4:1

Familiar Spirits

noun (plural)
fə-ˈmil-yər ˈspir-əts

1. A spirit or demon that serves or prompts an individual
2. An evil spirit believed to assist in occult practices, such as divination or communication with the dead

- **Leviticus 20:6:** If a person turns to mediums and necromancers, whoring after them, I will set my face against that person and will cut him off from among his people.
- **Leviticus 19:31:** Do not turn to mediums or necromancers; do not seek them out, and so make yourselves unclean by them: I am the Lord your God.
- **Leviticus 20:27:** A man or a woman who is a medium or a necromancer shall surely be put to death. They shall be stoned with stones; their blood shall be upon them.
- **Deuteronomy 18:10–14:** There shall not be found among you anyone who burns his son or his daughter as an offering, anyone who practices divination or tells fortunes or interprets omens, or a sorcerer, or a charmer or a medium or a necromancer or one who inquires of the dead, for whoever does these things is an abomination to the Lord. And because of these abominations, the Lord your God is driving them out before you. You shall be blameless before the Lord your God, for these nations, which you are about to dispossess, listen to fortune-tellers and to diviners. But as for you, the Lord your God has not allowed you to do this.

Reflections:

_____

_____

_____

_____

_____

_____

Prayer:

Heavenly Father,

I come before You in a posture of humility and reverence. Lord, I seek Your protection and guidance in a world filled with spiritual deception. Shield me, O God, from beings that monitor or prompt me toward deception. Holy Spirit, grant me the wisdom to discern Your voice above all other spirits. Sharpen my spiritual senses that I may recognize and resist the lure of familiar spirits.

Father, I repent and renounce any guidance, oaths, or incantations I have sought from familiar spirits, knowingly or unknowingly. Cleanse me from any spiritual contamination resulting from these interactions.

When culture promotes practices of channeling or communicating with the dead as harmless, grant me the strength and wisdom to stand firm in Your truth. Help me to be a light in the darkness, steering clear of such demonic practices and guiding others away from them.

Lord, guard my heart and mind against the allure of new age practices. Let me not be entertained by or curious about these deceptive schemes. Instead, fill me with a hunger for Your Word and Your presence.

I declare that I will seek guidance only from You, Lord. You are my God, and I will listen to no other voice. Help me to be blameless before You, rejecting all forms of divination, fortune-telling, and necromancy. Thank You for not allowing me to partake in these abominations. Keep me pure and undefiled, walking in the path You have set before me.

In Jesus' name I pray, Amen.

My own prayer:

_____

_____

_____

_____

Fasting

verb
'fast

1. To abstain from food
2. To refrain from certain pleasures or desires as an act of devotion, often for spiritual purposes

- **Matthew 6:16–18:** "And when you fast, do not look gloomy like the hypocrites, for they disfigure their faces that their fasting may be seen by others. Truly, I say to you, they have received their reward. But when you fast, anoint your head and wash your face, that your fasting may not be seen by others but by your Father who is in secret. And your Father who sees in secret will reward you."
- **Job 23:12:** I have not departed from the commandment of his lips; I have treasured the words of his mouth more than my portion of food.
- **Ezra 8:21,** 23: Then I proclaimed a fast there, at the river Ahava, that we might humble ourselves before our God, to seek from him a safe journey for ourselves, our children, and all our goods. So we fasted and implored our God for this, and he listened to our entreaty.
- **Acts 13:2–3:** While they were worshiping the Lord and fasting, the Holy Spirit said, "Set apart for me Barnabas and Saul for the work to which I have called them." Then after fasting and praying they laid their hands on them and sent them off.
- **Joel 2:12:** "Yet even now," declares the Lord, "return to me with all your heart, with fasting, with weeping, and with mourning."

Reflections:

_____
_____
_____
_____
_____
_____
_____

Prayer:

Heavenly Father,

I come before You in humility, seeking Your revelation, guidance, and wisdom. Lord, like Job, may I treasure Your words more than my daily bread. Grant me the discipline to embrace fasting not as a religious performance, but as a heartfelt sacrifice to draw closer to You.

Father, as I fast, help me to do so in secret, without a gloomy countenance or outward show. Let my fasting be seen only by You, my Father who sees in secret. Anoint my head and wash my face, that my devotion may be genuine and pleasing to You alone. Lord, I declare my desire to delight in a lifestyle of fasting and worship. May this sacred time bring me into sweet intimacy with You. As I humble myself before You, seeking Your will, listen to my entreaty as You did for Ezra.

Holy Spirit, speak to me during this fast. May it prepare and set me apart for the work to which You have called me. Let this time of fasting align my heart with Yours, that I may return to You wholeheartedly.

In Jesus' name I pray, Amen.

My own prayer:

_____
_____
_____
_____
_____
_____
_____
_____

Father

noun
ˈfä-thər

1. A male parent
2. The first person of the Holy Trinity

- **2 Corinthians 6:18**: And I will be a father to you, and you shall be sons and daughters to me, says the Lord Almighty.
- **Psalm 103:13:** As a father shows compassion to his children, so the Lord shows compassion to those who fear him.
- **Proverbs 23:24:** The father of the righteous will greatly rejoice; he who fathers a wise son will be glad in him.
- **Luke 15:20:** And he arose and came to his father. But while he was still a long way off, his father saw him and felt compassion, and ran and embraced him and kissed him.
- **Deuteronomy 22:30:** A man shall not take his father's wife, so that he does not uncover his father's nakedness.
- **Ephesians 6:4:** Fathers, do not provoke your children to anger, but bring them up in the discipline and instruction of the Lord.
- **Proverbs 20:7:** The righteous who walks in his integrity—blessed are his children after him!
- **Proverbs 22:6:** Train up a child in the way he should go; even when he is old he will not depart from it.
- **3 John 1:4**: I have no greater joy than to hear that my children are walking in the truth.

Reflections:

_____
_____
_____
_____
_____
_____

Prayer:

Heavenly Father,

I come before You in gratitude for the gift of fatherhood. Thank You for being the perfect example of a loving Father to us all.

Lord, help me to show compassion to my children as You show compassion to those who fear You. Grant me wisdom to bring up my children in the discipline and instruction of the Lord, without provoking them to anger. Father, may I walk in integrity so that my children may be blessed. Guide me as I train them in the way they should go, that even when they are old, they will not depart from it.

Give me the strength to run toward my children with open arms when they return to me, just as You welcome us with open arms when we turn to You. Lord, may my greatest joy be to hear that my children are walking in the truth. Help me to rejoice in their righteousness and wisdom, knowing that these are gifts from You.

Thank You for the privilege of being called Your child. May I reflect Your love and compassion in my role as a father.

In Jesus' name I pray Amen.

My own prayer:

_____
_____
_____
_____
_____
_____
_____

Favor

noun
ˈfā-vər

1. Friendly regard shown toward another, especially by a superior
2. Approving consideration or attention

- **Psalm 90:17:** Let the favor of the Lord our God be upon us, and establish the work of our hands upon us; yes, establish the work of our hands!
- **Psalm 5:12:** For you bless the righteous, O Lord; you cover him with favor as with a shield.
- **Ephesians 1:11–14:** In him we have obtained an inheritance, having been predestined according to the purpose of him who works all things according to the counsel of his will, so that we who were the first to hope in Christ might be to the praise of his glory. In him you also, when you heard the word of the truth, the gospel of your salvation, and believed in him, were sealed with the promised Holy Spirit, who is the guarantee of our inheritance until we acquire possession of it, to the praise of his glory.
- **Psalm 106:4:** Remember me, O Lord, when you show favor to your people; help me when you save them.
- **Isaiah 58:11:** And the Lord will guide you continually and satisfy your desire in scorched places and make your bones strong; and you shall be like a watered garden, like a spring of water whose waters do not fail.
- **Matthew 5:8:** "Blessed are the pure in heart, for they shall see God."
- **Psalm 84:11:** For the Lord God is a sun and shield; the Lord bestows favor and honor. No good thing does he withhold from those who walk uprightly.

Reflections:

_____
_____
_____
_____
_____
_____

Prayer:

Heavenly Father,

I come before You in righteousness, humbly seeking Your presence. Lord, I ask that Your favor be upon me and that You establish the work of my hands. I thank You, for You bless the righteous and cover them with favor as with a shield. I am grateful for the inheritance I have in You, the favor You show to Your people. Remember me, O Lord, when You show favor to Your people; help me when You save them.

Holy Spirit, I ask that You guide me continually. Satisfy my desires in scorched places and make my bones strong. Transform me to be like a watered garden, like a spring of water whose waters do not fail.

Keep my heart pure, O God, that I may see You. You are my sun and shield, bestowing favor and honor. I trust that You withhold no good thing from those who walk uprightly.

May Your favor rest upon me as I seek to honor You in all I do.

In Jesus' name I pray, Amen.

My own prayer:

_____
_____
_____
_____
_____
_____
_____
_____
_____

Favoritism

noun

ˈfā-v(ə-)rə-ti-zəm

1. Showing of special favor

- **James 2:9:** But if you show partiality, you are committing sin and are convicted by the law as transgressors.
- **Romans 2:11:** For God shows no partiality.
- **Acts 10:34:** So Peter opened his mouth and said: "Truly I understand that God shows no partiality."
- **Deuteronomy 10:17:** For the Lord your God is God of gods and Lord of lords, the great, the mighty, and the awesome God, who is not partial and takes no bribe.
- **James 2:5:** Listen, my beloved brothers, has not God chosen those who are poor in the world to be rich in faith and heirs of the kingdom, which he has promised to those who love him?
- **Galatians 3:28:** There is neither Jew nor Greek, there is neither slave nor free, there is no male and female, for you are all one in Christ Jesus.
- **Leviticus 19:15:** You shall do no injustice in court. You shall not be partial to the poor or defer to the great, but in righteousness shall you judge your neighbor.
- **John 3:16:** For God so loved the world, that he gave his only Son, that whoever believes in him should not perish but have eternal life.
- **Colossians 3:25:** For the wrongdoer will be paid back for the wrong he has done, and there is no partiality.

Reflections:

_____
_____
_____
_____
_____
_____

Prayer:

Heavenly Father,

I come before You acknowledging that You show no partiality. You are the God of gods and Lord of lords, great, mighty, and awesome, who takes no bribe and favors no one over another. I confess any instances where I have shown favoritism, recognizing it as sin. Help me to treat all people equally, as You do.

Lord, remind me that You have chosen those who are poor in the world to be rich in faith. Let me see others through Your eyes, not judging by outward appearances or status. I thank You that in Christ, there is neither Jew nor Greek, slave nor free, male nor female. We are all one in Him. Help me to embrace this truth in my interactions with others.

Grant me the wisdom to judge righteously, not being partial to the poor or deferring to the great. Let me reflect Your impartial love, which You demonstrated by giving Your Son for the whole world.

May I always remember that You will repay each person according to their deeds, without partiality. Let this motivate me to act justly and love mercy in all my dealings.

In Jesus' name I pray, Amen.

My own prayer:

_____

_____

_____

_____

_____

_____

Fear

noun
fir

1. An unpleasant, often strong emotion caused by anticipation or awareness of danger

- **Isaiah 41:10:** Fear not, for I am with you; be not dismayed, for I am your God; I will strengthen you, I will help you, I will uphold you with my righteous right hand.
- **Joshua 1:9:** Have I not commanded you? Be strong and courageous. Do not be frightened, and do not be dismayed, for the Lord your God is with you wherever you go.
- **Psalm 118:6:** The Lord is on my side; I will not fear. What can man do to me?
- **Psalm 23:4:** Even though I walk through the valley of the shadow of death, I will fear no evil, for you are with me; your rod and your staff, they comfort me.
- **Psalm 27:1:** The Lord is my light and my salvation; whom shall I fear? The Lord is the stronghold of my life; of whom shall I be afraid?
- **Psalm 34:4:** I sought the Lord, and he answered me and delivered me from all my fears.
- **Hebrews 13:6:** So we can confidently say, "The Lord is my helper; I will not fear; what can man do to me?"
- **Luke 12:32:** "Fear not, little flock, for it is your Father's good pleasure to give you the kingdom."
- **Psalm 56:4:** In God, whose word I praise, in God I trust; I shall not be afraid. What can flesh do to me?
- **2 Timothy** 1:7: For God gave us a spirit not of fear but of power and love and self-control.

Reflections:

_____
_____
_____
_____
_____
_____

Prayer:

Heavenly Father,

I come before You seeking courage and strength. Lord, You have not given me a spirit of fear, but of power, love, and self-control. Help me grow in faith, knowing that when I seek You, You answer and deliver me from all my fears. Teach me to fear not, for You are with me. I shall not be dismayed, for You are my God who strengthens and upholds me with Your righteous right hand.

O God, I no longer partner with fear. In You, whose Word I praise, I trust. I shall not be afraid, for what can mere flesh do to me? I proclaim that You are my helper; I will not fear. Even though I walk through the valley of the shadow of death, I fear no evil, for You are with me. Your rod and Your staff comfort me. You are my light and my salvation; whom shall I fear? You are the stronghold of my life; of whom shall I be afraid?

I trust in Your promise that it is Your good pleasure to give me the kingdom.

In Jesus' name I pray, Amen.

My own prayer:

_____

_____

_____

_____

_____

_____

_____

_____

Fire

noun
ˈfī(-ə)r

1. The phenomenon of combustion manifested in light, flame, and heat

- **Matthew 28:19:** "Therefore go and make disciples of all nations, baptizing them in the name of the Father and of the Son and of the Holy Spirit."
- **Luke 12:49:** "I came to cast fire on the earth, and would that it were already kindled!"
- **Luke 3:16:** John answered them all, saying, "I baptize you with water, but he who is mightier than I is coming, the strap of whose sandals I am not worthy to untie. He will baptize you with the Holy Spirit and fire."
- **Hebrews 12:29:** For our God is a consuming fire.
- **Isaiah 66:15–16:** For behold, the Lord will come in fire, and his chariots like the whirlwind, to render his anger in fury, and rebuke with flames of fire. For by fire will the Lord enter into judgment, and by his sword, with all flesh; and those slain by the Lord shall be many.

Reflections:

_____
_____
_____
_____
_____
_____
_____
_____
_____
_____

Prayer:

Heavenly Father,

I come before You in humility and reverence, acknowledging Your mighty power. Lord, may the fire of the Holy Spirit dwell in me all the days of my life. Keep the embers of Your presence ever-burning within me, ready to ignite a blaze of Your glory at any moment.

Father, let Your refining fire purify my heart, mind, and soul. As Your Word says, "Our God is a consuming fire." Consume all that is not of You within me. Grant me the strength to endure this purification process, remaining faithful through the flames of Your love.

Lord Jesus, You said You came to cast fire on the earth. Kindle that holy fire in me, that I may fulfill the great commission with passion and zeal. Empower me to make disciples of all nations, baptizing them in the name of the Father, Son, and Holy Spirit.

Holy Spirit, baptize me anew with Your fire, as John the Baptist foretold. May Your fire burn away all impurities and ignite a fervent love for You and for others.

In Jesus' name I pray, Amen.

My own prayer:

_____
_____
_____
_____
_____
_____
_____

Flesh

noun
flesh

1. The soft parts of the body of an animal and especially of a vertebrate
2. The physical nature of human beings

- **Romans 8:8:** Those who are in the flesh cannot please God.
- **Galatians 5:16:** But I say, walk by the Spirit, and you will not gratify the desires of the flesh.
- **Galatians 5:19–21:** Now the works of the flesh are evident: sexual immorality, impurity, sensuality, idolatry, sorcery, enmity, strife, jealousy, fits of anger, rivalries, dissensions, divisions, envy, drunkenness, orgies, and things like these. I warn you, as I warned you before, that those who do such things will not inherit the kingdom of God.
- **Colossians 3:11:** Here there is not Greek and Jew, circumcised and uncircumcised, barbarian, Scythian, slave, free; but Christ is all, and in all.
- **Romans 8:13:** For if you live according to the flesh you will die, but if by the Spirit you put to death the deeds of the body, you will live.
- **1 Corinthians 6:18:** Flee from sexual immorality. Every other sin a person commits is outside the body, but the sexually immoral person sins against his own body.
- **Matthew 26:41:** "Watch and pray that you may not enter into temptation. The spirit indeed is willing, but the flesh is weak."

Reflections:

_____
_____
_____
_____
_____
_____
_____

WARFARE BATTLECARDS

Prayer:

Heavenly Father,

I come before You in humility, recognizing my weakness and need for Your strength. Lord, I acknowledge Your Word that those in the flesh cannot please You. I desire to walk by Your Spirit and not gratify the desires of my flesh.

Father, help me resist the temptations of sexual immorality, impurity, and all other works of the flesh. Grant me the strength to flee from these sins that war against my soul. I know that if I live according to the flesh, I will die, but if by Your Spirit I put to death the deeds of the body, I will live.

Holy Spirit, empower me to be watchful and prayerful, for though my spirit is willing, my flesh is weak. May I find my identity in Christ alone, not in worldly distinctions.

Lord, I surrender my body, mind, and soul to You. Have Your way in me, that I may walk in the Spirit and inherit Your kingdom.

In Jesus' name, Amen.

My own prayer:

_____
_____
_____
_____
_____
_____
_____

Forgiveness

noun
fər-ˈgiv-nəs

1. The act of forgiving (ceasing to feel resentment against)

- **Matthew 6:14–15 (KJV):** "For if ye forgive men their trespasses, your heavenly Father will also forgive you: but if ye forgive not men their trespasses, neither will your Father forgive your trespasses."
- **Ephesians 4:31–32:** Let all bitterness and wrath and anger and clamor and slander be put away from you, along with all malice. Be kind to one another, tenderhearted, forgiving one another, as God in Christ forgave you.
- **1 John 1:9:** If we confess our sins, he is faithful and just to forgive us our sins and to cleanse us from all unrighteousness.
- **Luke 17:3–4:** "Pay attention to yourselves! If your brother sins, rebuke him, and if he repents, forgive him, and if he sins against you seven times in the day, and turns to you seven times, saying, 'I repent,' you must forgive him."
- **Colossians 3:13:** Bearing with one another and, if one has a complaint against another, forgiving each other; as the Lord has forgiven you, so you also must forgive.
- **Luke 6:37:** "Judge not, and you will not be judged; condemn not, and you will not be condemned; forgive, and you will be forgiven."

Reflections:

_____
_____
_____
_____
_____
_____
_____

Prayer:

Heavenly Father,

I come before You in humility, my heart is heavy with the burden of unforgiveness. Lord, I acknowledge my struggle to forgive those who have hurt me deeply.

Father, forgive me for the times I've acted as judge, deeming others' actions unforgivable. Help me to see my own need for Your forgiveness and to extend that same grace to others.

Holy Spirit, soften my heart. Remove from me all bitterness, wrath, anger, clamor, and slander. Fill me instead with kindness and tenderheartedness.

Lord, teach me to forgive as You have forgiven me. Grant me the strength to bear with others, to forgive repeatedly, just as You forgive me time and time again.

Help me, O God, to let go of worldly ideas of justice and embrace Your way of forgiveness. May my life reflect the freedom that comes from living in the grace of Your forgiveness.

In Jesus' name I pray, Amen.

My own prayer:

_____
_____
_____
_____
_____
_____
_____

Fortitude

noun
-fōr-tə-tüd

1. Strength of mind that enables a person to encounter danger or bear pain or adversity with courage

- **1 Timothy 6:11:** But as for you, O man of God, flee these things. Pursue righteousness, godliness, faith, love, steadfastness, gentleness.
- **2 Timothy 2:3:** Share in suffering as a good soldier of Christ Jesus.
- **1 Peter 1:5:** Who by God's power are being guarded through faith for a salvation ready to be revealed in the last time.
- **Revelation 2:17:** "He who has an ear, let him hear what the Spirit says to the churches. To the one who conquers, I will give some of the hidden manna, and I will give him a white stone, with a new name written on the stone that no one knows except the one who receives it."
- **Hebrews 12:7:** It is for discipline that you have to endure. God is treating you as sons. For what son is there whom his father does not discipline?
- **1 Peter 4:12:** Beloved, do not be surprised at the fiery trial when it comes upon you to test you, as though something strange were happening to you.
- **Proverbs 4:27:** Do not swerve to the right or to the left; turn your foot away from evil.
- **Proverbs 31:17:** She dresses herself with strength and makes her arms strong.

Reflections:

_____
_____
_____
_____
_____
_____
_____

Prayer:

Heavenly Father,

I come before You, seeking refuge and strength. Lord, dress me with Your might and make my arms strong for the tasks ahead. Grant me courage, Father, to share in suffering as a good soldier of Christ Jesus. Keep my feet steady on Your path, not swerving to the right or left, but turning away from evil.

Holy Spirit, prepare my heart for the trials that may come. Help me not to be surprised by fiery tests, but to recognize them as opportunities for growth in faith.

Lord, sharpen my discernment and increase my discipline. Open my ears to hear what the Spirit says, and nurture in me the perseverance to endure. Father, I ask that You guide me in pursuing righteousness, godliness, faith, love, steadfastness, and gentleness. Guard me through faith for the salvation that is to be revealed.

May I be counted among those who conquer, receiving the hidden manna and the white stone with a new name.

In Jesus' name I pray, Amen.

My own prayer:

_____
_____
_____
_____
_____
_____
_____

Freedom

noun
'frē-dəm

1. The quality or state of being free: such as the absence of necessity, coercion, or constraint in choice or action

- **Romans 8:2:** For the law of the Spirit of life has set you free in Christ Jesus from the law of sin and death.
- **John 8:32:** "And you will know the truth, and the truth will set you free."
- **John 8:36:** "So if the Son sets you free, you will be free indeed."
- **Galatians 5:1:** For freedom Christ has set us free; stand firm therefore, and do not submit again to a yoke of slavery.
- **Galatians 5:13:** For you were called to freedom, brothers. Only do not use your freedom as an opportunity for the flesh, but through love serve one another.
- **Isaiah 61:1:** The Spirit of the Lord God is upon me, because the Lord has anointed me to bring good news to the poor; he has sent me to bind up the brokenhearted, to proclaim liberty to the captives, and the opening of the prison to those who are bound.
- **Psalm 118:5:** Out of my distress I called on the Lord; the Lord answered me and set me free.

Reflections:

_____
_____
_____
_____
_____
_____
_____

Prayer:

Heavenly Father,

I come before You seeking everlasting freedom. Thank You for the liberty I have through Your Son, Jesus Christ, who has set me free from the law of sin and death. Lord, in my distress, I called to You, and You answered, setting me free. I am grateful for the truth that liberates my soul.

Help me, Father, to stand firm in the freedom Christ has won for me. Keep me from submitting again to the yoke of slavery. Remind me that I am called to freedom not for selfish pursuits, but to serve others in love.

Holy Spirit, anoint me as You did Isaiah, to bring good news to the poor, to bind up the brokenhearted, to proclaim liberty to captives, and to open prison doors for those who are bound.

May my life forever display the power of Your freedom, proclaiming that whom the Son sets free is free indeed.

In Jesus' name I pray, Amen.

My own prayer:

_____
_____
_____
_____
_____
_____
_____

Friendship

noun
ʹfren(d)-ship

1. The state of being friends

- **Proverbs 27:17:** Iron sharpens iron, and one man sharpens another.
- **1 Samuel 18:1**: As soon as he had finished speaking to Saul, the soul of Jonathan was knit to the soul of David, and Jonathan loved him as his own soul.
- **Acts 11:25–26:** So Barnabas went to Tarsus to look for Saul, and when he had found him, he brought him to Antioch. For a whole year they met with the church and taught a great many people. And in Antioch the disciples were first called Christians.
- **James 2:23:** And the Scripture was fulfilled that says, "Abraham believed God, and it was counted to him as righteousness"—and he was called a friend of God.
- **John 15:14–15:** "You are my friends if you do what I command you. No longer do I call you servants, for the servant does not know what his master is doing; but I have called you friends, for all that I have heard from my Father I have made known to you."

Reflections:

_____
_____
_____
_____
_____
_____
_____
_____
_____

Prayer:

Heavenly Father,

I come before You in gratitude and joy for the gift of friendship. Lord, Your Word shows us the beauty and importance of true companionship. Father, I thank You for the example of Jonathan and David, whose souls were knit together in loyal friendship. Help me to be a friend who sharpens others as iron sharpens iron, encouraging and challenging those around me to grow in faith and character.

Lord, I ask for a Barnabas in my life—someone who will support me, seek me out, and walk alongside me in all seasons. May I also be that kind of friend to others, offering support in trials and sharing in celebrations. Above all, Abba Father, I desire to be Your friend. Thank You for calling me not just a servant, but a friend through Christ. Help me to live up to this honor, walking closely with You and seeking Your will in all things. Guide me in nurturing deep, meaningful friendships that reflect Your love and bring glory to Your name.

In Jesus' name I pray, Amen.

My own prayer:

_____

_____

_____

_____

_____

_____

_____

_____

Fruit of the Spirit

noun
ˈfrüt əv _thə_ ˈspir-ət

1. The qualities or virtues that are the result of the Holy Spirit's work in a believer's life
2. The state of bearing fruit
3. A supernatural being or essence: such as

- **Galatians 5:22–23:** But the fruit of the Spirit is love, joy, peace, patience, kindness, goodness, faithfulness, gentleness, self-control; against such things there is no law.
- **Romans 8:9:** You, however, are not in the flesh but in the Spirit, if in fact the Spirit of God dwells in you. Anyone who does not have the Spirit of Christ does not belong to him.
- **1 Corinthians 12:13:** For in one Spirit we were all baptized into one body—Jews or Greeks, slaves or free—and all were made to drink of one Spirit.
- **Ephesians 1:13:** In him you also, when you heard the word of truth, the gospel of your salvation, and believed in him, were sealed with the promised Holy Spirit.

Reflections:

_____
_____
_____
_____
_____
_____
_____
_____
_____

Prayer:

Heavenly Father,

I come before You in humility and gratitude. Lord, I thank You for the gift of Your Holy Spirit, who dwells within me and seals me as Your own. Father, I ask that You cultivate in me the fruit of Your Spirit. May love, joy, and peace flourish in my heart. Grant me patience in trials and kindness toward others. Let Your goodness and faithfulness shine through me. Teach me gentleness in my words and actions and strengthen my self-control.

Holy Spirit, guide me to live not by the flesh, but by Your power. Help me to remember that I am no longer bound by the law of sin and death, but free in Christ Jesus.

Lord, unite me with all believers as one body in Your Spirit, regardless of our earthly differences. May my life be a testament to Your transforming work, bearing fruit that glorifies You.

In Jesus' name I pray, Amen.

My own prayer:

_____
_____
_____
_____
_____
_____
_____
_____

Generational Curse

noun

je-nə-ˈrā-sh(ə-)nəl ˈkərs

1. Generational consequences, the consequence of sinful actions and behavior, a concept of sowing and reaping passed down from one generation to the next
2. A concept in spiritual and religious contexts referring to negative patterns, behaviors, or consequences that are believed to be passed down from one generation to the next within a family lineage

- **Exodus 20:5:** You shall not bow down to them or serve them, for I the Lord your God am a jealous God, visiting the iniquity of the fathers on the children to the third and the fourth generation of those who hate me.
- **Numbers 14:18:** The Lord is slow to anger and abounding in steadfast love, forgiving iniquity and transgression, but he will by no means clear the guilty, visiting the iniquity of the fathers on the children, to the third and the fourth generation.
- **Deuteronomy 5:9:** You shall not bow down to them or serve them; for I the Lord your God am a jealous God, visiting the iniquity of the fathers on the children to the third and fourth generation of those who hate me.
- **2 Corinthians 5:17:** Therefore, if anyone is in Christ, he is a new creation. The old has passed away; behold, the new has come.
- **Romans 8:1:** There is therefore now no condemnation for those who are in Christ Jesus.
- **Romans 12:1:** I appeal to you therefore, brothers, by the mercies of God, to present your bodies as a living sacrifice, holy and acceptable to God, which is your spiritual worship.

Reflections:

_____
_____
_____
_____
_____

Prayer:

Heavenly Father,

I come before You in humble submission. Lord, I heed Your warning from Exodus and Deuteronomy, acknowledging that You are a jealous God who visits the iniquities of the fathers upon their children. I thank You, Abba, for Your patience, steadfast love, and forgiveness. Father, have mercy on my soul and my bloodline. Let these prayers cover generations past and future. I renounce any worship or alliances with other gods, cultural rituals, or séances that may have affected my lineage. Uproot all unrighteous systems, airways, destructive behaviors, curses, poverty, broken relationships, addictions, and oppression. By Your authority, I stand in the gap for my bloodline, repenting for such practices. I bind myself to Your truth and obey Your instructions, O God. I rejoice that in Christ, I am a new creation; the old has passed away. Thank You for Your mercies. I present my body as a living sacrifice, holy and acceptable to You, whom I worship all my days. In Jesus' name and by the authority of His blood, I pray, Amen.

My own prayer:

_____
_____
_____
_____
_____
_____
_____
_____
_____

Gentle

adjective
'jen-tel

1. Free from harshness, sternness, or violence

- **Proverbs 15:4:** A gentle tongue is a tree of life, but perverseness in it breaks the spirit.
- **Titus 3:2:** To speak evil of no one, to avoid quarreling, to be gentle, and to show perfect courtesy toward all people.
- **James 3:17:** But the wisdom from above is first pure, then peaceable, gentle, open to reason, full of mercy and good fruits, impartial and sincere.
- **Proverbs 15:1:** A soft answer turns away wrath, but a harsh word stirs up anger.
- **Ephesians 4:2:** With all humility and gentleness, with patience, bearing with one another in love.

Reflections:

_____
_____
_____
_____
_____
_____
_____
_____
_____
_____

Prayer:

Heavenly Father,

I come before You in humility, seeking Your wisdom and guidance. Lord, Your Word teaches that a gentle tongue is a tree of life, and I yearn to cultivate such gentleness in my speech and actions.

Father, forgive me for the times I have spoken harshly or acted in anger. I turn away from wrath and perverseness of tongue. Instead, grant me the grace to speak no evil, to avoid quarreling, and to show perfect courtesy to all people.

Holy Spirit, help gentleness to flourish within me. May my words be soft answers that turn away wrath. Teach me to be peaceable, open to reason, full of mercy, and sincere in all my interactions.

Lord, guide me to walk in humility and gentleness, with patience, bearing with others in love. Let my conduct reflect Your wisdom that is pure and full of good fruits.

In Jesus' name I pray, Amen.

My own prayer:

_____
_____
_____
_____
_____
_____
_____
_____
_____

GOD

noun
ʻgäd

1. The being perfect in power, wisdom, and goodness who is worshipped as a creator and ruler of the universe

- **Revelation 1:8:** "I am the Alpha and the Omega," says the Lord God, "who is and who was and who is to come, the Almighty."
- **John 3:16:** "For God so loved the world, that he gave his only Son, that whoever believes in him should not perish but have eternal life."
- **Isaiah 40:28:** Have you not known? Have you not heard? The Lord is the everlasting God, the Creator of the ends of the earth. He does not faint or grow weary; his understanding is unsearchable.
- **Psalm 18:30:** This God—his way is perfect; the word of the Lord proves true; he is a shield for all those who take refuge in him.
- **Zephaniah 3:17:** The Lord your God is in your midst, a mighty one who will save; he will rejoice over you with gladness; he will quiet you by his love; he will exult over you with loud singing.
- **Psalm 147:5:** Great is our Lord, and abundant in power; his understanding is beyond measure.
- **Romans 5:8:** But God shows his love for us in that while we were still sinners, Christ died for us.

Reflections:

_____
_____
_____
_____
_____
_____

WARFARE BATTLECARDS

Prayer:

Heavenly Father,

I come before You in reverence, acknowledging Your mighty names—Yahweh, Adonai, Elohim, El Shaddai, El Roi. You are the Alpha and Omega, who is and who was and who is to come, the Almighty. I declare my faith in You, the God who loves the world so much that You gave Your only Son for us. Thank You that through belief in Him, I have the promise of eternal life.

Lord, You are the everlasting God, the Creator of all. Your understanding is unsearchable, and You never grow weary. Your way is perfect, Your Word is true, and You are my shield and refuge. I am in awe that You, the mighty God, rejoice over me with gladness. Your power is abundant, and Your understanding is beyond measure.

Father, I am humbled by Your love, shown through Christ's sacrifice while I was still a sinner. My salvation rests in You alone. I declare myself Yours, O God. Guide me, protect me, and use me for Your glory.

In Jesus' name I pray, Amen.

My own prayer:

_____

_____

_____

_____

_____

_____

_____

Greed

noun
'grēd

1. A selfish and excessive desire for more of something than is needed

- **Luke 12:15:** And he said to them, "Take care, and be on your guard against all covetousness, for one's life does not consist in the abundance of his possessions."
- **Matthew 16:19–21:** "I will give you the keys of the kingdom of heaven, and whatever you bind on earth shall be bound in heaven, and whatever you loose on earth shall be loosed in heaven." Then he strictly charged the disciples to tell no one that he was the Christ. From that time Jesus began to show his disciples that he must go to Jerusalem and suffer many things from the elders and chief priests and scribes, and be killed, and on the third day be raised.
- **1 Timothy 6:9–10**: But those who desire to be rich fall into temptation, into a snare, into many senseless and harmful desires that plunge people into ruin and destruction. For the love of money is a root of all kinds of evils. It is through this craving that some have wandered away from the faith and pierced themselves with many pangs.
- **Proverbs 28:25:** A greedy man stirs up strife, but the one who trusts in the Lord will be enriched.
- **James 4:3:** You ask and do not receive, because you ask wrongly, to spend it on your passions.
- **Mark 8:36:** "For what does it profit a man to gain the whole world and forfeit his soul?"
- **Acts 20:35:** In all things I have shown you that by working hard in this way we must help the weak and remember the words of the Lord Jesus, how he himself said, 'It is more blessed to give than to receive.'"
- **Luke 6:38:** "Give, and it will be given to you. Good measure, pressed down, shaken together, running over, will be put into your lap. For with the measure you use it will be measured back to you."
- **Proverbs 11:24–25:** One gives freely, yet grows all the richer; another withholds what he should give, and only suffers want. Whoever brings blessing will be enriched, and one who waters will himself be watered.

Reflections:

Prayer:

Heavenly Father,

I come before You, burdened by the culture of materialism that surrounds me. Lord, in a world that constantly demands more, help me guard against covetousness. Remind me that life's value doesn't lie in the abundance of possessions.

Holy Spirit, purify my heart. Remove from me the desire for riches that leads to temptation and senseless wants. Shield me from the snares that could plunge me into ruin and destruction.

Father, instill in me the righteousness to work hard and help the weak, remembering Jesus' words that it is more blessed to give than to receive. I declare my trust in You, believing that as I give, it will be given back to me in good measure, pressed down, shaken together, and running over. Lord, I proclaim Your holy name. Raise me up to cling only to You, never forsaking my faith. Grant me a heart to freely pass blessings to others without hesitation, trusting that all my needs are met by You. Build in me a spirit of generosity, truly releasing me from the grip of greed.

In Jesus' name I pray, Amen.

My own prayer:

_____
_____
_____
_____
_____
_____
_____
_____

Draw near to God, and he will draw near to you. Cleanse your hands, you sinners, and purify your hearts, you double-minded. - James 4:8

Grief

noun
'grēf

1. Deep and poignant distress caused by or as if by bereavement

- **Matthew 5:4:** "Blessed are those who mourn, for they shall be comforted."
- **Psalm 30:5:** For his anger is but for a moment, and his favor is for a lifetime. Weeping may tarry for the night, but joy comes with the morning.
- **Ecclesiastes 7:2–3:** It is better to go to the house of mourning than to go to the house of feasting, for this is the end of all mankind, and the living will lay it to heart. Sorrow is better than laughter, for by sadness of face the heart is made glad.
- **Psalm 34:18:** The Lord is near to the brokenhearted and saves the crushed in spirit.
- **Romans 12:15:** Rejoice with those who rejoice, weep with those who weep.
- **Revelation 21:4:** He will wipe away every tear from their eyes, and death shall be no more, neither shall there be mourning, nor crying, nor pain anymore, for the former things have passed away.
- **Isaiah 41:10:** Fear not, for I am with you; be not dismayed, for I am your God; I will strengthen you, I will help you, I will uphold you with my righteous right hand.
- **2 Corinthians 7:10**: For godly grief produces a repentance that leads to salvation without regret, whereas worldly grief produces death.

Reflections:

_____
_____
_____
_____
_____
_____
_____

Prayer:

Heavenly Father,

I come before You in sorrow, stricken with grief. Lord, as I mourn, let Your comfort rest upon my soul. As I weep through the night, I thank You for the joy that comes in the morning. With my spirit crushed, I am soothed by Your presence, O God.

Grant me hope in this time when sorrow runs deep, helping me to see this grief as but a season, with times of rejoicing on the horizon. Wipe away every tear, my Lord. Let me not be dismayed, for You are my God. It is You who strengthens me, You who will help me, upholding me with Your righteous right hand.

Holy Spirit, let this grief produce a repentance that leads to salvation without regret. May I live in the freedom that Jesus Christ, my Savior—my shield, my restoration, and my hope—provides.

In Jesus' name I pray, Amen.

My own prayer:

_____
_____
_____
_____
_____
_____
_____
_____

Guilt

noun
'gilt

1. Feelings of deserving blame especially for imagined offenses or from a sense of inadequacy

- **Romans 2:23:** You who boast in the law dishonor God by breaking the law.
- **1 John 1:9**: If we confess our sins, he is faithful and just to forgive us our sins and to cleanse us from all unrighteousness.
- **2 Samuel 22:24**: I was blameless before him, and I kept myself from guilt.
- **Psalm 103:12:** As far as the east is from the west, so far does he remove our transgressions from us.
- **Romans 8:1:** There is therefore now no condemnation for those who are in Christ Jesus.
- **Micah 7:19:** He will again have compassion on us; he will tread our iniquities underfoot. You will cast all our sins into the depths of the sea.
- **Acts 8:22:** Repent, therefore, of this wickedness of yours, and pray to the Lord that, if possible, the intent of your heart may be forgiven you.
- **John 3:17:** "For God did not send his Son into the world to condemn the world, but in order that the world might be saved through him."

Reflections:

_____
_____
_____
_____
_____
_____
_____
_____

Prayer:

Heavenly Father,

I come before You in submission, seeking Your grace and mercy. Forgive me, Father, for my sins– every vile and wicked thing within my heart, mind, and soul. You are faithful and just, able to cleanse me from all unrighteousness.

Abba, I desire to be blameless before You, keeping myself from guilt. I thank You that You can remove my transgressions as far as the east is from the west. I declare myself a new creation in Christ Jesus, and I'm grateful for Your compassion, treading my iniquities underfoot and casting my sins into the depths of the sea. I repent from all wickedness, pressing into Your throne room, Lord.

Thank you for sending Your Son that through HIM we might be saved, rather than condemned. There is no condemnation for those in Christ Jesus, and I cling to this truth. Help me to live in the freedom of Your forgiveness, unburdened by guilt.

In Jesus' name I pray, Amen.

My own prayer:

_____

_____

_____

_____

_____

_____

_____

_____

Harmony

noun
'här-mə-nē

1. Agreement, accord
2. Internal calm

- **Psalm 133:1:** Behold, how good and pleasant it is when brothers dwell in unity!
- **Romans 12:16–18:** Live in harmony with one another. Do not be haughty, but associate with the lowly. Never be wise in your own sight. Repay no one evil for evil, but give thought to do what is honorable in the sight of all. If possible, so far as it depends on you, live peaceably with all.
- **1 Peter 3:8**: Finally, all of you, have unity of mind, sympathy, brotherly love, a tender heart, and a humble mind.
- **Romans 14:19:** So then let us pursue what makes for peace and for mutual upbuilding.
- **Philippians 2:2:** Complete my joy by being of the same mind, having the same love, being in full accord and of one mind.
- **John 17:21:** "That they may all be one, just as you, Father, are in me, and I in you, that they also may be in us, so that the world may believe that you have sent me."
- **Colossians 3:14:** And above all these put on love, which binds everything together in perfect harmony.

Reflections:

_____
_____
_____
_____
_____
_____
_____

Prayer:

Heavenly Father,

I come before You in song and praise, carrying a melody of harmony to Your feet. I sing praises for how good and pleasant it is when brothers dwell in unity. Lord, I renounce haughty speech and practices. Help me not to repay evil for evil, but to live in peace among others.

Holy Spirit, grant me unity of mind, a heart filled with sympathy, expressing brotherly love, tender in heart, and humble in posture. Let me pursue peace always for mutual upbuilding. Complete my joy by helping me be of the same mind with others, having the same love, being in full accord and of one mind.

Abba, dress me in Your love, which binds everything together in perfect harmony. May my life reflect the unity You desire for Your children, just as You, Father, are in Christ, and Christ in You.

Guide me to live peaceably with all, as far as it depends on me. Let my actions and words contribute to the harmony of Your body, the church.

In Jesus' name I pray, Amen.

My own prayer:

_____
_____
_____
_____
_____
_____
_____
_____

Harvest

verb
'här-vəst

1. To gather in (a crop) reap

- **2 Corinthians 9:10**: He who supplies seed to the sower and bread for food will supply and multiply your seed for sowing and increase the harvest of your righteousness.
- **Genesis 8:22:** While the earth remains, seedtime and harvest, cold and heat, summer and winter, day and night, shall not cease.
- **Proverbs 3:9:** Honor the Lord with your wealth and with the firstfruits of all your produce.
- **Galatians 6:9:** And let us not grow weary of doing good, for in due season we will reap, if we do not give up.
- **Luke 10:2:** And he said to them, "The harvest is plentiful, but the laborers are few. Therefore pray earnestly to the Lord of the harvest to send out laborers into his harvest."

Reflections:

_____
_____
_____
_____
_____
_____
_____
_____
_____
_____
_____

Prayer:

Heavenly Father,

I come before You in humility as Your servant. Lord, remind me of Your words as I seek a harvest. Grant me a heart to honor You with my wealth and first fruits.

Holy Spirit, let me not grow weary of doing good, for in due season I will reap if I do not give up. I ask for Your strength and courage to carry on, O God. How I long to be a laborer for Your divine harvest! Build me up so that I remain faithful to the call.

I pray earnestly to You, Lord of the harvest. Send me as a laborer for Your great harvest. While the earth remains, let me be mindful of Your faithfulness in seedtime and harvest, in all seasons. May I sow generously, trusting in Your provision and multiplication.

In Jesus' name I pray, Amen.

My own prayer:

_____
_____
_____
_____
_____
_____
_____
_____
_____

Haughty

adjective
'hȯ-tē

1. Blatantly and disdainfully proud: having or showing an attitude of superiority and contempt for people or things perceived to be inferior

- **Matthew 23:12:** "Whoever exalts himself will be humbled, and whoever humbles himself will be exalted."
- **James 4:6:** But he gives more grace. Therefore it says, "God opposes the proud but gives grace to the humble."
- **1 Peter 5:5**: Likewise, you who are younger, be subject to the elders. Clothe yourselves, all of you, with humility toward one another, for "God opposes the proud but gives grace to the humble."
- **Proverbs 16:18–19:** Pride goes before destruction, and a haughty spirit before a fall. It is better to be of a lowly spirit with the poor than to divide the spoil with the proud.
- **Proverbs 18:12:** Before destruction a man's heart is haughty, but humility comes before honor.
- **Proverbs 21:4:** Haughty eyes and a proud heart, the lamp of the wicked, are sin.

Reflections:

_____
_____
_____
_____
_____
_____
_____
_____

Prayer:

Heavenly Father,

I come before You in humble submission, recognizing Your sovereignty and my need for Your grace. Lord, Your Word teaches us that whoever exalts himself will be humbled, and whoever humbles himself will be exalted. In light of this truth, I renounce any haughty spirit within me. I acknowledge that God opposes the proud but gives grace to the humble. Father, help me to clothe myself with humility toward others, especially those You have placed in authority over me.

Holy Spirit, keep my heart teachable and guard me against pride. I understand that pride goes before destruction, and a haughty spirit before a fall. Instead, I choose to cultivate a lowly spirit, knowing it is better in Your eyes.

Lord, I seek Your honor rather than my own exaltation. Forgive me for the times when my heart has been haughty and my eyes proud. Create in me a clean heart, O God, and renew a right spirit within me.

May I walk in the grace that comes from true humility, always remembering that "humility comes before honor." Help me to reside in lowly places, serving others as Christ served us.

In Jesus' name I pray, Amen.

My own prayer:

_____

_____

_____

_____

_____

_____

_____

Health

noun
'helth

1. The condition of being sound in mind, body, or spirit

- **3 John 2:** Beloved, I pray that all may go well with you and that you may be in good health, as it goes well with your soul.
- **Matthew 4:23:** And he went throughout all Galilee, teaching in their synagogues and proclaiming the gospel of the kingdom and healing every disease and every affliction among the people.
- **Proverbs 3:8:** It will be healing to your flesh and refreshment to your bones.
- **Matthew 19:26:** But Jesus looked at them and said, "With man this is impossible, but with God all things are possible."

Reflections:

_____
_____
_____
_____
_____
_____
_____
_____
_____
_____

Prayer:

Heavenly Father,

I come before You seeking refreshment and good health. Thank You, Lord, that Your design for me is to be well and in good health, as it goes well with my soul. Help me to practice a healthy lifestyle, nourishing my body and soul with the riches of Your truth. As Jesus went about in synagogues teaching, proclaiming, and healing, may that be a sign of hope for good health to me.

O God, You are healing to my flesh and refreshment to my bones. With man, good health may sometimes seem impossible, yet with You, Lord, all things are possible. Grant me the wisdom to care for this body You've given me. When I face affliction or disease, remind me of Your power to heal and restore. May my health be a testament to Your goodness and grace.

In Jesus' name I pray, Amen.

My own prayer:

_____
_____
_____
_____
_____
_____
_____
_____
_____

Heart

noun
'härt

1. One's innermost character, feelings, or inclinations

- **Philippians 4:7:** And the peace of God, which surpasses all understanding, will guard your hearts and your minds in Christ Jesus.
- **Psalm 61:1–2:** Hear my cry, O God, listen to my prayer; from the end of the earth I call to you when my heart is faint. Lead me to the rock that is higher than I.
- **Psalm 51:10:** Create in me a clean heart, O God, and renew a right spirit within me.
- **Proverbs 4:23:** Keep your heart with all the vigilance, for from it flow the springs of life.
- **Hebrews 4:12:** For the word of God is living and active, sharper than any two-edged sword, piercing to the division of soul and of spirit, of joints and of marrow, and discerning the thoughts and intentions of the heart.

Reflections:

_____
_____
_____
_____
_____
_____
_____
_____
_____
_____

Prayer:

Heavenly Father,

I come before You in complete surrender. My Lord, Your peace which surpasses all understanding will guard my heart and mind in Christ Jesus. Hear my cry, O God, listen to my prayer. From the ends of the earth, I call to You when my heart is faint. Lead me to the rock that is higher than I.

As I lay prostrated at Your feet, create in me a clean heart and renew a right spirit within me, O God. I cast my cares and lay my burdens before You, opening myself to Your will. Have Your way within my heart, fill me with the truth of Your Word, and wrap me in Your loving arms.

Holy Spirit, teach me to guard my heart, keeping it with all vigilance, for from it flow the springs of life. Remind me daily that the Word of God is living and active, sharper than any two-edged sword, piercing to the division of soul and spirit, of joints and marrow, and discerning the thoughts and intentions of the heart. May I walk with a clean heart, building Your kingdom in love and truth.

In Jesus' name I pray, Amen.

My own prayer:

_____
_____
_____
_____
_____
_____
_____
_____

Help

verb
'help

1. To give assistance or support to (someone): to provide with something that is useful or necessary in achieving an end

- **Psalm 38:22:** Make haste to help me, O Lord, my salvation!
- **Psalm 35:2:** Take hold of shield and buckler and rise for my help!
- **Matthew 15:25:** But she came and knelt before him, saying, "Lord, help me."
- **Psalm 121:2:** My help comes from the Lord, who made heaven and earth.
- **Psalm 119:86:** All your commandments are sure; they persecute me with falsehood; help me!
- **Psalm 46:1:** God is our refuge and strength, a very present help in trouble.

Reflections:

_____
_____
_____
_____
_____
_____
_____
_____
_____
_____
_____

Prayer:

Heavenly Father,

I come before You in reverence of Your mighty power and unmatched grace and mercy. Father, make haste to help me, O Lord, my salvation. My Lord, I am in need of divine help. Take hold of shield and buckler, rise up for my help. As I kneel before You, O King, I cry out: HELP ME! You are my only hope, my refuge and strength in this very time of trouble.

My God, release Your holy angels as aid. My help comes from You, Lord, who made heaven and earth. All Your commands are sure; though the world may persecute me with falsehoods, help me!

You are my present help in trouble, my shield, and my defender. I trust in Your unfailing love and Your power to deliver me from all adversity. Guide me, protect me, and strengthen me, O Lord. Let Your help be swift and Your presence be nearby.

In Jesus' name I pray, Amen.

My own prayer:

_____
_____
_____
_____
_____
_____
_____
_____

Hindrance

noun
'hin-drən(t)s

1. The state of being interfered with, held back, or slowed down
2. The act of interfering with or slowing the progress of someone or something

- **Galatians 5:7:** You were running well. Who hindered you from obeying the truth?
- **1 Thessalonians 2:18**: Because we wanted to come to you—I, Paul, again and again—but Satan hindered us.
- **James 1:2–4:** Count it all joy, my brothers, when you meet trials of various kinds, for you know that the testing of your faith produces steadfastness. And let steadfastness have its full effect, that you may be perfect and complete, lacking in nothing.

Reflections:

_____
_____
_____
_____
_____
_____
_____
_____
_____
_____

Prayer:

Heavenly Father,

I come before You, renouncing my will and emotions, seeking Your counsel. O Lord, pave a way that I may walk in accordance with Your calling upon my life, observing Your faithful Scriptures. As I run well in my faith journey, let me not be hindered by those in opposition to You and Your call upon my destiny. Keep me alert to the delays and hindrances of the enemy in my comings and goings.

Holy Spirit, help me to count it all joy when I meet various kinds of trials, for I know that the testing of my faith produces steadfastness. Allow steadfastness to have its full effect in me, that I may be perfect and complete, lacking nothing.

Grant me discernment to recognize when Satan seeks to hinder Your work in my life. Strengthen me to persevere through obstacles, knowing that You use even hindrances to shape me according to Your will.

May I remain obedient to Your truth, undeterred by worldly influences or spiritual opposition. Let every hindrance become an opportunity for growth and a testimony to Your overcoming power.

In Jesus' name I pray, Amen.

My own prayer:

_____

_____

_____

_____

_____

_____

_____

Holy Spirit

noun

1. The third person of the Christian Trinity

- **John 14:26:** "But the Helper, the Holy Spirit, whom the Father will send in my name, he will teach you all things and bring to your remembrance all that I have said to you."
- **Acts 2:38:** And Peter said to them, "Repent and be baptized every one of you in the name of Jesus Christ for the forgiveness of your sins, and you will receive the gift of the Holy Spirit."
- **1 Corinthians 6:19**: Or do you not know that your body is a temple of the Holy Spirit within you, whom you have from God? You are not your own.
- **John 14:16–17:** "And I will ask the Father, and he will give you another Helper, to be with you forever, even the Spirit of truth, whom the world cannot receive, because it neither sees him nor knows him. You know him, for he dwells with you and will be in you."
- **Genesis 1:2:** The earth was without form and void, and darkness was over the face of the deep. And the Spirit of God was hovering over the face of the waters.
- **Romans 8:11:** If the Spirit of him who raised Jesus from the dead dwells in you, he who raised Christ Jesus from the dead will also give life to your mortal bodies through his Spirit who dwells in you.

Reflections:

_____
_____
_____
_____
_____
_____
_____
_____

Prayer:

Heavenly Father,

I come before You in submission to Your holiness. As Your Spirit hovered over the face of the waters at creation, I am in awe of Your power and presence. Thank You for the Helper, the Holy Spirit, who teaches me all things and brings to remembrance Your words. I repent, Lord, from anything unclean or worldly. As I walk in faith, declaring Jesus as my Lord, I receive Your gift of the Holy Spirit.

Grant me discipline, knowing my body is a temple of the Holy Spirit within me. I am not my own, but Yours. O Lord, how I yearn to dwell with You in spirit, recognizing that the world does not know You. May I no longer quench the Spirit who raised Jesus from the dead but allow Him to give life to my mortal body. Fill me with Your truth, power, and presence, Holy Spirit.

In Jesus' name I pray, Amen.

My own prayer:

_____
_____
_____
_____
_____
_____
_____
_____
_____
_____
_____

Honesty

noun
ˈä-nə-stē

1. Fairness and straightforwardness of conduct

- **John 8:32:** "And you will know the truth, and the truth will set you free."
- **Colossians 3:9:** Do not lie to one another, seeing that you have put off the old self with its practices.
- **2 Corinthians 8:21**: For we aim at what is honorable not only in the Lord's sight but also in the sight of man.
- **Proverbs 10:9:** Whoever walks in integrity walks securely, but he who makes his ways crooked will be found out.

Reflections:

_____
_____
_____
_____
_____
_____
_____
_____
_____
_____
_____
_____

Prayer:

Heavenly Father,

I come before You, seeking divine clarity and truth. For You are the author of truth, and it is by Your truth that I may be set free.

Holy Spirit, help me to walk in integrity. Forgive me for any faulty speech or practices. Grant me the eyes to see that I may not lie to another, remembering that I have put off the old self with its practices. May my choices lead to a life honorable not only in Your sight, Lord, but in the sight of man as well. I proclaim to walk in integrity, securely in faith, knowing You make crooked paths straight. Give me the courage to be honest in all my dealings, even when it's difficult. Let my words and actions align with Your truth, that I may be a reflection of Your character. May Your holy name be exalted and glorified through my commitment to honesty and integrity.

In Jesus' name I pray, Amen.

My own prayer:

_____
_____
_____
_____
_____
_____
_____
_____
_____
_____

Hope

verb
'hōp

1. To cherish a desire with anticipation: to want something to happen or be true

- **Romans 15:13:** May the God of hope fill you with all joy and peace in believing, so that by the power of the Holy Spirit you may abound in hope.
- **Hebrews 11:1:** Now faith is the assurance of things hoped for, the conviction of things not seen.
- **Romans 12:12:** Rejoice in hope, be patient in tribulation, be constant in prayer.
- **Romans 8:24–25:** For in this hope we were saved. Now hope that is seen is not hope. For who hopes for what he sees? But if we hope for what we do not see, we wait for it with patience.
- **Proverbs 23:18:** Surely there is a future, and your hope will not be cut off.

Reflections:

_____
_____
_____
_____
_____
_____
_____
_____
_____
_____

Prayer:

Heavenly Father,

I come before You, acknowledging You as the God of hope. I ask that You fill me with all joy and peace in believing, so that by the power of the Holy Spirit, I may abound in hope.

Lord, I am reminded that faith is the assurance of things hoped for, the conviction of things not seen. Strengthen my faith so that I may hold firmly to the hope You have set before me, trusting in Your promises even when I cannot see the outcome.

Help me to rejoice in hope, be patient in tribulation, and constant in prayer. In times of trial, may my heart remain steadfast, anchored by the hope I have in You.

I thank You, Father, for the hope in which I was saved. I recognize that hope that is seen is not hope, for who hopes for what he sees? But if I hope for what I do not see, I wait for it with patience. Grant me the patience to wait on Your perfect timing and the assurance that my hope in You will not be in vain.

Finally, I hold on to the promise that surely there is a future, and my hope will not be cut off. May this truth encourage me, knowing that my future is secure in Your hands.

In Jesus' name I pray, Amen.

My own prayer:

_____
_____
_____
_____
_____
_____

Humility

noun

hyü-ˈmi-lə-tē

1. Freedom from pride or arrogance: the quality or state of being humble

- **Proverbs 22:4:** The reward for humility and fear of the Lord is riches and honor and life.
- **Proverbs 11:2:** When pride comes, then comes disgrace, but with the humble is wisdom.
- **Colossians 3:12:** Put on then, as God's chosen ones, holy and beloved, compassionate hearts, kindness, humility, meekness, and patience.
- **Ephesians 4:2:** With all humility and gentleness, with patience, bearing with one another in love.
- **Proverbs 18:12:** Before destruction a man's heart is haughty, but humility comes before honor.

Reflections:

___

___

___

___

___

___

___

___

___

___

Prayer:

Heavenly Father,

I come before You in submission to Your Word and truth. I humbly acknowledge my need for Your guidance and grace. Lord, forgive me for any pride that has taken root in my speech, heart, and actions. I turn away from these destructive attitudes and behaviors, recognizing that when pride comes, disgrace follows.

Holy Spirit, fill me with Your presence. Keep me teachable and open to Your wisdom. Save me from my own self-importance and help me to put on compassion, kindness, humility, meekness, and patience as one of Your chosen ones. Teach me to bear with others in love, showing all humility and gentleness. Let me remember that humility comes before honor, and that the reward for humility and fear of You is riches, honor, and life.

Father, I renounce pride in all its forms. Help me to honor a life lived in humility rather than one driven by pride. May I decrease so that You may increase in my life.

In Jesus' name I pray, Amen.

My own prayer:

_____
_____
_____
_____
_____
_____
_____
_____

Hurt

verb
ˈhərt

1. To inflict with physical pain
2. To cause emotional pain or anguish to

- **Luke 6:27–28:** "But I say to you who hear, Love your enemies, do good to those who hate you, bless those who curse you, pray for those who abuse you."
- **Romans 3:23:** For all have sinned and fall short of the glory of God.
- **John 11:35:** Jesus wept.
- **1 Peter 4:1**: Since therefore Christ suffered in the flesh, arm yourselves with the same way of thinking, for whoever has suffered in the flesh has ceased from sin.

Reflections:

_____
_____
_____
_____
_____
_____
_____
_____
_____
_____
_____
_____

Prayer:

Heavenly Father,

I come before You, hurt! Just as Jesus wept, I weep at Your feet, O God. Help me to remain in faith and hope, remembering that vengeance is Yours. Grant me the strength to love my enemies and do good to those who have hurt me.

I acknowledge that all have sinned and fallen short of Your glory, including myself. I renounce any ideas of self-righteous justice or vengeance. Fill me with Your Holy Spirit, reminding me that Christ too has suffered. May I arm myself with the same way of thinking, knowing that whoever has suffered in the flesh has ceased from sin.

Heal my wounds, Lord, and help me to forgive as You have forgiven me. Let Your love flow through me, even in my hurt.

In Jesus' name I pray, Amen.

My own prayer:

_____
_____
_____
_____
_____
_____
_____
_____

Immorality

noun

,i-(,)mò-'ra-lə-tē

1. The quality or state of being immoral (not moral)
2. An immoral act or practice

- **1 Corinthians 6:18–19**: Flee from sexual immorality. Every other sin a person commits is outside the body, but the sexually immoral person sins against his own body. Or do you not know that your body is a temple of the Holy Spirit within you, whom you have from God? You are not your own,
- **Colossians 3:5:** Put to death therefore what is earthly in you: sexual immorality, impurity, passion, evil desire, and covetousness, which is idolatry.
- **Hebrews 4:15–16:** For we do not have a high priest who is unable to sympathize with our weaknesses, but one who in every respect has been tempted as we are, yet without sin. Let us then with confidence draw near to the throne of grace, that we may receive mercy and find grace to help in time of need.
- **2 Timothy 2:22**: So flee youthful passions and pursue righteousness, faith, love, and peace, along with those who call on the Lord from a pure heart.
- **Philippians 4:8:** Finally, brothers, whatever is true, whatever is honorable, whatever is just, whatever is pure, whatever is lovely, whatever is commendable, if there is any excellence, if there is anything worthy of praise, think about these things.

Reflections:

_____

_____

_____

_____

_____

_____

Prayer:

Heavenly Father,

I come before You in humility and reverence of Your almighty name. Lord, forgive me for the lack of morality in my ways. Help me to flee from any and all immorality.

Holy Spirit, teach me to honor my body as a holy temple with Your presence within. Grant me the courage and boldness to put to death what is earthly in me: sexual immorality, impurity, passion, evil desire, and covetousness, which is idolatry.

I look to the High Priest who sympathizes with my weakness, for I have sinned. Allow me to draw near to Your throne of grace that I may receive mercy and find grace to help in my time of need.

I pledge myself to whatever is honorable, just, pure, lovely, and commendable—mirroring excellence and all that is worthy of praise. Help me to think about these things which are pleasing to You, my God. Strengthen me to flee youthful passions and instead pursue righteousness, faith, love, and peace, along with those who call on You from a pure heart.

In Jesus' name I pray, Amen.

My own prayer:

_____
_____
_____
_____
_____
_____
_____

Infirmity

Noun

in-ˈfər-mə-tē

1. The condition of being feeble
2. Disease, malady

- **2 Corinthians 12:9–10**: But he said to me, "My grace is sufficient for you, for my power is made perfect in weakness." Therefore I will boast all the more gladly of my weaknesses, so that the power of Christ may rest upon me. For the sake of Christ, then, I am content with weaknesses, insults, hardships, persecutions, and calamities. For when I am weak, then I am strong.
- **Matthew 8:17:** This was to fulfill what was spoken by the prophet Isaiah: "He took our illnesses and bore our diseases."
- **Psalm 103:2–3:** Bless the Lord, O my soul, and forget not all his benefits, who forgives all your iniquity, who heals all your diseases.
- **Luke 13:11–13:** And behold, there was a woman who had had a disabling spirit for eighteen years. She was bent over and could not fully straighten herself. When Jesus saw her, he called her over and said to her, "Woman, you are freed from your disability." And he laid his hands on her, and immediately she was made straight, and she glorified God.

Reflections:

_____
_____
_____
_____
_____
_____
_____
_____

Prayer:

Heavenly Father,

I come before You, burdened, resting upon Your feet and calling Your holy name. My Lord, Your grace is sufficient, Your power is made perfect in my weakness. Therefore, I boast all the more of my weakness so that the power of Christ may rest upon me. For the sake of Christ, I am content with weaknesses, insults, hardships, persecutions, and calamities. For when I am weak, then I am strong. As the prophets spoke, Lord Jesus took our illnesses and bore our diseases. I proclaim with a shout: Bless the Lord, O my soul, and forget not all His benefits, who forgives all my iniquity, who heals all my diseases.

Abba, just as the woman with the disabling spirit, free me from this infirmity. Lay Your hands upon me, O God, that I too may stand straight in glorification of Your miraculous ways, confounding the wise and doubtful. In my weakness, let Your strength be perfected. In my illness, let Your healing power be manifested. May this trial become a testimony to Your glory and grace and my praise declare healing in the name of Jesus.

In Jesus' name I pray, Amen

My own prayer:

_____

_____

_____

_____

_____

_____

_____

Iniquity

noun
i-ˈni-kwə-tē

1. Gross injustice
2. A wicked act or thing

- **Psalm 32:5:** I acknowledge my sin to you, and I did not cover my iniquity; I said, "I will confess my transgressions to the Lord," and you forgave the iniquity of my sin.
- **Isaiah 59:2:** But your iniquities have made a separation between you and your God, and your sins have hidden his face from you so that he does not hear.
- **Proverbs 28:13:** Whoever conceals his transgressions will not prosper, but he who confesses and forsakes them will obtain mercy.
- **Isaiah 53:5:** But he was pierced for our transgressions; he was crushed for our iniquities; upon him was the chastisement that brought us peace, and with his wounds we are healed.
- **Psalm 119:11:** I have stored up your word in my heart, that I might not sin against you.
- **Romans 12:2:** Do not be conformed to this world, but be transformed by the renewal of your mind, that by testing you may discern what is the will of God, what is good and acceptable and perfect.

Reflections:

_____
_____
_____
_____
_____
_____
_____
_____
_____

Prayer:

Heavenly Father,

I come before You in humility, with a heart of repentance. I acknowledge my sin to You and do not cover my iniquity; rather, I say, "I will confess my transgressions to the Lord," and You forgive the iniquity of my sin. Forgive me, O Lord, for the times I have hidden my iniquity from You—as if You had not seen my wicked practices, every vile thought, twisted tongue, deep moral corruption, and crookedness of heart. Hear my cry for Your mercy. Wash me clean, O Lord. I surrender and call upon the name of Jesus Christ for purification and the washing away of my transgressions. By my Savior's blood, my iniquities are redeemed, my wounds are healed, and I am restored and made new, receiving His peace. My soul proclaims that I have stored up Your words in my heart so that I may not sin against You. Yielding to Your commands, Lord, and submitting to transformation by the renewing of my mind, may discernment be granted to know Your will—what is good, acceptable, and perfect. Holy Spirit, help me not to be conformed to this world, but to be continually transformed by Your Word and Your Spirit. Let Your truth guide my thoughts, words, and actions. In Jesus' name, and by the authority of His blood, I pray. AmenIn Jesus' name I pray, Amen.

My own prayer:

_____
_____
_____
_____
_____
_____
_____
_____
_____

Insecurity

noun

ˌin-si-ˈkyūr-ə-tē

1. A state or feeling of anxiety, fear, or self-doubt
2. Lack of dependability or certainty

- **Psalm 139:14:** I praise you, for I am fearfully and wonderfully made. Wonderful are your works; my soul knows it very well.
- **Isaiah 41:10:** Fear not, for I am with you; be not dismayed, for I am your God; I will strengthen you, I will help you, I will uphold you with my righteous right hand.
- **Philippians 4:13:** I can do all things through him who strengthens me.
- **1 John 4:18:** There is no fear in love, but perfect love casts out fear. For fear has to do with punishment, and whoever fears has not been perfected in love.
- **Matthew 7:24–25:** "Everyone then who hears these words of mine and does them will be like a wise man who built his house on the rock. And the rain fell, and the floods came, and the winds blew and beat on that house, but it did not fall, because it had been founded on the rock."

Reflections:

_____
_____
_____
_____
_____
_____
_____
_____

Prayer:

Heavenly Father,

I come before You in complete faith. I praise You, for I am fearfully and wonderfully made. How wonderful are Your works; my soul knows it very well. Lord, grant me discernment to know the difference between Your almighty divine security and the temporary security of this fallen world. In times when I am shaken by my circumstances, remind me to fear not, for You are with me. I shall not be dismayed, for You are my God. You will strengthen me, You will help me, You will uphold me with Your righteous right hand.

Holy Spirit, teach me to trust in the Lord, my one and only true security, for through Christ who strengthens me I can do all things. Build up my soul in perfect love, for love casts out fear. You are my Rock, O God, and it is on this rock I build my foundation. I renounce fear and control, yielding myself to You, my God. Let Your perfect love cast out all insecurity, replacing it with confidence in Your unfailing presence and power.

In Jesus' name I pray, Amen.

My own prayer:

_____

_____

_____

_____

_____

_____

_____

_____

Isolation

noun

ī-sə-ˈlā-shən

1. The condition of being isolated (alone)

- **Genesis 2:18:** The LORD God said, "It is not good for man to be alone. I will make a helper for him."
- **Proverbs 18:1:** Whoever isolates himself seeks his own desire; he breaks out against all sound judgment.
- **1 Corinthians 12:14**: For the body does not consist of one member but of many.
- **Genesis 2:18:** Then God said, "It is not good that the man should be alone; I will make him a helper fit for him."
- **Ecclesiastes 4:9–10:** Two are better than one, because they have a good reward for their toil. For if they fall, one will lift up his fellow. But woe to him who is alone when he falls and has not another to lift him up!
- **Hebrews 10:24–25:** And let us consider how to stir up one another to love and good works, not neglecting to meet together, as is the habit of some, but encouraging one another, and all the more as you see the Day drawing near.

Reflections:

_____

_____

_____

_____

_____

_____

_____

_____

Prayer:

Heavenly Father,

I come before You in humility. Lord, I recognize that it is not Your design for me to be alone, for in Your mighty power You declared it is not good for man to be alone, making a helper fit for him. Remove from me the deceptive thinking that I ought to remain in isolation, for the body does not consist of one member but of many. Rid me of the pride of isolation that seeks my own desire and leads to breaking out of sound judgment. As this fallen world tries to impart falsehoods regarding singleness and isolation, engrain into my soul that two are better than one, for there is good reward for our toil. For if one falls, the other will lift up his fellow.

Holy Spirit, teach me to consider others in love and good works, not neglecting to meet as is the habit of some. Let my life display encouragement to others, day by day drawing near to You. Grant me the wisdom to seek godly companionship and the courage to engage with Your body of believers. Help me to find my place in Your community, serving and being served, loving and being loved.

In Jesus' name I pray, Amen.

My own prayer:

_____
_____
_____
_____
_____
_____
_____
_____

Prayer:

Heavenly Father,

I come before You in unity with Your truth. God of hope, fill me with all joy and peace in believing, so that by the power of the Holy Spirit I may abound in hope. Lord, You make known to me the path of life; in Your presence is fullness of joy. At Your right hand are pleasures forevermore. Father, help me when my heart is crushed to recall Your words: Rejoice in the Lord always; again I will say, rejoice!

May I live by the fruit of the Spirit: love, joy, peace, patience, kindness, goodness, faithfulness, gentleness, and self-control. Help me focus on Your kingdom, not based on eating or drinking, but on righteousness, peace, and joy in the Holy Spirit.

Teach me to count it all joy when I face trials of various kinds. May I greatly rejoice in You, Lord, for You have clothed me with the garments of salvation and covered me with the robe of righteousness.

In Jesus' name I pray, Amen.

My own prayer:

_____
_____
_____
_____
_____
_____
_____
_____
_____
_____

Jealousy

noun
ˈje-lə-sē

1. A jealous disposition (disposed to suspect rivalry or unfaithfulness), attitude, or feeling

Zealous vigilance

- **Proverbs 14:30:** A tranquil heart gives life to the flesh, but envy makes the bones rot.
- **James 3:16:** For where jealousy and selfish ambition exist, there will be disorder and every vile practice.
- **Galatians 5:19–21:** Now the works of the flesh are evident: sexual immorality, impurity, sensuality, idolatry, sorcery, enmity, strife, jealousy, fits of anger, rivalries, dissensions, divisions, envy, drunkenness, orgies, and things like these. I warn you, as I warned you before, that those who do such things will not inherit the kingdom of God.
- **1 Corinthians 13:4**: Love is patient and kind; love does not envy or boast; it is not arrogant or rude.
- **Psalm 37:1–3:** Fret not yourself because of evildoers; be not envious of wrongdoers! For they will soon fade like the grass and wither like the green herb. Trust in the Lord, and do good; dwell in the land and befriend faithfulness.

Reflections:

_____
_____
_____
_____
_____
_____
_____

Prayer:

Heavenly Father,

I come before You in submission to Your Word and ways. Lord, I yearn to have a tranquil heart which gives life, ridding the envy from my heart that rots my bones. Remove every vile practice from me, plucking out jealousy and selfish ambition.

Holy Spirit, wash me clean, purify my heart so that I can live a life pleasing to God and inherit the kingdom. Keep me teachable, O God, acting with love and patience, not boasting or fueled with envy. I proclaim I will not fret over evildoers, nor be envious of wrongdoers, for they will soon fade like the grass and wither away like the green herb. I choose to trust in You, Lord, and to do good, dwelling in Your land and befriending faithfulness. Help me to embody the love that does not envy, that is patient and kind. Guard my heart against the works of the flesh–enmity, strife, jealousy, and fits of anger. Instead, fill me with Your peace and contentment.

In Jesus' name I pray, Amen.

My own prayer:

_____
_____
_____
_____
_____
_____
_____
_____

Jesus

noun
ˈjē-zəs

1. The highest human corporeal concept of the divine idea rebuking and destroying error and bringing to light man's immortality

- **John 3:16:** "For God so loved the world, that he gave his only Son, that whoever believes in him should not perish but have eternal life."
- **John 14:6:** Jesus said to him, "I am the way, and the truth, and the life. No one comes to the Father except through me."
- **John 1:14:** And the Word became flesh and dwelt among us, and we have seen his glory, glory as of the only Son from the Father, full of grace and truth.
- **Isaiah 9:6:** For to us a child is born, to us a son is given; and the government shall be upon his shoulder, and his name shall be called Wonderful Counselor, Mighty God, Everlasting Father, Prince of Peace.
- **John 8:58:** Jesus said to them, "Truly, truly, I say to you, before Abraham was, I am."
- **Romans 6:23:** For the wages of sin is death, but the free gift of God is eternal life in Christ Jesus our Lord.

Reflections:

_____
_____
_____
_____
_____
_____
_____
_____

Prayer:

Heavenly Father,

I come before You with exclamation of song and dance, in celebration and praise of Your holy name. I am in awe of Your love for the world, that You gave Your only Son so that whoever believes in Him should not perish but have eternal life.

Lord Jesus, I declare You are the way, the truth, and the life. No one comes to the Father except through You, O King Jesus. You are the Word made flesh, full of grace and truth, dwelling among us.

Just as Isaiah proclaimed: for us a child is born, to us a son is given, and the government shall be upon His shoulders. Your name is Wonderful Counselor, Mighty God, Everlasting Father, Prince of Peace. Jesus, You truly are the great I AM, there is no one like You, Lord. I heed Your Word, for the wages of sin is death, but the free gift of God is eternal life in You, Christ Jesus.

You are my Lord, and I am Your humble servant. Thank You for being the Almighty that rebukes and destroys error, bringing to light man's immortality. Help me to trust in You, to do good, and to dwell in Your land of faithfulness.

In Your precious name I pray, Amen.

My own prayer:

_____

_____

_____

_____

_____

_____

Jezebel

noun
ˈje-zə-bel

1. An impudent, shameless, or morally unrestrained woman

- **Revelation 2:20:** "But I have this against you, that you tolerate that woman Jezebel, who calls herself a prophetess and is teaching and seducing my servants to practice sexual immorality and to eat food sacrificed to idols."
- **Revelation 2:24–26:** "But to the rest of you in Thyatira, who do not hold this teaching, who have not learned what some call the deep things of Satan, to you I say, I do not lay on you any other burden. Only hold fast what you have until I come. The one who conquers and who keeps my works until the end, to him I will give authority over the nations."
- **1 John 4:1**: Beloved, do not believe every spirit, but test the spirits to see whether they are from God, for many false prophets have gone out into the world.
- **1 Thessalonians 4:3–7**: For this is the will of God, your sanctification: that you abstain from sexual immorality; that each one of you know how to control his own body in holiness and honor, not in the passion of lust like the Gentiles who do not know God; that no one transgress and wrong his brother in this matter, because the Lord is an avenger in all these things, as we told you beforehand and solemnly warned you. For God has not called us for impurity, but in holiness.
- **Psalm 91:2–4:** I will say to the Lord, "My refuge and my fortress, my God, in whom I trust." For he will deliver you from the snare of the fowler and from the deadly pestilence. He will cover you with his opinions, and under his wings you will find refuge; his faithfulness is a shield and buckler.
- **Ephesians 5:11:** Take no part in the unfruitful works of darkness, but instead expose them.

Reflections:

_____

_____

_____

_____

Prayer:

Heavenly Father,

I come before You in surrender and humility. Lord, the works of Jezebel have left my soul crushed and weary. Forgive me for knowingly or unknowingly aligning myself with the vices, practices, and contentions of Jezebel. I remove the impure desires to control, manipulate, silence others, and engage in seductive measures. I renounce idolatry, fantasies of power, and selfish ambitions.

Holy Spirit, fill me with Your precious Spirit, teach me to withstand the temptations to mimic the ancient entity, Jezebel.

Cleanse my hands, heart, and soul; make me a new creation in Christ Jesus. Lord, You are my refuge, and I choose Your ways over mine. It is You I trust, God, who will deliver me from the snares of Jezebel and all deadly pestilence.

Grant me discernment to test the spirits and recognize false prophets. Help me to abstain from sexual immorality and control my body in holiness and honor. I shall take no part in the unfruitful works of darkness but instead expose them.

In Jesus' name I pray Amen

My own prayer:

_____

_____

_____

_____

_____

_____

Joy

noun
jòi

1. The emotion evoked by well-being, success, or good fortune or by the prospect of possessing what one desires

- **Romans 15:13:** May the God of hope fill you with all joy and peace in believing, so that by the power of the Holy Spirit you may abound in hope.
- **Philippians 4:4:** Rejoice in the Lord always; again I will say, rejoice!
- **Galatians 5:22–23:** But the fruit of the Spirit is love, joy, peace, patience, kindness, goodness, faithfulness, gentleness, self-control; against such things there is no law.
- **Psalm 16:11:** You make known to me the path of life; in your presence there is fullness of joy; at your right hand are pleasures forevermore.
- **Isaiah 61:10:** I will greatly rejoice in the Lord; my soul shall exult in my God, for he has clothed me with the garments of salvation; he has covered me with the robe of righteousness, as a bridegroom decks himself like a priest with a beautiful headdress, and as a bride adorns herself with her jewels.
- **Romans 14:17:** For the kingdom of God is not a matter of eating and drinking but of righteousness and peace and joy in the Holy Spirit.
- **James 1:2:** Count it all joy, my brothers, when you meet trials of various kinds.

Reflections:

___

___

___

___

___

___

___

Justice

noun
ˈjə-stəs

1. The administration of law
2. The quality of being just, impartial, or fair

- **Isaiah 1:17:** Learn to do good; seek justice, correct oppression; bring justice to the fatherless, plead the widow's cause.
- **Micah 6:8:** He has told you, O man, what is good; and what does the Lord require of you but to do justice, and to love kindness, and to walk humbly with your God?
- **Proverbs 21:15:** When justice is done, it is a joy to the righteous but terror to evildoers.
- **Isaiah 30:18:** Therefore the Lord waits to be gracious to you, and therefore he exalts himself to show mercy to you. For the Lord is a God of justice; blessed are all those who wait for him.
- **Psalm 33:5:** He loves righteousness and justice; the earth is full of the steadfast love of the Lord.

Reflections:

_____
_____
_____
_____
_____
_____
_____
_____
_____

Prayer:

Heavenly Father,

I come before You in humility, seeking Your justice. Lord, in a world where evil is considered good and what is good by Your Word is considered evil, help me withstand. Remind me to do good, to seek justice, correct oppression, bring justice to the fatherless, and plead the widow's cause. Grant me the discipline to do justice, walk humbly, and display love and kindness.

Lord, just as You love righteousness and justice, help me to wait on You, not seeking my own justice. You desire to be gracious and show mercy; You are a God of justice. Blessed are those who wait for You. May Your righteousness flow through me like a river, and may I find joy in seeing justice done. Fill the earth with Your steadfast love as I strive to reflect Your justice in my actions.

In Jesus' name I pray, Amen.

My own prayer:

_____
_____
_____
_____
_____
_____
_____
_____
_____

Kindness

noun
ˈkīn(d)-nəs

1. The quality or state of being kind (of a sympathetic or helpful nature)
2. A kind deed

- **Ephesians 4:32:** Be kind to one another, tenderhearted, forgiving one another, as God in Christ forgave you.
- **Luke 6:35:** "But love your enemies, and do good, and lend, expecting nothing in return, and your reward will be great, and you will be sons of the Most High, for he is kind to the ungrateful and the evil."
- **Proverbs 11:17:** A man who is kind benefits himself, but a cruel man hurts himself.
- **Colossians 3:12:** Put on then, as God's chosen ones, holy and beloved, compassionate hearts, kindness, humility, meekness, and patience.
- **Proverbs 31:26:** She opens her mouth with wisdom, and the teaching of kindness is on her tongue.

Reflections:

_____
_____
_____
_____
_____
_____
_____
_____

Prayer:

Heavenly Father,

I come before You as a faithful servant. Lord, may I live by Your words, knowing that a man who is kind benefits himself, but a cruel man hurts himself. Forgive me for the times I have rationalized and cultivated a practice of unkindness.

Call to mind any impure motive or hindrance keeping me from a mouth filled with wisdom, teaching kindness with my tongue.

Holy Spirit, help me to love my enemies, do good, and lend expecting nothing in return. You have chosen me, God, and I shall put on compassion, kindness, humility, meekness, and patience all the days of my life. Not for my benefit, but for the building up of Your kingdom and to glorify Your holy name.

Teach me to be kind to others, tenderhearted, forgiving as You in Christ have forgiven me. May I reflect Your kindness, even to those who are ungrateful or evil. Shape my heart to be compassionate, my actions to be kind, and my words to be filled with wisdom and kindness. Let Your kindness flow through me to touch the lives of those around me.

In Jesus' name I pray, Amen.

My own prayer:

_____

_____

_____

_____

_____

_____

Kingdom

noun

'kiŋ-dəm

1. A politically organized community or major territorial unit having a monarchical form of government headed by a king or queen

- **Matthew 6:33:** "But seek first the kingdom of God and his righteousness, and all these things will be added to you."
- **1 Corinthians 4:20**: For the kingdom of God does not consist in talk but in power.
- **Psalm 145:13:** Your kingdom is an everlasting kingdom, and your dominion endures throughout all generations.
- **Romans 14:17–18:** For the kingdom of God is not a matter of eating and drinking but of righteousness and peace and joy in the Holy Spirit. Whoever thus serves Christ is acceptable to God and approved by men.

Reflections:

_____
_____
_____
_____
_____
_____
_____
_____
_____
_____

Prayer:

Heavenly Father,

I come before You in submission, seeking Your kingdom and Your righteousness above all else. Lord, I acknowledge that this world's conditions sway like the wind, pressed by man's wicked ideas and deceitful propaganda. Forgive me for aligning myself with the world. I pledge my allegiance to You and Your kingdom, which does not consist of talk but of power. Your kingdom is everlasting, and Your dominion endures throughout all generations.

Holy Spirit, keep me simple and teachable, pursuing the Kingdom of the Almighty. Help me to live in righteousness, peace, and joy in the Holy Spirit, serving Christ in a way that is acceptable to You and approved by others. May Your kingdom come in my life, not as a matter of eating and drinking, but as a transformative power that changes me from within. I trust that as I seek Your kingdom first, all other things I need will be added unto me.

In Jesus' name I pray Amen

My own prayer:

_____

_____

_____

_____

_____

_____

_____

_____

Lazy

adjective
ˈlā-zē

1. Disinclined to activity or exertion: not energetic or vigorous

- **Titus 2:5:** To be self-controlled, pure, working at home, kind, and submissive to their own husbands, that the word of God may not be reviled.
- **2 Timothy 2:6**: It is the hard-working farmer who ought to have the first share of the crops.
- **Proverbs 10:4:** A slack hand causes poverty, but the hand of the diligent makes rich.

Reflections:

_____
_____
_____
_____
_____
_____
_____
_____
_____
_____
_____
_____

Prayer:

Heavenly Father,

I come before You, acknowledging my struggle with laziness. Lord, forgive me for the times I have been disinclined to activity or exertion, lacking energy and vigor in my daily tasks and responsibilities. Help me to be self-controlled and pure in my actions, working diligently whether at home or elsewhere. Jesus deliver me from the spell keeping me bound to inaction. Teach me to be kind and submissive where appropriate, that Your Word may not be reviled because of my laziness.

Instill in me the spirit of the hard-working farmer, who rightfully earns the first share of the crops. May I approach my work and duties with enthusiasm and dedication, knowing that my efforts honor You. Grant me the strength to overcome my tendency toward idleness. Help me to productively use the gifts and talents You've given me, serving You and others with energy and purpose.

In Jesus' name I pray, Amen.

My own prayer:

_____
_____
_____
_____
_____
_____
_____
_____
_____

Legion

noun
'lē-jən

1. A large military force

- **Mark 5:9:** Then Jesus asked him, "What is your name?" "My name is Legion," he replied, "for we are many."
- **Romans 8:37:** No, in all these things we are more than conquerors through him who loved us.
- **Ephesians 6:11:** Put on the whole armor of God, so that you can take your stand against the devil's schemes.
- **James 4:7:** Submit yourselves therefore to God. Resist the devil, and he will flee from you.
- **1 Peter 5:8–9 (NIV)**: Be alert and of sober mind. Your enemy the devil prowls around like a roaring lion looking for someone to devour. Resist him, standing firm in the faith.
- **Psalm 18:2:** The Lord is my rock and my fortress and my deliverer, my God, my rock, in whom I take refuge.
- **Psalm 34:17:** When the righteous cry for help, the Lord hears and delivers them out of all their troubles.
- **Psalm 50:15:** Call upon me in the day of trouble; I will deliver you, and you shall glorify me.

Reflections:

_____
_____
_____
_____
_____
_____
_____
_____

Prayer:

Heavenly Father,

I come before You in submission, seeking deliverance. Lord, I am burdened and overrun in my soul, mind, and body by Legion. Forgive me for any idolatry or rebellion that has contributed to such torment. Liberate my soul, O Jesus. You are my rock and my fortress, in whom I take refuge. I cry out to Your holy name for help; deliver my soul. As You delivered the man possessed with just a command-"Come out, you unclean spirit!"-I trust that You can deliver me as well. Holy Spirit, fill me up. Gird up my legs so that I may stand with the full armor of God, submitting myself to God alone, resisting Legion. Guide me to live maturely through your scriptures. Grant me the strength to be alert and of sober mind, standing firm in my faith in You, my Savior.

Lord, I declare that in all these things, I am more than a conqueror through You who loves me. In the day of trouble, I call upon You, knowing You will deliver me, and I shall glorify Your name.

In Jesus' name, and by the authority of His blood, I pray. Amen

My own prayer:

_____
_____
_____
_____
_____
_____
_____
_____

Leviathan

noun

li-ˈvī-ə-thn

1. Sea monster defeated by Yahweh in various scriptural accounts
2. Something large or formidable

- **Psalm 74:14:** You crushed the heads of Leviathan; you gave him as food for the creatures of the wilderness.
- **Isaiah 27:1:** In that day the Lord with his hard and great and strong sword will punish Leviathan the fleeing serpent, Leviathan the twisting serpent, and he will slay the dragon that is in the sea.
- **1 John 5:4**: For everyone who has been born of God overcomes the world. And this is the victory that has overcome the world—our faith.
- **Romans 8:37:** No, in all these things we are more than conquerors through him who loved us.
- **Job 41:1:** Can you draw out Leviathan with a fishhook, or press down his tongue with a cord?
- **Job 41:33 (NIV)**: Nothing on earth is its equal—a creature without fear.

Reflections:

_____
_____
_____
_____
_____
_____
_____
_____

Prayer:

Heavenly Father,

I come before You, acknowledging Your supreme power over all creation, even the mightiest creatures like Leviathan. Lord, I am in awe of Your strength, for You alone can crush the heads of Leviathan and punish the fleeing serpent.

I renounce any fear or intimidation I may feel in the face of overwhelming challenges, remembering that through You, I am more than a conqueror. Help me to trust in Your victory, knowing that my faith in You overcomes the world.

Father, when I face seemingly unconquerable obstacles, remind me that nothing on earth is Your equal. Just as no one can draw out Leviathan with a hook, I cannot overcome my greatest battles alone. I need Your strength and Your sword.

Grant me the courage to face my own "Leviathans"—those fears, addictions, and struggles that seem too powerful to defeat. Help me remember that You have already won the victory, and through faith in You, I can overcome.

Thank You for Your love that makes me more than a conqueror.

In Your mighty name I pray, Amen.

My own prayer:

_____

_____

_____

_____

_____

Life

noun
'līf

1. The sequence of physical and mental experiences that make up the existence of an individual

- **Genesis 1:30:** "And to every beast of the earth and to every bird of the heavens and to everything that creeps on the earth, everything that has the breath of life, I have given every green plant for food." And it was so.
- **Genesis 2:7:** Then the Lord God formed the man of dust from the ground and breathed into his nostrils the breath of life, and the man became a living creature.
- **Leviticus 17:14:** For the life of every creature is its blood: its blood is its life. Therefore I have said to the people of Israel, 'You shall not eat the blood of any creature, for the life of every creature is its blood. Whoever eats it shall be cut off.'
- **Psalm 6:4:** Turn, O Lord, deliver my life; save me for the sake of your steadfast love.
- **Psalm 16:11:** You make known to me the path of life; in your presence there is fullness of joy; at your right hand are pleasures forevermore.
- **Psalm 86:2:** Preserve my life, for I am godly; save your servant, who trusts in you—you are my God.
- **Psalm 119:50:** This is my comfort in my affliction, that your promise gives me life.
- **John 14:6:** Jesus said to him, "I am the way, and the truth, and the life. No one comes to the Father except through me."

Reflections:

_____
_____
_____
_____
_____
_____

Prayer:

Heavenly Father,

I come before You in submission to Your mighty name as Creator and the Author of Life. You have given breath to every beast on earth, every bird of the heavens, and everything that creeps on the earth. You formed man from dust and breathed into his nostrils the breath of life, making him a living creature.

Lord, forgive me for the times I have taken life for granted, for passing it off as invaluable. Like David, I pray, "Turn, O Lord, deliver my life; save me for the sake of your steadfast love." Your promise gives me life and comfort in my affliction.

Jesus, You are the Way, the Truth, and the Life. No one comes to the Father except through You. Help me to remain faithful and discerning of those who seek to pervert or taint life.

May Your Holy Spirit flow through me all the days of my life so that others will desire to know the God whom I call Abba. Make known to me the path of life; in Your presence, there is fullness of joy.

Preserve my life, for I trust in You—You are my God. At Your right hand are pleasures forevermore, and I long to walk in Your ways.

In Jesus' name I pray, Amen

My own prayer:

_____
_____
_____
_____
_____
_____

Lonely

adjective
'lōn-lō

1. being without company
2. sad from being alone

- **Psalm 25:16:** "Turn to me and be gracious to me, for I am lonely and afflicted."
- **Psalm 23:4:** Even though I walk through the valley of the shadow of death, I will fear no evil, for you are with me; your rod and your staff, they comfort me.
- **Isaiah 41:10:** Fear not, for I am with you; be not dismayed, for I am your God; I will strengthen you, I will help you, I will uphold you with my righteous right hand.
- **Deuteronomy 31:6:** Be strong and courageous. Do not fear or be in dread of them, for it is the Lord your God who goes with you. He will not leave you or forsake you.
- **Matthew 28:20:** "Teaching them to observe all that I have commanded you. And behold, I am with you always, to the end of the age."
- **Psalm 68:6:** God settles the solitary in a home; he leads out the prisoners to prosperity, but the rebellious dwell in a parched land.
- **1 Peter 5:7:** Casting all your anxieties on him, because he cares for you.

Reflections:

_____
_____
_____
_____
_____
_____
_____
_____
_____

Prayer:

Heavenly Father,

I come before You in ruins, feeling lonely and afflicted. As I walk through this valley of loneliness, remind me that You are with me, comforting and guiding me. Father, on this isolating journey where no companion seems to understand or accept me, help me remember that You do. It is Your comfort I seek, and Your everlasting love is the banner I clothe myself with. Help me not to fear or be dismayed, for You are my God.

Lord, help me see rejection and loneliness as temporary, knowing You will never leave or forsake me. I take comfort in Your promise to be with me always, to the very end of the age.

Holy Spirit, grant me strength and courage during this lonely time. Remind me that You set the lonely in families. I cast all my anxieties on You, trusting in Your care for me.

In Jesus' name I pray, Amen.

My own prayer:

_____

_____

_____

_____

_____

_____

_____

_____

Loss

noun
'lòs

1. The act or fact of being unable to keep or maintain something or someone

- **Acts 27:10:** "Sirs, I perceive that the voyage will be with injury and much loss, not only of the cargo and the ship, but also of our lives."
- **Philippians 3:8:** Indeed, I count everything as loss because of the surpassing worth of knowing Christ Jesus my Lord. For his sake I have suffered the loss of all things and count them as rubbish, in order that I may gain Christ.

Reflections:

_____
_____
_____
_____
_____
_____
_____
_____
_____
_____
_____

Prayer:

Heavenly Father,

I come before You with a heavy heart, acknowledging the losses in my life. Like Paul warned of the perilous voyage, I too have faced journeys filled with injury and loss. Yet, Lord, I am reminded of the words in Philippians, that knowing You surpasses all else.

Father, help me to count all my losses as gain for the sake of Christ. When I feel the sting of loss, be it material possessions, relationships, or dreams, remind me that these things are temporary. Grant me the strength to view my losses through Your eternal perspective. Lord, I confess there are times when I cling too tightly to worldly things. Teach me to hold loosely to what I have, knowing that You are my greatest treasure. Help me to trust in Your plan, even when it involves loss, knowing that You work all things for the good of those who love You. May I, like Paul, come to a place where I can count all things as loss for the surpassing worth of knowing You, Jesus Christ, my Lord. Let every loss in my life draw me closer to You, deepening my faith and reliance on Your grace.

In Jesus' name I pray, Amen.

My own prayer:

_____

_____

_____

_____

_____

_____

_____

Love

noun
'ləv

1. Strong affection for another arising out of kinship or personal ties
2. An assurance of affection

- **Deuteronomy 6:5:** You shall love the LORD your God with all your heart and with all your soul and with all your might.
- **Deuteronomy 7:9:** Know therefore that the LORD your God is God, the faithful God who keeps covenant and steadfast love with those who love him and keep his commandments, to a thousand generations.
- **Joshua 23:11:** Be very careful, therefore, to love the LORD your God.
- **Mark 12:30–31:** "And you shall love the LORD your God with all your heart and with all your soul and with all your mind and with all your strength.' The second is this: 'You shall love your neighbor as yourself.' There is no other commandment greater than these."
- **John 14:15:** "If you love me, you will keep my commandments."
- **1 Corinthians 13:4–7**: Love is patient and kind; love does not envy or boast; it is not arrogant or rude. It does not insist on its own way; it is not irritable or resentful; it does not rejoice at wrongdoing, but rejoices with the truth. Love bears all things, believes all things, hopes all things, endures all things.

Reflections:

_____
_____
_____
_____
_____
_____
_____

Prayer:

Heavenly Father,

I come before You, basking in the splendor that is Your love. Lord, You have displayed Your everlasting love to me; You are a faithful and gracious God. Father, as the world has redefined love, I stand firm on Your truth. Love is patient and kind; it does not envy or boast, it is not arrogant or rude. It does not insist on its own way; it is not irritable or resentful; it does not rejoice at wrongdoing but rejoices with the truth. Love bears all things, believes all things, hopes all things, endures all things.

May my life always display such acts of love, not just to the lovable but to the unlovable just the same. Forgive me for the times that I have negotiated, manipulated, or compromised love. I declare that I will keep Your commandments even when it is challenging. I shall love the Lord my God with all my heart, with all my soul, with all my mind, and with all my strength. And I shall love my neighbor as myself, for there is no commandment greater than these.

Help me, Lord, to be very careful to love You, my God, with every fiber of my being. Let Your steadfast love flow through me to others, that I may be a living testament to Your covenant of love that endures for a thousand generations.

In Jesus' name, Amen

My own prayer:

_____

_____

_____

_____

_____

_____

Lukewarm

adjective
'lük-'wȯrm

1. Moderately warm
2. Lacking conviction

- **Revelation 3:15–16:** "I know your works: you are neither cold nor hot. Would that you were either cold or hot! So, because you are lukewarm, and neither hot nor cold, I will spit you out of my mouth."
- **1 Kings 18:21 (NIV):** Elijah went before the people and said, "'How long will you waver between two opinions? If the Lord is God, follow him; but if Baal is God, follow him.'"
- **Matthew 5:37:** "Let what you say be simply 'Yes' or 'No'; anything more than this comes from evil."
- **James 1:8 (NIV):** Such a person is double-minded and unstable in all they do.

Reflections:

_____
_____
_____
_____
_____
_____
_____
_____
_____
_____
_____
_____

Prayer:

Heavenly Father,

I come before you in submission. Lord, as the world provides endless options of compromise teach me to remain bold and firm, with my "yes" and my "no". When I am presented with a matter that befuddles me, Lord, may I come to you first seeking righteous wisdom and council. May I not let my decision toss and turn like the wind. Holy Spirit, fill me with the truth of God's Word and commands, with a heart of obedience so that I remain faithful to the Lord God, uncompromised by the demands of man and this wicked world.

Like Elijah challenged the people, I ask myself: How long will I waver between two opinions? Help me to choose You wholeheartedly, to follow You alone with passion and conviction.

Holy Spirit, grant me a heart of obedience so that I remain faithful to You, Lord God, uncompromised by the demands of man and this world's temptations. When I face decisions that confuse me, may I come to You first, seeking righteous wisdom and counsel. Keep me from being double-minded and unstable.

Ignite in me a fervent faith that is neither lukewarm nor apathetic. May my life reflect a passionate commitment to You that impacts the world around me.

In Jesus' name, Amen.

My own prayer:

_____
_____
_____
_____
_____
_____

Lust

noun
'ləst

1. Usually intense or unbridled sexual desires

- **Proverbs 11:6:** The righteousness of the upright delivers them, but the treacherous are taken captive by their lust.
- **2 Peter 2:10**: And especially those who indulge in the lust of defiling passion and despise authority. Bold and willful, they do not tremble as they blaspheme the glorious ones.
- **Leviticus 18:20–23:** You shall not lie sexually with your neighbor's wife, and so make yourself unclean with her. You shall not give any of your children to offer them to Molech, and so profane the name of your God: I am the Lord. You shall not lie with a male as with a woman; it is an abomination. And you shall not lie with any animal and so make yourself unclean with it, neither shall any woman give herself to an animal to lie with it: it is perversion.
- **Galatians 5:19–21:** Now the works of the flesh are evident: sexual immorality, impurity, sensuality, idolatry, sorcery, enmity, strife, jealousy, fits of anger, rivalries, dissentions, divisions, envy, drunkenness, orgies, and things like these.
- **2 Timothy 2:22**: So flee youthful passions and pursue righteousness, faith, love, and peace, along with those who call on the Lord from a pure heart.
- **1 Corinthians 6:18**: Flee from sexual immorality. Every other sin a person commits is outside the body, but the sexually immoral person sins against his own body.
- **2 Corinthians 10:5**: We destroy arguments and every lofty opinion raised against the knowledge of God, and take every thought captive to obey Christ.

Reflections:

_____
_____
_____
_____
_____

Prayer:

Heavenly Father,

I come before You in humility, acknowledging my struggle with lustful thoughts and desires. Lord, Your Word says that the righteousness of the upright delivers them, but the treacherous are taken captive by their lust. Help me to become righteous in Your sight. Cleanse my soul from the wicked cravings of lust. Break the hold of defiling passions that lead me to despise Your authority. May Your Holy Spirit purify and cleanse my heart, removing the hunger for lustful practices.

Grant me the strength to flee youthful passions and pursue righteousness, faith, love, and peace. Help me to make no provision for the flesh, to gratify its desires. Instead, let me walk by the Spirit, so I will not gratify the desires of the flesh. May I grow in self-control and discipline, living a life of purity and righteousness that is pleasing to You. Teach me to honor my body as a temple of the Holy Spirit. Let me serve You, Lord, rather than my fleshly appetites.

Give me the courage to make a covenant with my eyes, that I may not gaze upon that which would lead me into temptation. Help me to take every thought captive to obey Christ. May I lead a humble life of prayer and fasting, overcoming lustful desires.

In Jesus' name I pray, Amen

My own prayer:

_____
_____
_____
_____
_____
_____
_____

Lying

adjective
'lī-iŋ

1. Marked by or containing untrue statements

- **Proverbs 12:10:** Whoever is righteous has regard for the life of his beast, but the mercy of the wicked is cruel.
- **Proverbs 12:22:** Lying lips are an abomination to the Lord, but those who act faithfully are his delight.
- **2 Corinthians 11:31**: The God and Father of the Lord Jesus, he who is blessed forever, knows that I am not lying.
- **Matthew 5:37:** "Let what you say be simply 'Yes' or 'No'; anything more than this comes from evil."

Reflections:

_____
_____
_____
_____
_____
_____
_____
_____
_____
_____

Prayer:

Heavenly Father,

I come before You in humility, acknowledging my struggle with truthfulness. Lord, Your Word tells us that lying lips are an abomination to You, and I confess the times I have fallen short of Your standard of honesty. Forgive me for the lies I have told, whether big or small, to others or to myself. Cleanse my heart and my lips, that I may be counted among those who act faithfully and are Your delight.

Grant me the courage to speak truth, even when it's difficult. Help me to remember that You, the God and Father of the Lord Jesus, know all things and cannot be deceived. Instill in me a deep respect for honesty, not only in my words but in all my actions. May I regard the lives of others with righteousness and show true mercy, not the false kindness that comes from deceit. Guide me to be a person of integrity, whose words and deeds align with Your truth. Let my 'yes' be yes and my 'no' be no, as Your Son Jesus taught us.

In Jesus' name I pray, Amen.

My own prayer:

_____
_____
_____
_____
_____
_____
_____
_____

Malice

noun
'ma-ləs

1. Desire to cause pain, injury, or distress to another

- **1 Peter 2:1**: So put away all malice and all deceit and hypocrisy and envy and all slander.
- **Colossians 3:8:** But now you must put them all away: anger, wrath, malice, slander, and obscene talk from your mouth.
- **Ephesians 4:31:** Let all bitterness and wrath and anger and clamor and slander be put away from you, along with all malice.
- **Psalm 41:5:** My enemies say of me in malice, "'When will he die, and his name perish?'"

Reflections:

_____
_____
_____
_____
_____
_____
_____
_____
_____
_____
_____

Prayer:

Heavenly Father,

I come before You in submission. Lord, remove this chain from me, free my heart from all malice, deceit, hypocrisy, envy, and slander. Help me put away anger, wrath, and obscene talk from my mouth. Pluck out this bitterness that rots my soul, O God. Cleanse me with Your Holy Spirit. Do not let my name perish, but instead let it be a blessing. Plant in me living waters that thrive with peace, joy, patience, unity, and self-control.

Grant me the strength to be kind to others, tenderhearted, and forgiving, even as You have forgiven me in Christ. Let no corrupt word proceed from my mouth, but only what is good for necessary edification. Help me to avoid those who cause divisions and create obstacles contrary to Your teachings. Instead, fill me with Your love, that I may not harbor hatred or malice in my heart.

In Jesus' name I pray, Amen.

My own prayer:

_____
_____
_____
_____
_____
_____
_____
_____

Manipulate

verb

mə-'ni-pyə-lāt

1. To treat or operate with or as if with the hands or by mechanical means, especially in a skillful manner
2. To change by artful or unfair means so as to serve one's purpose

- **Proverbs 11:3 (NIV)**: The integrity of the upright guides them, but the unfaithful are destroyed by their duplicity.
- **Leviticus 19:35 (NIV)**: Do not use dishonest standards when measuring length, weight or quantity.
- **Proverbs 16:28 (NIV)**: A perverse person stirs up conflict, and a gossip separates close friends.
- **Proverbs 15:4**: A gentle tongue is a tree of life, but perverseness in it breaks the spirit.
- **Romans 16:18 (NIV)**: For such people are not serving our Lord Christ, but their own appetites. By smooth talk and flattery they deceive the minds of naive people.

Reflections:

Prayer:

Heavenly Father,

I come before You in humility, seeking deliverance. Lord, when the world and its culture use manipulative practices as standard, help me to stand firm, remaining in unity with Your Word and truth, not consenting to the viles that prowl around me. Let integrity guide me, allowing the unfaithful to be destroyed by their own duplicity. Forgive me for any time I have used dishonest measures, stirred up conflict, or engaged in gossip that separated close friends.

Holy Spirit, teach me to impart a tongue that brings healing like a tree of life. Grant me the discipline to serve the Lord, not my own appetites. Keep me from using smooth talk and flattery to deceive the minds of naive people. May my words and actions reflect Your truth and love, never crushing the spirit of others through deceit. Help me to measure all things honestly, in my dealings with others and in my own heart. Guard me against perversity that stirs up conflict, and instead, let me be an instrument of Your peace and reconciliation.

In Jesus' name I pray, Amen.

My own prayer:

_____

_____

_____

_____

_____

_____

_____

Marriage

noun
'mer-ij

1. The state of being united as spouses in a consensual and contractual relationship recognized by law

- **Genesis 2:24:** Therefore a man shall leave his father and his mother and hold fast to his wife, and they shall become one flesh.
- **Ephesians 5:33:** However, let each one of you love his wife as himself, and let the wife see that she respects her husband.
- **Ephesians 5:28:** In the same way husbands should love their wives as their own bodies. He who loves his wife loves himself.
- **Ephesians 5:25:** Husbands, love your wives, as Christ loved the church and gave himself up for her.
- **Ephesians 5:22–23:** Wives, submit to your own husbands, as to the Lord. For the husband is the head of the wife even as Christ is the head of the church, his body, and is himself its Savior.
- **Matthew 19:6:** "So they are no longer two but one flesh. What therefore God has joined together, let not man separate."
- **Hebrews 13:4:** Let marriage be held in honor among all, and let the marriage bed be undefiled, for God will judge the sexually immoral and adulterous.

Reflections:

_____
_____
_____
_____
_____
_____

Prayer:

Heavenly Father,

I come before You with gratitude for the sacred gift of marriage. Lord, help me to honor this covenant You have established, to leave behind my old life and hold fast to my spouse, becoming one flesh as You intended. Grant me the strength to love my wife as Christ loved the church, sacrificially and unconditionally. Help me to cherish her as my own body, recognizing that in loving her, I love myself.

Holy Spirit, guide me in respecting my husband and submitting to him as unto You, Lord. May our relationship reflect the beautiful mystery of Christ and the church.

Father, protect our marriage from temptation and division. Let us honor our marriage bed, keeping it pure and undefiled. Remind us daily that what You have joined together, no man should separate. Give us wisdom to navigate the challenges of married life, always turning to You for guidance and strength. May our union be a testament to Your love and grace in this world.

In Jesus' name I pray, Amen.

My own prayer:

_____
_____
_____
_____
_____
_____
_____

Medicine

noun

'me-di-sən

1. A substance or preparation used in treating disease
2. The science and art dealing with the maintenance of health and the prevention, alleviation, or cure of disease

- **Proverbs 17:22 (NIV)**: A cheerful heart is good medicine, but a crushed spirit 'dries up the bones.
- **Ezekiel 47:12:** And on the banks, on both sides of the river, there will grow all kinds of trees for food. Their leaves will not wither, nor their fruit fail, but they will bear fresh fruit every month, because the water for them flows from the sanctuary. Their fruit will be for food, and their leaves for healing.
- **Isaiah 38:21:** Now Isaiah had said, "Let them take a cake of figs and apply it to the boil, that he may recover."
- **Luke 5:31:** And Jesus answered them, "Those who are well have no need of a physician, but those who are sick."
- **Colossians 4:14:** Luke, the beloved physician, greets you, as does Demas.

Reflections:

___
___
___
___
___
___
___
___

Prayer:

Heavenly Father,

I come before You with gratitude. Thank You, Lord, for the gift of medicine and healing that You have provided. As Your Word says, "A cheerful heart is good medicine," and I am grateful for the joy and laughter You bring into my life, even in difficult times.

Yahweh-Rapha, let me be reminded that, as Hezekiah turned his face to the wall and prayed to You, You heard his weeping and guided Isaiah to use a poultice for healing. Lord, just as You showed Ezekiel trees with leaves for healing, I trust in Your provision of natural remedies and healing power. Thank You for the wisdom You have given to physicians and researchers who develop treatments to ease our suffering. Help me to be open to the various ways You may choose to bring healing into my life-whether through medical treatments, natural remedies, or Your divine intervention.

Jesus, You taught us that those who are well do not need a physician, but those who are sick. Grant me the wisdom to seek appropriate medical care when needed, trusting that You are able to work through healthcare professionals to bring about healing. I am thankful for the example of Luke, the beloved physician.

Help me to recognize and appreciate You, God, as the ultimate healer of every disease-physical, spiritual, and emotional. May I see the medical profession as a noble calling and be truly grateful for those who dedicate their lives to healing others, knowing that all healing ultimately comes from You.

In Jesus' name, and by the power of His blood, I pray. Amen.

My own prayer:

_____

_____

_____

Memory

noun
'mem-rē

1. The power or process of reproducing or recalling what has been learned and retained especially through associative mechanisms

- **Proverbs 10:7:** The memory of the righteous is a blessing, but the name of the wicked will rot.
- **Ecclesiastes 9:5:** For the living know that they will die, but the dead know nothing, and they have no more reward, for the memory of them is forgotten.
- **Matthew 26:13:** "Truly, I say to you, wherever this gospel is proclaimed in the whole world, what she has done will also be told in memory of her."

Reflections:

_____
_____
_____
_____
_____
_____
_____
_____
_____
_____
_____
_____

Prayer:

Heavenly Father,

I come before You in humility, seeking Your guidance for my memory. Lord, help me remain righteous so that my memory will be a blessing, not that of the wicked which rots away. Release me from the grip of using memory to haunt or scold others. Free me from tormenting thoughts that rob and steal my peace. Liberate my memory, Lord, so that it recalls fruitful experiences, healed from all painful recollections once used to hurt me.

May my life be an example remembered as pleasing to You, giving all to You in faith–body, mind, and soul. Help me to store up Your Word in my heart, that I might not sin against You. Let my memory be a tool for Your glory, recalling Your faithfulness and steadfast love. Grant me the wisdom to forget what should be forgotten and remember what should be remembered. May I use the gift of memory to comfort others, to grow in faith, and to proclaim Your goodness.

In Jesus' name I pray, Amen.

My own prayer:

_____

_____

_____

_____

_____

_____

_____

_____

Mental Illness

noun

1. Any of a broad range of medical conditions that are marked primarily by sufficient disorganization of personality, mind, or emotions to impair normal psychological functioning

- **Psalm 34:17–20:** When the righteous cry for help, the Lord hears and delivers them out of all their troubles. The Lord is near to the brokenhearted and saves the crushed in spirit. Many are the afflictions of the righteous, but the Lord delivers him out of them all.
- **Philippians 4:6–7:** Do not be anxious about anything, but in everything by prayer and supplication with thanksgiving let your requests be made known to God. And the peace of God, which surpasses all understanding, will guard your hearts and your minds in Christ Jesus.
- **2 Timothy 1:7:** For God gave us a spirit not of fear but of power and love and self-control.
- **1 Peter 5:7:** Casting all your anxieties on him, because he cares for you.
- **Joshua 1:9:** "Have I not commanded you? Be strong and courageous. Do not be frightened, and do not be dismayed, for the Lord your God is with you wherever you go."

Reflections:

_____
_____
_____
_____
_____
_____
_____
_____
_____

Prayer:

Heavenly Father,

I come before You in submission, seeking clarity. My Lord, deliver me from the clamor within my thoughts. Quiet the noise between my ears, break this hold over my mind. Forgive me for any gateways I have allowed to access my mind. Release me from such agony, O God. You did not create such a majestic vessel that is my brain to torment me. Make me clean, O God, so that my cries may be heard; deliver me from my fears. As I wait by the still waters, Lord, restore my soul!

Teach me not to be anxious but in everything to come to You in prayer and supplication. Help me to take every thought captive and make it obedient to Christ Jesus. Fill me with Your Holy Spirit, for You did not give me a spirit of fear but of power, love, and self-control. My God, thank You for restoring me to a sound mind, for I know the authority of the blood of Jesus Christ. I declare Your command: I will remain strong and courageous. I will not be frightened or dismayed, for You are my God, and You are with me always.

In Jesus' name I pray, Amen.

My own prayer:

_____

_____

_____

_____

_____

_____

_____

Mercy

noun
'mər-sē

1. Compassion or forbearance shown especially to an offender or to one subject to one's power

- **Psalm 123:3:** Have mercy upon us, O Lord, have mercy upon us, for we have had more than enough of contempt.
- **Job 19:21:** Have mercy on me, have mercy on me, O you my friends, for the hand of God has touched me!
- **Matthew 5:7:** "Blessed are the merciful, for they shall receive mercy."
- **Job 8:5:** If you will seek God and plead with the Almighty for mercy.
- **Psalm 119:156:** Great is your mercy, O Lord; give me life according to your rules.
- **James 2:13:** For judgment is without mercy to one who has shown no mercy. Mercy triumphs over judgment.

Reflections:

_____
_____
_____
_____
_____
_____
_____
_____
_____

Prayer:

Heavenly Father,

I come before You, seeking Your mercy in my life. Lord, I echo the words of the psalmist, "Have mercy upon us, O Lord, have mercy upon us," for I have faced more than enough contempt and hardship. I acknowledge my need for Your compassion and grace. Like Job, I cry out, "Have mercy on me!" I feel the weight of Your hand upon me, and I ask for relief and healing in my spirit.

Thank You for the promise that blessed are the merciful, for they shall receive mercy. Help me to embody this truth in my own life. Teach me to extend mercy to others as I have received it from You. Lord, I seek You earnestly, pleading with You for mercy in my struggles. Great is Your mercy, O Lord, give me life according to Your rules and guide me in Your ways.

I am reminded that judgment is without mercy to those who show no mercy. Let my heart overflow with compassion and understanding toward others, so that I may also receive Your mercy. Thank You for being a God of mercy who hears my cries and responds with love.

In Jesus' name I pray, Amen.

My own prayer:

_____
_____
_____
_____
_____
_____
_____

Molech

noun
'ma-lek

1. A Semitic god to whom children were sacrificed

- **Leviticus 18:21:** You shall not give any of your children to offer them to Molech, and so profane the name of your God: I am the Lord.
- **Leviticus 20:3:** I myself will set my face against that man and will cut him off from among his people, because he has given one of his children to Molech, to make my sanctuary unclean and to profane my holy name.
- **Psalm 127:3:** Behold, children are a heritage from the Lord, the fruit of the womb a reward.
- **Matthew 18:10:** "See that you do not despise one of these little ones. For I tell you that in heaven their angels always see the face of my Father who is in heaven."
- **John 14:15:** "If you love me, you will keep my commandments."
- **1 Samuel 15:20:** And Saul said to Samuel, "I have obeyed the voice of the Lord; I have gone on the mission on which the Lord sent me. I have brought Agag the king of Amalek, and I have devoted the Amalekites to destruction."

Reflections:

_____
_____
_____
_____
_____
_____
_____
_____
_____

Prayer:

Heavenly Father,

I come before You with a heavy heart, recognizing the gravity of Your commands against child sacrifice. Lord, forgive me for the times I have profaned Your holy name by valuing worldly things above the precious children You have entrusted to my care. Help me to see children as You do–a heritage and reward from You. Strengthen me to protect and cherish these little ones, never despising or neglecting them. May I always remember that their angels see Your face in heaven.

Father, purify my heart from any idolatry that would lead me to sacrifice what is precious to You. Let me not be like those who offered their children to Molech, but instead may I offer my whole life in obedience to Your commands. Grant me wisdom and courage to stand against modern forms of child sacrifice in our society. Help me to be a voice for the voiceless and to honor the sanctity of life You have created.

In Jesus' name I pray, Amen.

My own prayer:

_____
_____
_____
_____
_____
_____
_____
_____
_____

Mother

noun
'mə-thər

1. A female parent

- **Exodus 20:12:** Honor your father and your mother, that your days may be long in the land that the LORD your God is giving you.
- **Ephesians 6:2:** "Honor your father and mother" (this is the first commandment with a promise).
- **Proverbs 31:25–30:** Strength and dignity are her clothing, and she laughs at the time to come. She opens her mouth with wisdom, and the teaching of kindness is on her tongue. She looks well to the ways of her household and does not eat the bread of idleness. Her children rise up and call her blessed; her husband also, and he praises her: "Many women have done excellently, but you surpass them all." Charm is deceitful, and beauty is vain, but a woman who fears the LORD is to be praised.
- **Proverbs 23:25:** Let your father and mother be glad; let her who bore you rejoice.
- **Titus 2:3–5:** Older women likewise are to be reverent in behavior, not slanderers or slaves to much wine. They are to teach what is good, and so train the young women to love their husbands and children, to be self-controlled, pure, working at home, kind, and submissive to their own husbands, that the word of God may not be reviled.
- **Proverbs 1:8:** Hear, my son, your father's instruction, and forsake not your mother's teaching.
- **Proverbs 23:22:** Listen to your father who gave you life, and do not despise your mother when she is old.
- **3 John 4:** I have no greater joy than to hear that my children are walking in the truth.

Reflections:

_____

_____

_____

_____

Prayer:

Heavenly Father

I come before You with a heart full of gratitude for the gift of motherhood. Lord, help me to honor my mother as You have commanded, that my days may be long in the land You have given me. As a mother, I thank You for the strength and dignity You have clothed me with, for the wisdom and kindness that flow from my lips. May my children rise up and call me blessed, recognizing the excellence with which I have lived, a life in fear of You, O God.

Father, grant me the grace to bring joy to my mother's heart, to listen to her teachings, and to never despise her, especially in her old age. For those who are mothers, I pray that You would help them to be reverent in behavior, teaching what is good, and training the younger generation in love and godliness.

Lord, for mothers everywhere who may feel overwhelmed or as though they are failing at motherhood, I ask that You wrap them in Your comforting embrace. Remind them that Your grace is sufficient and that their labor in raising children is not in vain. Fill them with Your wisdom and strength and give them the courage to press on with unwavering faith. May they find their greatest joy in seeing their children walk in Your truth.

In Jesus' name I pray, Amen.

My own prayer:

_____

_____

_____

_____

_____

_____

Murder

noun
ˈmər-dər

1. The crime of unlawfully and unjustifiably killing a person

- **Exodus 20:13:** You shall not murder.
- **Leviticus 24:17:** Whoever takes a human life shall surely be put to death.
- **1 John 3:15**: Everyone who hates his brother is a murderer, and you know that no murderer has eternal life abiding in him.
- **Matthew 5:21:** "You have heard that it was said to those of old, 'You shall not murder; and whoever murders will be liable to judgment."
- **1 John 3:12**: We should not be like Cain, who was of the evil one and murdered his brother. And why did he murder him? Because his own deeds were evil and his brother's righteous.

Reflections:

_____
_____
_____
_____
_____
_____
_____
_____
_____
_____

Prayer:

Heavenly Father,

I come before You in obedience to Your Word. As the world calls for its own justice and evil practices deemed as just and fair, etch on my soul Your firm and sound word, "You shall not murder." Lord, forgive me for the times I have rationalized murder as just and fair, using my own reasoning as clearance to harbor thoughts of taking a life. Abba, have mercy on me, for Your judgment is valid. Remind me not to be like Cain, who was evil for he was after his own desires. Keep me simple and free from hate, murderous thoughts, and bitterness. Cleanse my heart from any hatred toward others, for I know that whoever hates his brother is a murderer in Your eyes.

Holy Spirit, guide my thoughts and actions to reflect Your love and respect for all human life. Help me to value and protect the sanctity of life, from conception to natural death. Cleanse me from all unrighteousness, save my soul, O God. May my hands, heart, and mind be pure before You.

In Jesus' name I pray, Amen.

My own prayer:

_____
_____
_____
_____
_____
_____
_____

Naive

adjective
nä-'ēv

1. Marked by unaffected simplicity
2. Deficient in worldly wisdom or informed judgment

- **2 Timothy 3:5**: Having the appearance of godliness, but denying its power. Avoid such people.
- **Romans 16:18:** For such persons do not serve our Lord Christ, but their own appetites, and by smooth talk and flattery they deceive the hearts of the naive.
- **Proverbs 14:15:** The simple believes everything, but the prudent gives thought to his steps.
- **Isaiah 11:2:** And the Spirit of the Lord shall rest upon him, the Spirit of wisdom and understanding, the Spirit of counsel and might, the Spirit of knowledge and the fear of the Lord.
- **1 John 4:1**: Beloved, do not believe every spirit, but test the spirits to see whether they are from God, for many false prophets have gone out into the world.
- **Matthew 6:33:** "But seek first the kingdom of God and his righteousness, and all these things will be added to you."

Reflections:

_____
_____
_____
_____
_____
_____
_____
_____

Prayer:

Heavenly Father,

I come before You in humility. Lord, help me to be aware of practices that appear godly yet deny the power of Your Holy Spirit. Teach me to serve You and Your body, not my own appetites with smooth talk and flattery that deceive hearts. Keep me prudent, O God, that I may not believe everything. Grant me discernment to test every spirit, to know whether they are from You, for many false prophets are in the world.

I seek Your kingdom first and Your righteousness. May the Spirit of wisdom, understanding, counsel, might, knowledge, and the fear of the Lord rest upon me. Help me give thought to my steps and avoid those who have only the appearance of godliness.

In Jesus' name I pray, Amen.

My own prayer:

_____
_____
_____
_____
_____
_____
_____
_____
_____

Narcissism

noun
ˈnä-sə-ˌsi-zəm

1. Egoism, egocentrism
2. Love of or sexual desire for one's own body

- **2 Timothy 3:1–5**: But understand this, that in the last days there will come times of difficulty. For people will be lovers of self, lovers of money, proud, arrogant, abusive, disobedient to their parents, ungrateful, unholy, heartless, unappeasable, slanderous, without self-control, brutal, not loving good, treacherous, reckless, swollen with conceit, lovers of pleasure rather than lovers of God, having the appearance of godliness, but denying its power. Avoid such people.
- **Romans 16:17–19:** I appeal to you, brothers, to watch out for those who cause divisions and create obstacles contrary to the doctrine that you have been taught; avoid them. For such persons do not serve our Lord Christ, but their own appetites, and by smooth talk and flattery they deceive the hearts of the naive.
- **1 Peter 5:5–6:** Likewise, you who are younger, be subject to the elders. Clothe yourselves, all of you, with humility toward one another, for "'God opposes the proud but gives grace to the humble.'" Humble yourselves, therefore, under the mighty hand of God so that at the proper time he may exalt you.
- **Philippians 2:3–4:** Do nothing from selfish ambition or conceit, but in humility count others more significant than yourselves. Let each of you look not only to his own interests, but also to the interests of others.

Reflections:

_____
_____
_____
_____
_____
_____

Prayer:

Heavenly Father,

I come before You with a heavy heart, recognizing the challenges of living in a world embracing self-centeredness as the norm. Lord, protect me from those who are lovers of self, proud, and arrogant. Grant me discernment to recognize and avoid those who cause divisions and create obstacles contrary to Your teachings. Father, clothe me with humility. Help me to resist the temptation of narcissism that plagues our world. May I never be swollen with conceit or love pleasure more than I love You.

Holy Spirit, guide me to do nothing from selfish ambition. Teach me to count others as more significant than myself, looking not only to my own interests but also to the interests of others.

Lord, I humbly ask for Your grace to navigate relationships with those who display narcissistic tendencies. Give me wisdom to set healthy boundaries and the strength to avoid those who do not serve You but their own appetites.

In Jesus' name I pray Amen.

My own prayer:

_____
_____
_____
_____
_____
_____
_____

Neglect

verb
ni-'glekt

1. To give little attention or respect to
2. To leave undone or unattended to especially through carelessness

- **Hebrews 2:1–3:** Therefore we must pay much closer attention to what we have heard, lest we drift away from it. For since the message declared by angels proved to be reliable, and every transgression or disobedience received a just retribution, how shall we escape if we neglect such a great salvation?
- **Hebrews 6:12:** So that you may not be sluggish, but imitators of those who through faith and patience inherit the promises.
- **2 Chronicles 29:11**: My sons, do not now be negligent, for the Lord has chosen you to stand in his presence, to minister to him and to be his ministers and make offerings to him.
- **Proverbs 24:30–34:** I passed by the field of a sluggard, by the vineyard of a man lacking sense, and behold, it was all overgrown with thorns; the ground was covered with nettles, and its stone wall was broken down. Then I saw and considered it; I looked and received instruction. A little sleep, a little slumber, a little folding of the hands to rest, and poverty will come upon you like a robber, and want like an armed man.
- **Ecclesiastes 9:10:** Whatever your hand finds to do, do it with your might, for there is no work or thought or knowledge or wisdom in Sheol, to which you are going.
- **James 1:22:** But be doers of the word, and not hearers only, deceiving yourselves.

Reflections:

_____
_____
_____
_____
_____
_____

Prayer:

Heavenly Father,

I come before You with a heavy heart, recognizing my tendency to neglect the precious gifts You've given me. Lord, I confess that I've often drifted away from Your Word, paying less attention than I should to Your teachings. Forgive me for the times I've been sluggish in my faith, neglecting the great salvation You've offered. I've allowed the field of my spiritual life to become overgrown with thorns, its walls broken down through my negligence.

Holy Spirit, stir within me a renewed passion for Your presence. Help me to stand firm, ministering to You with diligence and care. Let me not be a hearer only, but a doer of Your Word. Grant me the strength to do whatever my hand finds to do with all my might. May I imitate those who through faith and patience inherit Your promises.

Lord, I commit to paying closer attention to Your voice, to nurturing the vineyard of my soul with care and dedication. Help me to be vigilant against the creeping neglect that can rob me of the fullness of life in You.

In Jesus' name I pray, Amen.

My own prayer:

_____
_____
_____
_____
_____
_____
_____

Noble

adjective
ˈnō-bəl

1. possessing outstanding qualities

- **Isaiah 32:8:** But he who is noble plans noble things, and on noble things he stands.
- **Philippians 4:8:** Finally, brothers, whatever is true, whatever is honorable, whatever is just, whatever is pure, whatever is lovely, whatever is commendable, if there is any excellence, if there is anything worthy of praise, think about these things.
- **2 Peter 1:5**: For this very reason, make every effort to supplement your faith with virtue, and virtue with knowledge.
- **2 Peter 1:3**: His divine power has granted to us all things that pertain to life and godliness, through the knowledge of him who called us to his own glory and excellence.
- **Job 40:10:** Adorn yourself with majesty and dignity; clothe yourself with glory and splendor.
- **1 Timothy 3:4**: He must manage his own household well, with all dignity keeping his children submissive.

Reflections:

_____
_____
_____
_____
_____
_____
_____
_____
_____

Prayer:

Heavenly Father,

I come before You in meekness. Lord, as the world presents platforms of idolatry, selfish pursuits, and worldly pleasures, I separate myself from such vices, seeking Your nobility. For by Your Word, whoever is noble plans noble things, and on noble things I shall stand.

Holy Spirit, teach me to pursue Your truth, whatever is honorable, whatever is pure, whatever is lovely, whatever is commendable. When the world shouts of fame, give me the courage and dignity to make every effort to supplement my faith with virtue and virtue with Your knowledge. May I adorn myself not with the trappings of this world but with majesty and dignity, clothing myself in glory and splendor. I proclaim to manage my household well, with dignity, keeping my children submissive. Grant me Your divine power to attain all things that pertain to life and godliness, through the knowledge of Him who called me to His own glory and excellence.

In Jesus' name I pray, Amen.

My own prayer:

_____
_____
_____
_____
_____
_____
_____
_____

Occult

adjective
ə-ˈkəlt

1. Hidden or concealed from view
2. Matters regarded as involving the action or influence of supernatural or supernormal powers or some secret knowledge of them

- **Deuteronomy 18:10–14:** There shall not be found among you anyone who burns his son or his daughter as an offering, anyone who practices divination or tells fortunes or interprets omens, or a sorcerer or a charmer or a medium or a necromancer or one who inquires of the dead, for whoever does these things is an abomination to the Lord. And because of these abominations, the Lord your God is driving them out before you. You shall be blameless before the Lord your God, for these nations, which you are about to dispossess, listen to fortune-tellers and to diviners. But as for you, the Lord your God has not allowed you to do this.
- **Leviticus 19:31:** Do not turn to mediums or necromancers; do not seek them out, and so make yourselves unclean by them: I am the Lord your God.
- **Leviticus 20:6:** If a person turns to mediums and necromancers, whoring after them, I will set my face against that person and will cut him off from among his people.
- **1 Samuel 15:23**: For rebellion is as the sin of divination, and presumption is as iniquity and idolatry. Because you have rejected the word of the Lord, he has also rejected you from being king.
- **Acts 19:18–19:** Also many of those who were now believers came, confessing and divulging their practices. And a number of those who had practiced magic arts brought their books together and burned them in the sight of all. And they counted the value of them and found it came to fifty thousand pieces of silver.
- **Hebrews 11:1:** Now faith is the assurance of things hoped for, the conviction of things not seen.
- **Proverbs 3:5–6:** Trust in the Lord with all your heart, and do not lean on your own understanding. In all your ways acknowledge him, and he will make straight your paths.
- **2 Corinthians 5:7**: For we walk by faith, not by sight.

Reflections:

Prayer:

Heavenly Father,

I come before You in humility, bowing at Your throne in submission for myself and standing in the gap on behalf of the generations before and after me. I renounce all occult practices, forms of iniquity, corrupt speech, idols, and traditions that have tainted my life and lineage. Lord, call to my attention any vile conduct, possession, or relationship that is counterfeit or occultic in nature, so that I may rid my life and household of such ways.

I proclaim You as my Lord and Savior, acknowledging that Jesus Christ is the way, the truth, and the life. Holy Spirit, help me not to lean on my own understanding, but to trust in the Lord with all my heart. Guide me to acknowledge Your ways in all things, knowing You will make my paths straight. Teach me to test every spirit, yielding with discernment. I declare that I walk by faith, not by sight. I reject all forms of rebellion and its practices, committing to follow Your Word and truth all the days of my life.

May my faith be the assurance of things hoped for and the conviction of things not seen. Thank You, Lord, for restoration and freedom through the blood of Jesus Christ.

In Jesus' name, and by the authority of His blood, I pray. Amen

My own prayer:

_____
_____
_____
_____
_____
_____
_____

"And all the trees of the field shall know that I am the Lord; I bring low the high tree, and make high the low tree, dry up the green tree, and make the dry tree flourish. I am the Lord; I have spoken, and I will do it." - Ezekiel 17:24

Offense

noun
ə-'fen(t)s

1. Something that outrages the moral or physical senses
2. The act of displeasing or affronting

- **Proverbs 18:19:** A brother offended is more unyielding than a strong city, and quarreling is like the bars of a castle.
- **Proverbs 19:11:** Good sense makes one slow to anger, and it is his glory to overlook an offense.
- **Ecclesiastes 7:21–22:** Do not take to heart all the things that people say, lest you hear your servant cursing you. Your heart knows that many times you yourself have cursed others.
- **Leviticus 19:18:** You shall not take vengeance or bear a grudge against the sons of your own people, but you shall love your neighbor as yourself: I am the Lord.
- **Ephesians 4:2–3:** With all humility and gentleness, with patience, bearing with one another in love, eager to maintain the unity of the Spirit in the bond of peace.

Reflections:

___
___
___
___
___
___
___
___
___

Prayer:

Heavenly Father,

I come before You in humility, seeking Your grace and mercy. Lord, forgive me, for offense has ruled and reigned in my heart. As I have used offense as a means to serve my ambitions and pride, remind me of Your truth. Help me remember that a brother offended is more unyielding than a strong city, and quarreling is like the bars of a castle. Grant me good sense to be slow to anger and the wisdom to overlook an offense. Father, rid me of such vile practices and schemes. Teach me to guard my heart against all the things that people say and to refrain from taking vengeance or bearing grudges against others.

Holy Spirit, help me to love my neighbor as myself, acting in all humility and gentleness, with patience, and bearing with one another in love. Make me eager to maintain the unity of the Spirit in the bond of peace. May Your love and forgiveness flow through me, transforming my heart and my relationships.

In Jesus' name I pray, Amen.

My own prayer:

_____
_____
_____
_____
_____
_____
_____
_____
_____
_____

Oppression

noun
ə-'pre-shən

1. Unjust or cruel exercise of authority or power
2. A sense of being weighed down in body or mind

- **Psalm 9:9:** The LORD is a stronghold for the oppressed, a stronghold in times of trouble.
- **Isaiah 1:17:** Learn to do good; seek justice, correct oppression; bring justice to the fatherless, plead the widow's cause.
- **Psalm 72:4:** May he defend the cause of the poor of the people, give deliverance to the children of the needy, and crush the oppressor!
- **John 8:36:** "So if the Son sets you free, you will be free indeed."
- **Galatians 5:1:** For freedom Christ has set us free; stand firm therefore, and do not submit again to a yoke of slavery.

Reflections:

_____
_____
_____
_____
_____
_____
_____
_____
_____

Prayer:

Heavenly Father,

I come before You in humility, prostrating myself in submission to Your glory. Lord, this oppression has become too heavy a weight for me to bear. I lay it at Your feet, for You are the stronghold for the oppressed and a refuge in times of trouble. Grant me courage and strength to seek justice, correct oppression, bring justice to the fatherless, and plead the widow's cause. It is Your Son Jesus Christ who sets me free, and indeed free I will be.

O God, You defend the cause of the poor, deliver the children of the needy, and crush the oppressor. Holy Spirit, help me stand firm in the freedom Christ has given me, never again submitting to a yoke of slavery. May Your justice reign, and may I be an instrument of Your compassion for the oppressed. Thank you Lord for the freedom indeed given through the blood of Jesus Christ.

In Jesus' name I pray, Amen.

My own prayer:

_____
_____
_____
_____
_____
_____
_____
_____
_____

Orphan

noun
ʹȯr-fən

1. A child deprived by death of one or usually both parents

- **Psalm 146:9:** The Lord watches over the sojourners; he upholds the widow and the fatherless, but the way of the wicked he brings to ruin.
- **James 1:27:** Religion that is pure and undefiled before God the Father is this: to visit orphans and widows in their affliction, and to keep oneself unstained from the world.
- **John 14:18:** "I will not leave you as orphans; I will come to you."
- **John 14:6–7:** Jesus said to him, "I am the way, and the truth, and the life. No one comes to the Father except through me. If you had known me, you would have known my Father also. From now on you do know him and have seen him."
- **Romans 8:15:** For you did not receive the spirit of slavery to fall back into fear, but you have received the Spirit of adoption as sons, by whom we cry, "Abba! Father!"
- **1 John 3:1**: See what kind of love the Father has given to us, that we should be called children of God; and so we are. The reason why the world does not know us is that it did not know him.

Reflections:

_____
_____
_____
_____
_____
_____
_____

Prayer:

Heavenly Father,

I come before You in reverence and gratitude for Your favor toward orphans. I am eternally grateful to be adopted into Your kingdom, receiving an inheritance through faith in Jesus Christ. Thank You that You will not leave me as an orphan, O God. You watch over the sojourners and uphold the fatherless. I renounce any wickedness in me.

Lord Jesus, You are the way, the truth, and the life. No one comes to the Father except through You. Be exalted, O God, above the heavens! Let Your glory be over all the earth! I praise You that I have not received a spirit of slavery to fall back into fear, but the Spirit of adoption, by whom I cry, "Abba, Father!" Thank You for calling me Your child. Remind me to stay close to You alone, for the world does not know me because it did not know You.

In Jesus' name I pray, Amen.

My own prayer:

_____
_____
_____
_____
_____
_____
_____
_____

Pain

noun
ˈpān

1. A localized or generalized unpleasant bodily sensation or complex of sensations that causes mild to severe physical discomfort and emotional distress
2. Mental or emotional distress or suffering

- **1 Peter 4:12–19**: Beloved, do not be surprised at the fiery trial when it comes upon you to test you, as though something strange were happening to you. But rejoice insofar as you share Christ's sufferings, that you may also rejoice and be glad when his glory is revealed. If you are insulted for the name of Christ, you are blessed, because the Spirit of glory and of God rests upon you. But let none of you suffer as a murderer or a thief or an evildoer or as a meddler. Yet if anyone suffers as a Christian, let him not be ashamed, but let him glorify God in that name. For it is time for judgment to begin at the household of God, and if it begins with us, what will be the outcome for those who do not obey the gospel of God? And if the righteous is scarcely saved, what will become of the ungodly and the sinner? Therefore let those who suffer according to God's will entrust their souls to a faithful Creator while doing good.
- **Revelation 21:4:** He will wipe away every tear from their eyes, and death shall be no more, neither shall there be mourning, nor crying, nor pain anymore, for the former things have passed away.
- **Psalm 147:3:** He heals the brokenhearted and binds up their wounds.
- **Psalm 34:18:** The Lord is near to the brokenhearted and saves the crushed in spirit.
- **James 1:2–4:** Count it all joy, my brothers, when you meet trials of various kinds, for you know that the testing of your faith produces steadfastness. And let steadfastness have its full effect, that you may be perfect and complete, lacking in nothing.
- **Psalm 30:5:** For his anger is but for a moment, and his favor is for a lifetime. Weeping may tarry for the night, but joy comes with the morning.

Reflections:

Prayer:

Heavenly Father,

I come before You, broken and hurting. As I lay prostrate at Your feet, weeping from the pain I have endured, help me remain faithful. I take comfort in knowing You are near the brokenhearted, binding up my wounds. Lord, I trust that You will wipe away every tear from my eyes, and death shall be no more. Neither shall there be mourning, nor crying, nor pain anymore, for the former things will pass away. Though this suffering feels endless, I remember Your anger is but for a moment, and Your favor is for a lifetime. This weeping may tarry for the night, but joy comes with the morning.

Holy Spirit, help me count it all joy, even this pain, for I know the testing of my faith produces steadfastness. Let steadfastness have its full effect, that I may be perfect and complete, lacking nothing. Grant me the strength to see this suffering as an opportunity to grow in faith and truly understand why Christ must be where my hope rests. May I not become bitter but instead allow my faith to make me better.

In Jesus' name I pray, Amen.

My own prayer:

_____

_____

_____

_____

_____

_____

_____

_____

"Do not turn to mediums or seek out spiritists, for you will be defiled by them. I am the Lord your God." - Leviticus 19:31

Passion

noun
ʻpa-shən

1. The sufferings of Christ between the night of the Last Supper and his death
2. Intense, driving, or overmastering feeling or conviction

- **Galatians 5:16:** But I say, walk by the Spirit, and you will not gratify the desires of the flesh.
- **Galatians 5:24:** And those who belong to Christ Jesus have crucified the flesh with its passions and desires.
- **1 Corinthians 10:31**: So, whether you eat or drink, or whatever you do, do all to the glory of God.
- **Romans 12:11:** Do not be slothful in zeal, be fervent in spirit, serve the Lord.
- **Matthew 6:21:** "For where your treasure is, there your heart will be also."
- **Colossians 3:5:** Put to death therefore what is earthly in you: sexual immorality, impurity, passion, evil desire, and covetousness, which is idolatry.
- **Mark 12:30:** "And you shall love the Lord your God with all your heart and with all your soul and with all your mind and with all your strength."

Reflections:

_____
_____
_____
_____
_____
_____
_____
_____
_____
_____

Prayer:

Heavenly Father,

I come before You in joy and zeal, honoring Your precious name. Lord, let my flesh die so that I may walk in the Spirit, no longer gratifying the desires of the flesh. Grant me strength and courage to crucify my flesh with its passions and desires. Forgive me for the moments and seasons when I have fed my flesh rather than obeying Your truth. Holy Spirit, bring to my attention any treasures I have put before You, my God. Put to death what is earthly in me: sexual immorality, impurity, evil desires, and covetousness, which is idolatry.

I declare my love for You, Lord, giving You my full heart, soul, mind, and strength. May I remain zealous for You, fervent in spirit, serving You in all I do. Let my passion be for building Your kingdom according to Your will, not mine.

In Jesus' name I pray, Amen.

My own prayer:

_____
_____
_____
_____
_____
_____
_____
_____
_____
_____

Patience

noun

'pā-shən(t)s

1. The capacity, habit, or fact of being patient (not hasty)

- **Romans 12:12:** Rejoice in hope, be patient in tribulation, be constant in prayer.
- **Ephesians 4:2:** With all humility and gentleness, with patience, bearing with one another in love.
- **Psalm 37:7:** Be still before the LORD and wait patiently for him; fret not yourself over the one who prospers in his way, over the man who carries out evil devices!
- **Isaiah 40:31:** But they who wait for the LORD shall renew their strength; they shall mount up with wings like eagles; they shall run and not be weary; they shall walk and not faint.
- **Ecclesiastes 7:8:** Better is the end of a thing than its beginning, and the patient in spirit is better than the proud in spirit.
- **Galatians 5:22–23:** But the fruit of the Spirit is love, joy, peace, patience, kindness, goodness, faithfulness, gentleness, self-control; against such things there is no law.

Reflections:

_____
_____
_____
_____
_____
_____
_____
_____

Prayer:

Heavenly Father,

I come before You in submission to Your truth. Help me to be still before You and wait patiently, not fretting over those who prosper through evil means. Grant me the strength to rejoice in hope, be patient in tribulation, and remain constant in prayer. May I bear with others in love, showing patience in all my interactions.

Lord, I yearn for the discipline to wait on You, trusting that You will renew my strength. Help me to mount up on wings like eagles, that I may run and not grow weary, walk and not faint. Remind me, O God, that the end of a thing is better than its beginning, and that patience in spirit surpasses pride. Abba, may my patient soul bear the fruit of Your Spirit–love, joy, peace, patience, kindness, goodness, and faithfulness. Let this patience sustain me through the journey You have ordained for me.

In Jesus' name I pray, Amen.

My own prayer:

_____
_____
_____
_____
_____
_____
_____
_____

Peace

noun
'pēs

1. A state of tranquility or quiet
2. Freedom from disquieting or oppressive thoughts or emotions

- **John 14:27:** "Peace I leave with you; my peace I give to you. Not as the world gives do I give to you. Let not your hearts be troubled, neither let them be afraid."
- **Isaiah 26:3:** You keep him in perfect peace whose mind is stayed on you, because he trusts in you.
- **Colossians 3:15:** And let the peace of Christ rule in your hearts, to which indeed you were called in one body. And be thankful.
- **Philippians 4:6–7:** Do not be anxious about anything, but in everything by prayer and supplication with thanksgiving let your requests be made known to God. And the peace of God, which surpasses all understanding, will guard your hearts and your minds in Christ Jesus.
- **Psalm 34:14:** Turn away from evil and do good; seek peace and pursue it.

Reflections:

_____
_____
_____
_____
_____
_____
_____
_____
_____

Prayer:

Heavenly Father,

I come before You in humility and faith. Thank You for the peace You have given me that calms my troubled heart and dispels my fears. Lord, let Your peace that surpasses all understanding guard my heart and mind in Christ Jesus. Keep my mind focused on You, for in You I find perfect peace.

Holy Spirit, let the peace of Christ rule in my heart. I am grateful to be called into one body with fellow believers. Help me turn away from evil and pursue good, actively seeking and chasing after peace. In anxious times, remind me to bring everything to You in prayer with thanksgiving.

Thank You, Lord, for Your everlasting peace that transcends all circumstances.

In Jesus' name I pray, Amen.

My own prayer:

_____
_____
_____
_____
_____
_____
_____
_____
_____

Persecution

noun

ˌper-si-ˈkyü-shən

1. The act or practice of persecuting (harassing or punishing) especially those who differ in origin, religion, or social outlook

- **2 Timothy 3:12**: Indeed, all who desire to live a godly life in Christ Jesus will be persecuted.
- **John 15:18:** "If the world hates you, know that it has hated me before it hated you."
- **Matthew 5:44:** "But I say to you, Love your enemies and pray for those who persecute you."
- **Matthew 5:10:** "Blessed are those who are persecuted for righteousness' sake, for theirs is the kingdom of heaven."
- **Luke 6:22:** "Blessed are you when people hate you and when they exclude you and revile you and spurn your name as evil, on account of the Son of Man!"

Reflections:

_____
_____
_____
_____
_____
_____
_____
_____
_____
_____
_____

Prayer:

Heavenly Father,

I come before You in distress, seeking refuge. As I strive to live a godly life in Christ Jesus, I face persecution. When the world hates me, help me remember it hated You first.

Holy Spirit, grant me peace to guard my heart, enabling me to love my enemies and pray for those who persecute me. Your kingdom is what I seek, Father, not this world's approval.

Thank You, Lord, for the blessing You promise when people hate, exclude, revile, and spurn my name as evil on account of the Son of Man. Grant me strength to endure, knowing that my reward is great in heaven. Help me to rejoice in my sufferings for Your sake, remembering that I share in Christ's sufferings. May my response to persecution be a testimony of Your love and grace.

In Jesus' name I pray, Amen.

My own prayer:

_____
_____
_____
_____
_____
_____
_____
_____
_____
_____

Perseverance

noun

,pər-sə-ˈvir-ən(t)s

1. Continued effort to do or achieve something despite difficulties, failure, or opposition

- **Galatians 6:9:** And let us not grow weary of doing good, for in due season we will reap, if we do not give up.
- **Hebrews 12:1:** Therefore, since we are surrounded by so great a cloud of witnesses, let us also lay aside every weight, and sin which clings so closely, and let us run with endurance the race that is set before us.
- **James 1:12:** Blessed is the man who remains steadfast under trial, for when he has stood the test he will receive the crown of life, which God has promised to those who love him.
- **2 Thessalonians 3:13**: As for you, brothers, do not grow weary in doing good.
- **Ephesians 6:18:** Praying at all times in the Spirit, with all prayer and supplication. To that end, keep alert with all perseverance, making supplication for all the saints.
- **Romans 12:12:** Rejoice in hope, be patient in tribulation, be constant in prayer.

Reflections:

_____
_____
_____
_____
_____
_____
_____
_____

Prayer:

Heavenly Father,

I come before You in humility, seeking refreshment. Lord, may I persist in doing good knowing in due season I will reap a harvest if I do not give up. Thank You, Lord, that I am surrounded by a great cloud of brothers and sisters in Christ. Help me lay aside every weight and sin which clings so closely and let me run with endurance the race that is set before me.

Abba, let me stand firm on the hope that the one who remains steadfast under trial will be blessed, for when I have stood the test, I will receive the crown of life which You have promised to those who love You.

Holy Spirit, help me to always pray in the Spirit with supplications, keeping alert with all perseverance, making supplication for the saints. May I remain steadfast in hope, patient in tribulation, and constant in prayer.

In Jesus' name I pray, Amen.

My own prayer:

_____
_____
_____
_____
_____
_____
_____
_____

Pornography

noun

pȯr-ˈnä-grə-fē

1. The depiction of erotic behavior intended to cause sexual excitement

- **Matthew 5:27–28:** "You have heard that it was said, 'You shall not commit adultery.' But I say to you that everyone who looks at a woman with lustful intent has already committed adultery with her in his heart."
- **1 Corinthians 6:18**: Flee from sexual immorality. Every other sin a person commits is outside the body, but the sexually immoral person sins against his own body.
- **Job 31:1:** I have made a covenant with my eyes; how then could I gaze at a virgin?
- **Romans 12:12:** Rejoice in hope, be patient in tribulation, be constant in prayer.
- **2 Corinthians 12:9**: But he said to me, "My grace is sufficient for you, for my power is made perfect in weakness." Therefore I will boast all the more gladly of my weaknesses, so that the power of Christ may rest upon me.
- **Psalm 119:37:** Turn my eyes from looking at worthless things; and give me life in your ways.
- **1 Corinthians 10:13**: No temptation has overtaken you that is not common to man. God is faithful, and he will not let you be tempted beyond your ability, but with the temptation he will also provide the way of escape, that you may be able to endure it.

Reflections:

_____
_____
_____
_____
_____
_____
_____
_____

Prayer:

Heavenly Father,

I come before You in submission, seeking Your substance. Lord, tear down the idol of pornography in my life. Create in me clean hands and a pure heart, helping me see others as Your sons and daughters, wholesome and good.

Holy Spirit, grant me the strength to flee from sexual immorality, knowing it is a sin against my own body. Give me courage to resist such carnality, remaining fervent in prayer and patient in tribulation.

Father, Your grace is sufficient for me. Your power is made perfect in my weakness. Let Your power rest upon me, O God, as I cling to this hope. Forgive me for using my eyes, mouth, and body for pornographic purposes, perverting Your divine creation. I acknowledge that no temptation has overtaken me that is not common to man. You are faithful, God, and will not let me be tempted beyond my ability. With temptation, provide me a way of escape. Purify me, my Lord and Savior, that I may go and sin no more, testifying to the grace and mercy at Your hands.

In Jesus' name I pray, Amen.

My own prayer:

_____
_____
_____
_____
_____
_____
_____
_____

Power

noun
'paū(-ə)r

1. The ability to act or produce an effect
2. Possession of control, authority, or influence over others

- **Acts 1:8:** But you will receive power when the Holy Spirit has come upon you, and you will be my witnesses in Jerusalem and in all Judea and Samaria, and to the end of the earth.
- **2 Timothy 1:7-8**: For God gave us a spirit not of fear but of power and love and self-control. Therefore do not be ashamed of the testimony about our Lord, nor of me his prisoner, but share in suffering for the gospel by the power of God,
- **Colossians 1:11:** Being strengthened with all power, according to his glorious might, for all endurance and patience with joy.
- **Psalm 62:11:** Once God has spoken; twice have I heard this: that power belongs to God.
- **Job 26:14:** Behold, these are but the outskirts of his ways, and how small a whisper do we hear of him! But the thunder of his power who can understand?
- **Jeremiah 32:17:** Ah, Lord God! It is you who have made the heavens and the earth by your great power and by your outstretched arm! Nothing is too hard for you.

Reflections:

___

___

___

___

___

___

___

WARFARE BATTLECARDS

Prayer:

Heavenly Father,

I come before You in reverence and awe of Your endless divine power. Lord, remind me daily that You have given me a spirit of power, love, and self-control, not of fear. Strengthen me with all power according to Your glorious might, granting me endurance and patience with joy. I acknowledge that all power belongs to You, O God. I praise You for Your wondrous power that made the heavens and earth by Your outstretched arm. Nothing is too hard for You, Lord.

Holy Spirit, work within me. May I walk in Your power and love, building Your kingdom and being a witness for You in all the earth. Therefore, declaring of the testimony about You, Lord, sharing in the gospel by the power of God.

In Jesus' name I pray, Amen.

My own prayer:

_____
_____
_____
_____
_____
_____
_____
_____
_____
_____

Praise

verb
'prāz

1. To express a favorable judgment of
2. To glorify especially by the attribution of perfections

- **Psalm 150:** Praise the Lord! Praise God in his sanctuary; praise him in his mighty heavens! Praise him for his mighty deeds; praise him according to his excellent greatness! Praise him with trumpet sound; praise him with lute and harp! Praise him with tambourine and dance; praise him with strings and pipe! Praise him with sounding cymbals; praise him with loud clashing cymbals! Let everything that has breath praise the Lord! Praise the Lord!
- **Psalm 34:1:** I will bless the Lord at all times; his praise shall continually be in my mouth.
- **Psalm 145:1–2:** I will extol you, my God and King, and bless your name forever and ever. Every day I will bless you and praise your name forever and ever.
- **1 Chronicles 16:25**: For great is the Lord, and greatly to be praised, and he is to be held in awe above all gods.

Reflections:

_____
_____
_____
_____
_____
_____
_____
_____

Prayer:

Heavenly Father,

I come before You with a heart overflowing with praise and thanksgiving. Lord, You are worthy of all glory and honor. Let my every word, thought, and action be a melody of praise to Your holy name. Jesus, there is none like You. Your goodness, faithfulness, love, grace, and mercy are beyond compare.

When I was silent, You gave me a voice. When my heart was broken, You restored its rhythm. When I struggled for breath, You breathed new life into me. How great You are, O God! I declare with the psalmist, "I will bless the LORD at all times; His praise shall continually be in my mouth." For You are great and greatly to be praised, to be held in awe above all.

I will extol You, my God and King, and bless Your name forever and ever. Every day I will bless You and praise Your name, for You are worthy of endless adoration. Let everything within me cry out, "Holy, holy, holy is Your name!" May my life be a constant song of praise to You, echoing the words of the psalmist, "Praise the Lord! Praise God in His sanctuary; praise Him in His mighty heavens! Praise Him for His mighty deeds; praise Him according to His excellent greatness!"

In Jesus' name I pray, Amen.

My own prayer:

_____

_____

_____

_____

_____

_____

_____

Prayer

noun
'prer

1. An address to God or a god in word or thought
2. A religious service consisting chiefly of prayers

- **1 Thessalonians 5:17**: Pray without ceasing.
- **Matthew 6:9:** "Pray then like this: Our Father in heaven, hallowed be your name."
- **Matthew 6:6:** "But when you pray, go into your room and shut the door and pray to your Father who is in secret. And your Father who sees in secret will reward you."
- **Ephesians 6:18:** Praying at all times in the Spirit, with all prayer and supplication. To that end, keep alert with all perseverance, making supplication for all the saints.
- **James 5:16:** Therefore, confess your sins to one another and pray for one another, that you may be healed. The prayer of a righteous person has great power as it is working.

Reflections:

_____
_____
_____
_____
_____
_____
_____
_____
_____
_____
_____

Prayer:

Heavenly Father,

I come before You in humility, seeking to align my prayer life with Your will. Lord, teach me to pray without ceasing, as Your Word instructs. Grant me the discipline to enter the secret place, closing the door behind me, rather than seeking the approval of others through public displays of piety. Let my prayers be sincere and heartfelt, not empty phrases or vain repetitions.

Holy Spirit, guide me to always pray in the Spirit, with all prayer and supplication. Help me remain alert and to persevere in prayer, not just for myself, but for all the saints.

Father, I confess my sins before You, knowing that the prayer of a righteous person has great power. May my prayers be a reflection of a humble and contrite heart. Teach me to pray as Jesus taught:

Our Father in heaven, Hallowed be Your name.

Your kingdom come, Your will be done, on earth as it is in heaven.

Give us this day our daily bread,

And forgive us our debts, as we also have forgiven our debtors.

And lead us not into temptation, but deliver us from evil.

Lord, help me to forgive others, just as You have forgiven me. May my prayer life be a testament to Your grace and mercy.

In Jesus' name I pray, Amen.

My own prayer:

**You are a hiding place for me; you preserve me from trouble; you surround me with shouts of deliverance.
- Psalm 32:7**

Pride

noun
ˈprīd

1. The quality or state of being proud: such as a exaggerated self-esteem

- **Proverbs 16:18:** Pride goes before destruction, and a haughty spirit before a fall.
- **Proverbs 11:2:** When pride comes, then comes disgrace, but with the humble is wisdom.
- **Proverbs 29:23:** One's pride will bring him low, but he who is lowly in spirit will obtain honor.
- **Proverbs 8:13:** The fear of the Lord is hatred of evil. Pride and arrogance and the way of evil and perverted speech I hate.
- **James 4:6:** But he gives more grace. Therefore it says, "God opposes the proud, but gives grace to the humble."
- **Romans 12:16:** Live in harmony with one another. Do not be haughty, but associate with the lowly. Never be wise in your own sight.

Reflections:

_____
_____
_____
_____
_____
_____
_____
_____
_____
_____

Prayer:

Heavenly Father,

I come before Your throne in humility and surrender. Lord, I renounce pride in all its forms—its lofty ideas, vain imaginations, and self-serving agendas. Father, cleanse my heart and prune me like a branch, that I may bear fruit for Your glory, not my own. Holy Spirit, teach me to die to my carnal nature and embrace true humility.

Grant me the courage to break ties with pride, just as Paul silenced his temptations. Let me heed Your warning that pride goes before destruction, and a haughty spirit before a fall. Instill in me a fear of the Lord that hates evil, pride, and arrogance. Give me the discipline to live in harmony with others, not seeking to exalt myself, but to be a peacemaker focused on Your business rather than my own. May I never be wise in my own sight but always seek Your wisdom and grace. For You oppose the proud but give grace to the humble.

In Jesus' name I pray, Amen.

My own prayer:

_____
_____
_____
_____
_____
_____
_____
_____
_____

Profanity

noun
prō-ˈfa-nə-tē

1. The quality or state of being profane (obscene or vulgar)
2. The use of profane language

- **Exodus 20:7:** You shall not take the name of the Lord your God in vain, for the Lord will not hold him guiltless who takes his name in vain.
- **James 3:10:** From the same mouth come blessing and cursing. My brothers, these things ought not to be so.
- **Psalm 34:13:** Keep your tongue from evil and your lips from speaking deceit.
- **Matthew 15:11:** "It is not what goes into the mouth that defiles a person, but what comes out of the mouth; this defiles a person."
- **1 Thessalonians 5:22**: Abstain from every form of evil.
- **Revelation 4:8:** And the four living creatures, each of them with six wings, are full of eyes all around and within, and day and night they never cease to say, "Holy, holy, holy, is the Lord God Almighty, who was and is and is to come!"
- **Proverbs 18:21:** Death and life are in the power of the tongue, and those who love it will eat its fruits.

Reflections:

_____
_____
_____
_____
_____
_____
_____
_____

Prayer:

Heavenly Father,

I come before You, seeking Your refreshment and purity. Your name is above all names, unmatched in holiness. As the living creatures proclaim day and night, "Holy, holy, holy, is the Lord God Almighty, who was and is and is to come!" Lord, I acknowledge that life and death are in the power of the tongue. I repent of any misuse of Your name and any profane or slanderous speech. Help me keep my tongue from evil and my lips from deceit.

Holy Spirit, purify my heart. May my words be wholesome, righteous, and encouraging to others, bringing life rather than death.

Thank You, Jesus, for making me a new creation. Guide me to seek Your presence and abstain from all forms of evil, that I may use my tongue to glorify You.

In Your holy name I pray, Amen.

My own prayer:

_____
_____
_____
_____
_____
_____
_____
_____
_____

Prosperity

noun
prä-ˈsper-ə-tē

1. The condition of being successful or thriving

- **Matthew 25:14–30:** "For it will be like a man going on a journey, who called his servants and entrusted to them his property. To one he gave five talents, to another two, to another one, to each according to his ability. Then he went away. He who had received the five talents went at once and traded with them, and he made five talents more. So also he who had the two talents made two talents more. But he who had received the one talent went and dug in the ground and hid his master's money. Now after a long time the master of those servants came and settled accounts with them. And he who had received the five talents came forward, bringing five talents more, saying, 'Master, you delivered to me five talents; here, I have made five talents more.' His master said to him, 'Well done, good and faithful servant. You have been faithful over a little; I will set you over much. Enter into the joy of your master.' And he also who had the two talents came forward, saying, 'Master, you delivered to me two talents; here I have made two talents more.' His master said to him, 'Well done, good and faithful servant. You have been faithful over a little; I will set you over much. Enter into the joy of your master.' He also who had received the one talent came forward saying, 'Master, I knew you to be a hard man, reaping where you did not sow, and gathering where you scattered no seed, so I was afraid, and I went and hid your talent in the ground. Here, you have what is yours.' But his master answered him, 'You wicked and slothful servant! You knew that I reap where I have not sown and gather where I scattered no seed? Then you ought to have invested my money with the bankers, and at my coming I should have received what was my own with interest. So take the talent from him and give it to him who has ten talents. For to everyone who has, more will be given, and he will have an abundance. But from the one who has not, even what he has will be taken away. And cast the worthless servant into the outer darkness. In that place there will be weeping and gnashing of teeth.'"
- **Proverbs 3:9–10:** Honor the Lord with your wealth and with the firstfruits of all your produce; then your barns will be filled with plenty, and your vats will be bursting with wine.
- **Psalm 1:3:** He is like a tree planted by streams of water that yields its fruit in its season, and its leaf does not wither. In all that he does, he prospers.
- **Joshua 1:8:** This Book of the Law shall not depart from your mouth, but you shall meditate on it day and night, so that you may be careful to do according to all that is written in it. For

then you will make your way prosperous, and then you will have good success.
- **1 Timothy 6:17–19**: As for the rich in this present age, charge them not to be haughty, nor to set their hopes on the uncertainty of riches, but on God, who richly provides us with everything to enjoy. They are to do good, to be rich in good works, to be generous and ready to share, thus storing up treasure for themselves as a good foundation for the future, so that they may take hold of that which is truly life.

Reflections:

Prayer:

Heavenly Father,

I come before You with a heart of honor and praise, humbly seeking Your favor and guidance in matters of prosperity. Lord, help me to honor You with my wealth and with the first fruits of all my produce. I trust in Your promise that as I do so, my barns will be filled with plenty. Father, make me like a tree planted by streams of water, yielding fruit in its season, with leaves that do not wither. In all that I do, may I prosper according to Your will.

Holy Spirit, place the Word of God in my mouth all the days of my life. Help me to meditate on Your law, day and night, that I may be careful to do all that is written in it. Through this, I trust that You will make my way prosperous and grant me good success.

Lord, if You bless me with riches, guard my heart against haughtiness. Help me not to set my hopes on the uncertainty of wealth, but on You, God, who richly provides us with everything to enjoy. Guide me to be rich in good works, generous and ready to share, storing up treasure in heaven. Father, make me a good and faithful servant with whatever You entrust to me. Whether it be little or much, help me to use it wisely for Your glory. Let me not be like the one who hid his talent in fear, but like those who multiplied what was given to them. I pray for discernment to see any errors in my ways and to recognize potential threats to the prosperity You provide. May all areas of my life glorify You, my King.

In Jesus' name I pray, Amen.

My own prayer:

_____

_____

_____

_____

"... He will wipe every tear from their eyes. There will be no more death or mourning or crying or pain, for the old order of things has passed away." - Revelation 21:4

Protection

noun
prə-ˈtek-shən

1. Supervision or support of one that is smaller and weaker

- **Psalm 32:7:** You are a hiding place for me; you preserve me from trouble; you surround me with shouts of deliverance.
- **Psalm 46:1:** God is our refuge and strength, a very present help in trouble.
- **Isaiah 54:17:** No weapon that is fashioned against you shall succeed, and you shall refute every tongue that rises against you in judgment. This is the heritage of the servants of the Lord and their vindication from me, declares the Lord.
- **Psalm 91:** He who dwells in the shelter of the Most High will abide in the shadow of the Almighty. I will say to the Lord, "My refuge and my fortress, my God, in whom I trust." For he will deliver you from the snare of the fowler and from the deadly pestilence. He will cover you with his pinions, and under his wings you will find refuge; his faithfulness is a shield and buckler. You will not fear the terror of the night, nor the arrow that flies by day, nor the pestilence that stalks in darkness, nor the destruction that wastes at noonday. A thousand may fall at your side, ten thousand at your right hand, but it will not come near you. You will only look with your eyes and see the recompense of the wicked. Because you have made the Lord your dwelling place—the Most High, who is my refuge—no evil shall be allowed to befall you, no plague come near your tent. For he will command his angels concerning you to guard you in all your ways. On their hands they will bear you up, lest you strike your foot against a stone. You will tread on the lion and the adder; the young lion and the serpent you will trample underfoot. "Because he holds fast to me in love, I will deliver him; I will protect him, because he knows my name. When he calls to me, I will answer him; I will be with him in trouble; I will rescue him and honor him. With long life I will satisfy him and show him my salvation."

Reflections:

_____

_____

_____

_____

Prayer:

Heavenly Father,

I come before You with urgency, seeking Your divine protection. Lord, I acknowledge Your mighty ways, that You fight battles beyond my comprehension, commanding chariots of fire and angels at Your will. Father, I run to You seeking shelter. You are my covering, my refuge, and my fortress. I declare that You are my God, in whom I trust. Deliver me from the snares of the enemy and from deadly perils.

Cover me with Your pinions, Lord, and let me find refuge under Your wings. Be my shield and buckler. Remove from me the fear of night terrors and dangers that lurk in darkness or strike by day. Most High God, I make You my dwelling place. Command Your angels concerning me, to guard me in all my ways. Let no evil befall me, nor any plague come near my dwelling. Lord, I hold fast to You in love. Answer me when I call, be with me in trouble, rescue and honor me. Surround me with shouts of deliverance, preserving me from all harm. I declare that no weapon formed against me shall prosper, and I shall refute every tongue that rises against me in judgment. This is my heritage as Your servant, O Lord.

In the mighty name of Jesus I pray, Amen.

My own prayer:

_____
_____
_____
_____
_____
_____
_____
_____

Provision

noun

prə-'vi-zhən

1. The act or process of providing (supplying)
2. The fact or state of being prepared beforehand

- **Matthew 6:23:** "But if your eye is bad, your whole body will be full of darkness. If then the light in you is darkness, how great is the darkness!"
- **Philippians 4:19:** And my God will supply every need of yours according to his riches in glory in Christ Jesus.
- **John 3:16:** "For God so loved the world, that he gave his only Son, that whoever believes in him should not perish but have eternal life."
- **1 Timothy 5:8**: But if anyone does not provide for his relatives, and especially for members of his household, he has denied the faith and is worse than an unbeliever.
- **Mark 12:43:** And he called his disciples to him and said to them, "Truly, I say to you, this poor widow has put in more than all those who are contributing to the offering box."
- **Matthew 6:26:** "Look at the birds of the air: they neither sow nor reap nor gather into barns, and yet your heavenly Father feeds them. Are you not of more value than they?"

Reflections:

_____
_____
_____
_____
_____
_____
_____

Prayer:

Heavenly Father,

I come before You in full faith, trusting in Your miraculous ways and provision. Lord, help me to have eyes full of generosity and remove any darkness that keeps me from prioritizing heavenly treasures. Remind me, O God, of the faith of the poor widow who gave her last penny. Grant me such trust and devotion. Help me to believe wholeheartedly that You will supply every need according to Your riches in glory in Christ Jesus.

Thank You, Lord, for giving Your Son to be my Savior. I repent and renounce any doubt or lack of faith in Your great provision. Just as You feed the birds of the air, I trust that You care even more for me, Your child. Grant me the wisdom and means to provide for my relatives, trusting in You completely. Let my actions reflect my faith, that I may not deny You through neglect of my responsibilities. Lord, I surrender to You as my ultimate provider. May my eyes be clear, my body full of light, and my heart set on Your kingdom. Help me to give generously, trusting in Your abundant provision.

In Jesus' name I pray, Amen.

My own prayer:

_____
_____
_____
_____
_____
_____
_____
_____

Purification

noun

pyūr-ə-fə-ˈkā-shən

1. The act or instance of purifying or of being purified

- **Matthew 5:8:** "Blessed are the pure in heart, for they shall see God."
- **Psalm 51:10:** Create in me a clean heart, O God, and renew a right spirit within me.
- **1 John 1:9**: If we confess our sins, he is faithful and just to forgive us our sins and to cleanse us from all unrighteousness.

Reflections:

___

___

___

___

___

___

___

___

___

___

___

___

___

Prayer:

Heavenly Father,

I come before You in humility, giving reverence to Your almighty power. Lord, I confess every impurity in me and my bloodline, and I renounce any affiliation with the world that separates me from You. Father, I acknowledge the importance of purifying myself both spiritually and physically, not for the presence or performance of others, but to keep a pure and clean heart in communion with You, O God.

Your Word says, "Blessed are the pure in heart, for they shall see God." Holy Spirit, I pray that You create in me a clean and pure heart. Renew a right spirit within me, Lord. Jesus, I humbly ask You to baptize me with fresh spiritual waters, cleansing me from all impurities. If I confess my sins, I know You are faithful and just to forgive me and cleanse me from all unrighteousness.

Lord, help me to obey Your truth and ways above the clamor of a society and culture screaming for my consumption and focus. Grant me the strength to resist worldly temptations and maintain my purity in thought, word, and deed. Jesus, I acknowledge You as my Savior, and it is You whom I seek all the days of my life. May my purified heart allow me to see You more clearly and serve You more faithfully.

In Jesus' name I pray, Amen.

My own prayer:

_____
_____
_____
_____
_____
_____
_____

Quick Temper

noun

1. A tendency to get angry very quickly and easily

- **James 1:20:** For the anger of man does not produce the righteousness of God.
- **Proverbs 22:24–25:** Make no friendship with a man given to anger, nor go with a wrathful man, lest you learn his ways and entangle yourself in a snare.
- **Proverbs 19:11:** Good sense makes one slow to anger, and it is his glory to overlook an offense.
- **Proverbs 14:29:** Whoever is slow to anger has great understanding, but he who has a hasty temper exalts folly.
- **Proverbs 16:32:** Whoever is slow to anger is better than the mighty, and he who rules his spirit than he who takes a city.
- **Proverbs 15:18:** A hot-tempered man stirs up strife, but he who is slow to anger quiets contention.

Reflections:

_____
_____
_____
_____
_____
_____
_____
_____
_____

Prayer:

Heavenly Father,

I come before You in humility, with a posture of repentance. Lord, I acknowledge my struggle with a quick temper and seek Your divine guidance. King Jesus, Your Word says that the anger of man does not produce the righteousness of God. Oh, how I seek to be righteous in You, Father. Grant me the discernment to see the snare I have entangled myself in through my hasty anger. Forgive me, Lord, for my quick temper. I renounce the spirit of anger and any words or actions taken out in anger. I turn away from folly and seek Your understanding instead.

Holy Spirit, teach me to be even-tempered and self-controlled. Help me to be slow to anger, for I know that this demonstrates great understanding. Renew my heart to be a peacemaker, leaving envy, strife, and pride behind.

Father, give me the strength to rule my spirit, for Your Word says this is better than conquering a city. Help me to quiet contention rather than stir up strife. May I learn to overlook offenses, finding glory in patience and forbearance. Lord, guide me to cultivate friendships that encourage peace and self-control, rather than those that might lead me further into anger and wrath.

In Jesus' name I pray, Amen.

My own prayer:

_____

_____

_____

_____

_____

_____

_____

Rebellion

noun
ri-ˈbel-yən

1. Opposition to one in authority or dominance
2. An instance of such defiance or resistance

- **Proverbs 17:11:** An evil man seeks only rebellion, and a cruel messenger will be sent against him.
- **Hebrews 3:8:** Do not harden your hearts as in the rebellion, on the day of testing in the wilderness.
- **Job 34:37:** For he adds rebellion to his sin; he claps his hands among us and multiplies his words against God.
- **Jeremiah 33:8:** I will cleanse them from all the guilt of their sin against me, and I will forgive all the guilt of their sin and rebellion against me.
- **1 Samuel 15:23**: For rebellion is as the sin of divination, and presumption is as iniquity and idolatry. Because you have rejected the word of the Lord, he has also rejected you from being king.
- **Isaiah 63:10:** But they rebelled and grieved his Holy Spirit; therefore he turned to be their enemy, and himself fought against them.
- **Deuteronomy 31:27:** For I know how rebellious and stubborn you are. Behold, even today while I am yet alive with you, you have been rebellious against the Lord. How much more after my death!
- **James 4:7:** Submit yourselves therefore to God. Resist the devil, and he will flee from you.
- **Proverbs 28:9:** If one turns away his ear from hearing the law, even his prayer is an abomination.
- **Psalm 107:11:** For they had rebelled against the words of God and spurned the counsel of the Most High.

Reflections:

_____

_____

_____

Prayer:

Heavenly Father,

I come before You ready to obey Your truth and forsake a rebellious heart, I come before You. With a repentant heart, I acknowledge my rebellion and disobedience. Lord, I renounce all evil ways in me and my bloodline. Before You, O God, I submit myself. Soften my heart to Your Word and truth. Open my ears to hear Your voice clearly, muting the chaos of the world and those who seek to destroy me. Holy Spirit, cleanse me from rebellion and sinful disobedience. I take heed of Your instruction: "Rebellion is as the sin of divination, and presumption is as iniquity and idolatry." I will not reject Your Word, Lord, lest I be rejected by You. Teach me to resist the devil so that he must flee from me and my bloodline. Cleanse me from all the guilt of my sin and rebellion against You. Purify my heart and restore me to Your fellowship, according to Your faithful word.

Save my soul, O God, from the evil ones. Choosing to listen and obey, my ear is turned to hear Your truth. No longer spurning the counsel of the Most High, but seeking to walk in Your ways.

In Jesus' name, and by the authority of His blood, I pray. Amen

My own prayer:

_____

_____

_____

_____

_____

_____

_____

_____

Rebuild

verb
rē-'bild

1. To make extensive repairs to
2. To restore to a previous state

- **Isaiah 61:4:** They shall build up the ancient ruins; they shall raise up the former devastations; they shall repair the ruined cities, the devastations of many generations.
- **1 Peter 2:5**: You yourselves like living stones are being built up as a spiritual house, to be a holy priesthood, to offer spiritual sacrifices acceptable to God through Jesus Christ.
- **Jeremiah 31:4:** Again I will build you, and you shall be built, O virgin Israel! Again you shall adorn yourself with tambourines and shall go forth in the dance of the merrymakers.
- **Proverbs 3:5–6:** Trust in the Lord with all your heart, and do not lean on your own understanding. In all your ways acknowledge him, and he will make straight your paths.
- **James 1:5:** If any of you lacks wisdom, let him ask of God, who gives generously to all without reproach, and it will be given to him.

Reflections:

_____

_____

_____

_____

_____

_____

_____

_____

Prayer:

Heavenly Father,

I come before You in full faith, trusting Your will and direction for my life. Lord, grant me the vision to see the areas that need rebuilding, and place hope in my heart to undertake this task. Father, whether it be physical or spiritual reconstruction, help me focus on the mission to rebuild and persevere. Like living stones, build me up as part of Your spiritual house, to offer sacrifices acceptable to You through Jesus Christ.

Lord, I trust You with my whole heart and lean not on my own understanding. In all my ways, I acknowledge You, knowing You will make my paths straight. Grant me the wisdom to seek You rather than worldly solutions or my own will. As You promised to rebuild Israel, I pray for Your restoring power in my life and community. May You raise up former devastations and repair what has been ruined. I ask for the strength to rebuild and the discernment to recognize the sources, places, and means You provide for this purpose. If I lack wisdom, I ask You, knowing You give generously to all without finding fault.

In Jesus' name I pray, Amen.

My own prayer:

_____
_____
_____
_____
_____
_____
_____
_____

Redemption

noun
ri-'dem(p)-shən

1. The action or process of saving or being saved from sin, error, or evil
2. The action of regaining or gaining possession of something in exchange for payment, or clearing a debt

- **Ephesians 1:7:** In him we have redemption through his blood, the forgiveness of our trespasses, according to the riches of his grace.
- **Ephesians 4:30:** And do not grieve the Holy Spirit of God, by whom you were sealed for the day of redemption.
- **Psalm 111:9:** He sent redemption to his people; he has commanded his covenant forever. Holy and awesome is his name!
- **Romans 3:23–24:** For all have sinned and fall short of the glory of God, and are justified by his grace as a gift, through the redemption that is in Christ Jesus.
- **1 John 1:9:** If we confess our sins, he is faithful and just to forgive us our sins and to cleanse us from all unrighteousness.
- **Acts 3:17:** And now, brothers, I know that you acted in ignorance, as did also your rulers.
- **John 3:16:** "For God so loved the world, that he gave his only Son, that whoever believes in him should not perish but have eternal life."

Reflections:

_____
_____
_____
_____
_____
_____
_____

Prayer:

Heavenly Father,

I come before You in humility and reverence, acknowledging Your redemptive power. Thank You for the precious blood of Jesus through which redemption exists, granting forgiveness for my trespasses.

Father, I am grateful for the redemption You've sent to Your people, establishing a new and everlasting covenant. Holy and awesome is Your name, Lord.

O God, strengthen my faith that I may never doubt the power of Your redemption. Help me fully embrace the truth that I am justified by Your grace as a gift, through the redemption of Jesus Christ.

I renounce any lies I once held that dismissed the power of Your redemption through grace. Holy Spirit, I surrender to Your ways, releasing myself from grieving Your will and purpose in my life.

My Lord may my soul, mind, and spirit forever proclaim: For God so loved me that He gave His only Son, that as I believe in Him, I shall not perish but have eternal life.

Thank You for Your unfailing love and the redemption that sets me free. May I live each day in the truth of Your redeeming grace, sharing this good news with others.

In Jesus' name I pray, Amen.

My own prayer:

_____

_____

_____

_____

_____

Rejection

noun
ri-ˈjek-shən

1. The action of rejecting: state of being rejected
2. Something rejected

- **Lamentations 3:31–32:** For the Lord will not cast off forever, for, though he cause grief, he will have compassion according to the abundance of his steadfast love.
- **John 15:18:** "If the world hates you know that it has hated me before it hated you."
- **Psalm 27:10:** For my father and my mother have forsaken me, but the Lord will take me in.
- **Psalm 118:22:** The stone that the builders rejected has become the cornerstone.
- **Psalm 94:14:** For the Lord will not forsake his people; he will not abandon his heritage.
- **Luke 10:16:** "The one who hears you hears me, and the one who rejects you rejects me, and the one who rejects me rejects him who sent me."
- **Romans 8:31:** What shall we say to these things? If God is for us who can be against us?

Reflections:

_____
_____
_____
_____
_____
_____
_____
_____
_____
_____

WARFARE BATTLECARDS

Prayer:

Heavenly Father,

I come before You in humility, seeking Your compassion as I've experienced the grief of being cast off. Lord, as the world hates me, I'm comforted knowing it hated You first. When my father and mother have forsaken me, I rejoice that You will take me in!

Thank You, Father, that You have not abandoned me. Help me guard my heart, giving it fully to You rather than leaving it open for people's rejection. Forgive me for the days I've worn rejection as a method of seeking attention and comfort, instead of coming to You, my Lord.

Remind me, O God, that it is only Your acceptance I truly need, not that of people. As I walk in relationship with You, let my soul and spirit know deeply that the one who hears Christ hears me also, and the one who rejects me rejects You and Your Father.

Let me stand firm on Your truth: If God is for us, who can be against us? Help me see those who have been rejected with Your eyes of compassion. Prepare my heart to display Your love with open arms, knowing I carry Your goodness to pour out to those around me.

Lord, though You may allow grief, I trust in Your abundant steadfast love and compassion. Let me always remember that the stone the builders rejected has become the cornerstone. May this truth strengthen me in times of rejection.

In Jesus' name I pray, Amen.

My own prayer:

_____

_____

_____

_____

Religion

noun
ri-ˈli-jən

1. A particular system of faith and worship
2. The belief in and worship of a superhuman power or god, often in organized practices and doctrines

- **James 1:26:** If anyone thinks he is religious and does not bridle his tongue but deceives his heart, this person's religion is worthless.
- **Matthew 7:5:** "You hypocrite, first take the log out of your own eye, and then you will see clearly to take the speck out of your brother's eye."
- **Matthew 23:13:** "But woe to you, scribes and Pharisees, hypocrites! For you shut the kingdom of heaven in people's faces. For you neither enter yourselves nor allow those who would enter to go in."
- **Matthew 23:27:** "Woe to you, scribes and Pharisees, hypocrites! For you are like whitewashed tombs, which outwardly appear beautiful, but within are full of dead men's bones and all uncleanness."
- **Matthew 6:1:** "Beware of practicing your righteousness before other people in order to be seen by them, for then you will have no reward from your Father who is in heaven."
- **1 John 4:20:** If anyone says, "I love God," and hates his brother, he is a liar; for he who does not love his brother whom he has seen cannot love God whom he has not seen.
- **Titus 1:16:** They profess to know God, but they deny him by their works. They are detestable, disobedient, unfit for any good work.
- **Romans 10:3:** For, being ignorant of the righteousness of God, and seeking to establish their own, they did not submit to God's righteousness.
- **Luke 12:2:** "Nothing is covered up that will not be revealed, or hidden that will not be known."

Reflections:

Prayer:

Heavenly Father,

I come before You in humility, seeking Your grace. Lord, forgive me for being deceived by the religions of this world and the false religion I've created in my own heart to suit myself above a true relationship with You.

Father, I repent of my hypocritical ways—having a log in my eye yet remarking on the specks in others', shutting down the heavens in people's faces, and performing righteousness to be seen by others rather than to honor You.

O God, transform my heart. Rid me of any hatred toward my brothers and sisters, so that when I proclaim my love for You and profess You as Lord, it is pure and righteous.

Holy Spirit, help me to bridle my tongue and guard my heart from self-deception. Uncover any unclean, hypocritical, or religious acting spirit in me so that I may be purified.

Lord, I submit to Your righteousness rather than seeking to establish my own. Help me to practice my faith genuinely, not for the approval of others but for Your glory alone.

Reveal to me, Father, anything that is hidden or covered up in my heart. May I strive to be more than a whitewashed tomb, beautiful on the outside but full of uncleanness within.

Grant me the grace to love my brothers and sisters genuinely, knowing that I cannot truly love You if I harbor hatred for them.

In Jesus' name I pray, Amen.

My own prayer:

Renounce

verb

ri-ˈnau̇n(t)s

1. To say formally or publicly that one no longer believes in or supports something
2. To give up or reject something, especially a claim, right, or position

- **Titus 2:12:** Training us to renounce ungodliness and worldly passions, and to live self-controlled, upright, and godly lives in the present age.
- **2 Corinthians 4:2:** But we have renounced disgraceful, underhanded ways. We refuse to practice cunning or to tamper with God's word, but by the open statement of the truth we would commend ourselves to everyone's conscience in the sight of God.
- **Job 27:5:** Far be it from me to say that you are right; till I die I will not put away my integrity from me.
- **Romans 10:9:** Because, if you confess with your mouth that Jesus is Lord and believe in your heart that God raised him from the dead, you will be saved.
- **James 4:7:** Submit yourselves therefore to God. Resist the devil, and he will flee from you.
- **Joshua 24:15:** And if it is evil in your eyes to serve the Lord, choose this day whom you will serve, whether the gods your fathers served in the region beyond the River, or the gods of the Amorites in whose land you dwell. But as for me and my house, we will serve the Lord.

Reflections:

_____
_____
_____
_____
_____
_____
_____

Prayer:

Heavenly Father,

I come before You in humility, seeking Your ways. With a sincere heart, I renounce the things of this world—ungodliness and its passions, disgrace and underhanded ways. Instead, I choose to live a life that is self-controlled and upright in Your sight.

Lord, I refuse to practice cunning or tamper with Your word. Rather, I commit to openly stating Your truth, commending myself to Your presence. I will not put away my integrity, but hold fast to it until my last breath.

With my mouth, I confess that Jesus is Lord, and I believe in my heart that You, God, raised Him from the dead. I submit myself fully to You, resisting the devil, knowing that he must flee from Your presence in me.

Holy Spirit, fill me anew with Your power as I renounce the false gods of this region and those my forefathers may have served. I declare that I and my house will serve You, Lord, not just today but for a thousand generations to come.

Grant me the strength to live a godly life in this present age, always keeping my eyes fixed on You. May my life be a testament to Your transforming power and grace.

In Jesus' name I pray, Amen.

My own prayer:

_____

_____

_____

_____

_____

Restore

verb

ri-ˈstȯr

1. To bring back to a former or original state
2. To give something back to its rightful owner or place

- **Psalm 126:4:** Restore our fortunes, O Lord, like streams in the Negeb!
- **Psalm 51:12:** Restore to me the joy of your salvation, and uphold me with a willing spirit.
- **Jeremiah 30:17:** For I will restore health to you, and your wounds I will heal, declares the Lord, because they have called you an outcast: 'It is Zion, for whom no one cares!'
- **Psalm 23:3:** He restores my soul. He leads me in paths of righteousness for his name's sake.
- **Ruth 4:15:** He shall be to you a restorer of life and a nourisher of your old age, for your daughter-in-law who loves you, who is more to you than seven sons, has given birth to him.
- **Psalm 71:20–21:** You who have made me see many troubles and calamities will revive me again; from the depths of the earth you will bring me up again. You will increase my greatness and comfort me again.
- **2 Chronicles 7:14:** If my people who are called by my name humble themselves, and pray and seek my face and turn from their wicked ways, then I will hear from heaven and will forgive their sin and heal their land.

Reflections:

_____
_____
_____
_____
_____
_____
_____

Prayer:

Heavenly Father,

I come before You, seeking restoration, knowing You are the God who restores fortunes like streams in the desert. Father, restore to me the joy of Your salvation and uphold me with a willing spirit.

Forgive me for the doubts that have dismissed the power of Your desire to restore me to good health. Let me walk in renewed faith, fueled by the Holy Spirit, knowing You will restore every moment, thought, relationship, finances, and season stolen from me by my adversaries.

Lord, gird up my legs to stand firm, trusting that You will increase my greatness and comfort me once again. Each day, I humble myself before You, call upon Your name, pray, and seek Your face, turning from wicked ways. I trust that You will hear me, forgive me, and heal the land.

Thank You for being my restorer of life and the nourisher of my soul. Lead me in paths of righteousness for Your name's sake, restoring my soul along the way.

Even when I have seen many troubles and calamities, I trust that You will revive me again, bringing me up from the depths. Your restoration power knows no bounds, and I place my hope fully in You.

In Jesus' name I pray, Amen.

My own prayer:

_____

_____

_____

_____

_____

_____

Revelation

noun

ˌre-və-ˈlā-shən

1. The divine or supernatural disclosure to humans of something relating to human existence or the world
2. A surprising and previously unknown fact, especially one made known in a dramatic way

- **Psalm 119:105:** Your word is a lamp to my feet and a light to my path.
- **John 16:13:** "When the Spirit of truth comes, he will guide you into all the truth, for he will not speak on his own authority, but whatever he hears he will speak, and he will declare to you the things that are to come."
- **Genesis 37:5–8:** Now Joseph had a dream, and when he told it to his brothers they hated him even more. He said to them, "Hear this dream that I have dreamed: Behold, we were binding sheaves in the field, and behold, my sheaf arose and stood upright. And behold, your sheaves gathered around it and bowed down to my sheaf." His brothers said to him, "Are you indeed to reign over us? Or are you indeed to rule over us?" So they hated him even more for his dreams and for his words.
- **Acts 9:3–6:** Now as he went on his way, he approached Damascus, and suddenly a light from heaven flashed around him. And falling to the ground, he heard a voice saying to him, "Saul, Saul, why are you persecuting me?" And he said, "Who are you, Lord?" And he said, "I am Jesus, whom you are persecuting. But rise and enter the city, and you will be told what you are to do."
- **Mark 4:24:** And he said to them, "Pay attention to what you hear. With the measure you use, it will be measured to you, and still more will be added to you."
- **Romans 10:17:** So faith comes from hearing, and hearing through the word of Christ.
- **John 10:27:** "My sheep hear my voice, and I know them, and they follow me."
- **1 John 4:1:** Beloved, do not believe every spirit, but test the spirits to see whether they are from God, for many false prophets have gone out into the world.
- **Revelation 1:1:** The revelation of Jesus Christ, which God gave him to show to his servants the things that must soon take place. He made it known by sending his angel to his servant John.
- **Acts 13:2:** While they were worshiping the Lord and fasting, the Holy Spirit said, "Set apart for me Barnabas and Saul for the work to which I have called them."

Prayer:

Heavenly Father,

I come before You in humility, seeking Your presence and divine revelation. May Your Word be a lamp to my feet and a light to my path, guiding me above all worldly distractions competing for my affections.

Lord, protect my dreams from self-deception and false messengers. Let my dreams serve Your purpose, as they did for Joseph, preparing me for Your will and what is to come.

Forgive me, Father, for the times I've sought revelation from worldly or wicked sources. Like Paul's Damascus Road experience, I surrender to Your life-changing revelation. Guide me along the course You've set for me.

Help me pay attention to what I hear, knowing the measure I use will be used for me. Solidify my faith, reminding me that revelation comes through Your Word. I am Your sheep; help me recognize and follow Your voice always.

Grant me discernment to test every spirit and revelation, ensuring it truly comes from You, Holy God. May I be open to Your guidance through the Holy Spirit, as You directed Barnabas and Saul.

Let me be not deceived by false prophets, but always seek the truth that comes from You alone. May the revelation of Jesus Christ be the foundation of my understanding and faith.

In Jesus' name I pray, Amen.

My own prayer:

_____

_____

_____

_____

Revenge

noun
ri-ˈvenj

1. The action of inflicting harm or hurt on someone for an injury or wrong suffered at their hands
2. The desire to retaliate or get back at someone for a perceived wrong

- **Romans 12:19:** Beloved, never avenge yourselves, but leave it to the wrath of God, for it is written, "Vengeance is mine, I will repay, says the Lord."
- **1 Peter 3:9:** Do not repay evil for evil or reviling for reviling, but on the contrary, bless, for to this you were called, that you may obtain a blessing.
- **Leviticus 19:18:** You shall not take vengeance or bear a grudge against the sons of your own people, but you shall love your neighbor as yourself: I am the Lord.
- **Mark 11:25:** "And whenever you stand praying, forgive, if you have anything against anyone, so that your Father also who is in heaven may forgive you your trespasses."
- **Proverbs 20:22:** Do not say, "I will repay evil"; wait for the Lord, and he will deliver you.
- **Matthew 5:7:** "Blessed are the merciful, for they shall receive mercy."
- **Proverbs 10:12:** Hatred stirs up strife, but love covers all offenses.

Reflections:

_____
_____
_____
_____
_____
_____
_____
_____

Prayer:

Heavenly Father,

I come before You in humility, acknowledging my need for Your guidance and grace. Lord, as my heart carries the passion and pursuits fueling acts of revenge, whether by my own hands or through misguided prayers, deliver me from such vile thoughts and intentions. I recognize that vengeance is Yours alone, and wrath belongs to You, God.

Help me, Father, to not repay evil for evil or reviling for reviling. Instead, grant me the strength to wait on You, Lord. Prepare my heart to bless my enemies, not bearing grudges against Your people. Teach me to forgive, so that I may also be forgiven.

I renounce all ploys of hatred and strife, choosing instead to offer mercy to those on whom I once sought revenge. Holy Spirit, fill me with a merciful posture, keeping me aligned with God's ways rather than seeking my own vindication.

Lord, when I stand praying, remind me to forgive if I have anything against anyone. Let Your love flow through me to cover all offenses. May I be counted among the merciful, knowing that they shall receive mercy.

In moments of hurt and anger, help me remember that hatred stirs up strife, but love covers all offenses. Grant me the patience to wait for Your deliverance rather than taking matters into my own hands.

In Jesus' name I pray, Amen.

My own prayer:

_____

_____

_____

_____

Rude

adjective
'rüd

1. Offensively impolite or disrespectful
2. Lacking refinement or sophistication, often expressed in an abrupt or coarse manner

- **Philippians 2:3:** Do nothing from selfish ambition or conceit, but in humility count others more significant than yourselves.
- **Titus 3:2:** To speak evil of no one, to avoid quarreling, to be gentle, and to show perfect courtesy toward all people.
- **Proverbs 15:1:** A soft answer turns away wrath, but a harsh word stirs up anger.
- **Proverbs 29:11:** A fool gives full vent to his spirit, but a wise man quietly holds it back.
- **John 17:17:** "Sanctify them in the truth; your word is truth."
- **Ephesians 4:31–32:** Let all bitterness and wrath and anger and clamor and slander be put away from you, along with all malice. Be kind to one another, tenderhearted, forgiving one another, as God in Christ forgave you.

Reflections:

_____
_____
_____
_____
_____
_____
_____
_____
_____
_____

Prayer:

Heavenly Father,

I come before You in humility, renouncing selfish ambition and conceit. Help me live by Your words, to consider others above myself, to speak evil of no one, to avoid quarreling, and to move in gentleness, showing perfect courtesy toward all people.

Forgive me, Lord, for buying into the notion that harsh words and anger are valid means to communicate with Your people. Holy Spirit, instill in me self-control, that I may no longer be a fool who gives in to a harsh tongue. Sanctify me in Your truth; Your Word is truth.

Remove all bitterness from me, Lord. Help me put away slander, wrath, anger, clamor, and malice. Instead, let me operate in kindness, being tenderhearted and forgiving toward others, just as You have forgiven me in Christ.

Teach me, Father, to give soft answers that turn away wrath, rather than harsh words that stir up anger. When my spirit is vexed, grant me the wisdom to hold it back quietly instead of giving it full vent.

May my words and actions reflect Your love and grace, considering others more significant than myself. Let my gentleness and courtesy be evident to all, as a testament to Your transforming power in my life.

In Jesus' name I pray, Amen.

My own prayer:

_____

_____

_____

_____

_____

_____

_____

Rumination

noun
ˌrü-mə-ˈnā-shən

1. The action or process of thinking deeply about something
2. The act of repeatedly thinking about or dwelling on something, often to the point of obsession

- **Isaiah 43:18–19:** Remember not the former things, nor consider the old things. Behold, I am doing a new thing; now it springs forth, do you not perceive it? I will make a way in the wilderness and rivers in the desert.
- **Philippians 4:6–8:** Do not be anxious about anything, but in everything by prayer and supplication with thanksgiving let your requests be made known to God. And the peace of God, which surpasses all understanding, will guard your hearts and your minds in Christ Jesus. Finally, brothers, whatever is true, whatever is honorable, whatever is just, whatever is pure, whatever is lovely, whatever is commendable, if there is any excellence, if there is anything worthy of praise, think about these things.
- **Matthew 6:34:** "Therefore do not be anxious about tomorrow, for tomorrow will be anxious for itself. Sufficient for the day is its own trouble."
- **Psalm 119:15:** I will meditate on your precepts and fix my eyes on your ways.
- **Psalm 119:105:** Your word is a lamp to my feet and a light to my path.

Reflections:

_____
_____
_____
_____
_____
_____
_____

WARFARE BATTLECARDS

Prayer:

Heavenly Father,

I come before You in humility, seeking clarity and peace of mind. Lord, clear my thoughts of former things and old memories that keep me bound to the past. Help me to behold the new things You are bringing forth in my life. Grant me the perception to see the ways You are making in the wilderness and the rivers You are creating in the desert of my circumstances.

Father, I surrender to You the ruminating thoughts that creep into my days and nights, pulling me back in time rather than allowing me to live in the present moment You have set before me. Holy Spirit, guide me to meditate on Your Word, fixing my eyes on Your ways. Let Your Word be the lamp to my feet and the light to my path, illuminating the way forward.

Lord, I ask that You renew my mind, aligning my thoughts with Christ. Tear down the circus of rumination in my mind, replacing it with Your truth and promises. Help me to focus on whatever is true, honorable, just, pure, lovely, and commendable.

When anxiety threatens to overwhelm me, remind me to bring everything to You in prayer with thanksgiving. May Your peace, which surpasses all understanding, guard my heart and mind in Christ Jesus.

In Jesus' name I pray, Amen.

My own prayer:

_____
_____
_____
_____
_____

Safety

noun
'sāf-tē

1. The condition of being protected from harm or danger
2. The state of being free from injury, loss, or risk

- **Psalm 4:8:** In peace I will both lie down and sleep; for you alone, O Lord, make me dwell in safety.
- **Proverbs 18:10:** The name of the Lord is a strong tower; the righteous man runs into it and is safe.
- **Proverbs 1:32:** For the simple are killed by their turning away, and the complacency of fools destroys them.
- **Psalm 91:1–2:** He who dwells in the shelter of the Most High will abide in the shadow of the Almighty. I will say to the Lord, "My refuge and my fortress, my God, in whom I trust."

Reflections:

_____
_____
_____
_____
_____
_____
_____
_____
_____
_____
_____

Prayer:

Heavenly Father,

I come before You seeking refuge and safety. My God, as I search the lands for shelter, remind me that You are the safest haven one can dwell in, the strongest tower of protection.

May I become righteous in Your ways, obedient to Your words, always running to You for safety. Holy Spirit, remove the old trenches, hideouts, and burrows I once ran to for shelter, foolishly straying away from my Lord. Let these false refuges crumble, that I may fully embrace Your protection.

Let my soul rest in You alone as the Most High, abiding in the shadow of the Almighty. O Lord, I declare: You are my refuge, my fortress, my God in whom I trust. In peace, I will both lie down and sleep, for You alone, O Lord, make me dwell in safety.

In every circumstance, help me remember that my ultimate security is found in You. Whether in times of peace or trouble, may I always seek the shelter of Your presence.

In Jesus' name I pray, Amen.

My own prayer:

_____

_____

_____

_____

_____

_____

_____

Salt

verb
'sȯlt

1. To treat, provide, or season with common salt
2. To give flavor or piquancy to (something, such as a story)

- **Matthew 5:13:** "You are the salt of the earth, but if salt has lost its taste, how shall its saltiness be restored? It is no longer good for anything except to be thrown out and trampled under people's feet."
- **Leviticus 2:13:** You shall season all your grain offerings with salt. You shall not let the salt of the covenant with your God be missing from your grain offering; with all your offerings you shall offer salt.
- **Genesis 19:26:** But Lot's wife, behind him, looked back and she became a pilar of salt.
- **Mark 9:50:** "Salt is good, but if the salt has lost its saltiness, how will you make it salty again? Have salt in yourselves, and be at peace with one another."
- **Colossians 4:6:** Let your speech always be gracious, seasoned with salt, so that you may know how you ought to answer each person.
- **Numbers 18:19:** All the holy contributions that the people of Israel present to the LORD I give to you, and to your sons and daughters with you, as a perpetual due. It is a covenant of salt forever before the LORD for you and you offspring with you.

Reflections:

_____
_____
_____
_____
_____
_____
_____

Prayer:

Heavenly Father,

I come before You in need of flavoring, for as You have spoken, I am the salt of the earth. Lord, may I keep my tastiness to be used in enhancing Your kingdom, not to be thrown out and trampled under people's feet.

Let me remain in season with You and Your commands, acknowledging my covenant with You. Holy Spirit, forgive me for the times I've looked back, rather than ahead to what You have for me. May I never become a pillar of salt, frozen in the past, but always move forward in Your will.

Help me, Father, to let my speech always be gracious, seasoned with salt, so that I may know how to speak to each person. Grant me wisdom to answer others in a way that reflects Your love and truth.

I declare that every contribution of my soul contains salt, presenting to You a holy offering. May I never let the salt of our covenant be missing from my life and actions.

Lord, help me to have salt in myself, to be at peace with others, and to be a preserving and flavoring influence in this world. When I feel my saltiness fading, restore me, that I may continue to be effective for Your kingdom.

In Jesus' name I pray, Amen.

My own prayer:

_____
_____
_____
_____
_____
_____

Salvation

noun

sal-'vā-shən

1. The act of being saved or protected from harm, risk, or destruction
2. In a religious context, deliverance from sin and its consequences, through faith in Jesus Christ

- **Genesis 49:18:** I wait for your salvation, O Lord.
- **Psalm 38:22:** Make haste to help me, O Lord, my salvation!
- **Ephesians 2:8–9:** For by grace you have been saved through faith. And this is not your own doing; it is the gift of God, not a result of works, so that no one may boast.
- **Titus 3:5:** He saved us, not because of works done by us in righteousness, but according to his own mercy, by the washing of regeneration and renewal of the Holy Spirit.
- **John 14:6:** Jesus said to him, "I am the way, and the truth, and the life. No one comes to the Father except through me."
- **Romans 10:9:** If you confess with your mouth that Jesus is Lord and believe in your heart that God raised him from the dead, you will be saved.
- **Psalm 37:29:** The righteous shall inherit the land and dwell upon it forever.

Reflections:

_____
_____
_____
_____
_____
_____
_____
_____

Prayer:

Heavenly Father,

I come before You in humility, acknowledging that my salvation comes from You alone. Lord, I wait for Your salvation, trusting in Your perfect timing and plan for my life.

I renounce all previous acts, rituals, or assemblies that called forth false doctrines and false hope of security. Forgive me for pursuing idols instead of seeking Jesus as my Savior. I now declare my faith in His resurrection and confess that Jesus is Lord.

Thank You, Father, for the gift of salvation by Your grace through faith. I recognize that this is not my own doing, nor the result of any works, but solely Your gift to me. I am grateful for Your mercy, which saves me through the washing of regeneration and renewal by the Holy Spirit.

Lord, cleanse me and help me live righteously, that I may inherit the land and dwell upon it forever. May my life be a testament to Your transforming power and grace.

Holy Spirit, guide me in this journey of faith, assuring me of my salvation and helping me grow in righteousness and true holiness. I trust in Jesus as the way, the truth, and the life, knowing that through Him alone I can come to the Father.

In Jesus' name I pray, Amen.

My own prayer:

_____
_____
_____
_____
_____

Sanctification

noun

ˌsaŋ(k)-tə-fə-ˈkā-shən

1. The process of being made holy, set apart for God's purposes
2. The act of growing in spiritual maturity and moral purity through the work of the Holy Spirit

- **2 Timothy 2:21:** Therefore, if anyone cleanses himself from what is dishonorable, he will be a vessel for honorable use, set apart as holy, useful to the master of the house, ready for every good work.
- **1 Thessalonians 4:3, 7:** For this is the will of God, your sanctification: that you abstain from sexual immorality. . .. For God has not called us for impurity, but in holiness.
- **1 Thessalonians 5:23:** Now may the God of peace himself sanctify you completely, and may your whole spirit and soul and body be kept blameless at the coming of our Lord Jesus Christ.
- **1 Corinthians 1:30:** And because of him you are in Christ Jesus, who became to us wisdom from God, righteousness and sanctification and redemption.
- **Romans 6:22:** But now that you have been set free from sin and have become slaves of God, the fruit you get leads to sanctification and its end, eternal life.
- **Hebrews 12:14:** Strive for peace with everyone, and for the holiness without which no one will see the Lord.
- **2 Corinthians 7:1:** Since we have these promises, beloved, let us cleanse ourselves from every defilement of body and spirit, bringing holiness to completion in the fear of God.
- **1 Peter 1:2:** According to the foreknowledge of God the Father, in the sanctification of the Spirit, for obedience to Jesus Christ and for sprinkling with his blood: May grace and peace be multiplied to you.

Reflections:

_____

_____

_____

_____

Prayer:

Heavenly Father,

I come before You in humility, seeking cleansing to be an honorable vessel, set apart as holy, useful to You, the master of the house, and ready for every good work.

Lord, help me yield to Your will, adhering to sanctification and abstaining from sexual immorality. I acknowledge that You have called me to holiness, not impurity. May the God of peace Himself sanctify me completely, and may my whole spirit, soul, and body be kept blameless at the coming of our Lord Jesus Christ.

Thank You, Lord, that I am in Christ Jesus, who became my wisdom, righteousness, sanctification, and redemption. Help me to forever hold true to Your promises, cleansing myself from every defilement of body and spirit.

Holy Spirit, guide me in the process of sanctification. As I have been set free from sin and become a slave to God, may the fruit of my life lead to sanctification and its end, eternal life.

Father, multiply Your grace and peace in my life as I pursue sanctification. May my life be a testament to Your transforming power, reflecting Your holiness in all I do.

In Jesus' name I pray, Amen.

My own prayer:

_____

_____

_____

_____

_____

Satan

noun
'sā-tən

1. The adversary or enemy of God and mankind, often depicted as the embodiment of evil and opposition to God's will
2. A fallen angel who leads forces of rebellion against God

- **1 Peter 5:8:** Be sober-minded; be watchful. Your adversary the devil prowls around like a roaring lion, seeking someone to devour.
- **1 John 3:8:** Whoever makes a practice of sinning is of the devil, for the devil has been sinning from the beginning. The reason the Son of God appeared was to destroy the works of the devil.
- **James 4:7:** Submit yourselves therefore to God. Resist the devil, and he will flee from you.
- **1 Timothy 5:15:** For some have already strayed after Satan.
- **Zechariah 3:2:** And the Lord said to Satan, "The Lord rebuke you, O Satan! The Lord who has chosen Jerusalem rebuke you! Is not this a brand plucked from the fire?"

Reflections:

_____
_____
_____
_____
_____
_____
_____
_____
_____

Prayer:

Heavenly Father,

I come before You, acknowledging Your mighty power and authority over all. Lord, grant me the discipline to be sober-minded and watchful, for I know my adversary, the devil, prowls around like a roaring lion, seeking to devour.

Forgive me, Father, for any time I have made sinning a practice in my life. I thank You that Jesus came to destroy the works of the devil, and I claim that victory in my life today.

I submit myself fully to You, God, resisting the devil with the assurance that he must flee. Holy Spirit, grant me the courage to remain steadfast in Christ, no longer straying after Satan's deceptions.

Should I encounter the imps of Satan, remind me of Your powerful words, O God: "The Lord rebukes you, O Satan!" Let me stand firm in the knowledge that Satan's defeat is certain and the fire awaits him.

Lord, keep me vigilant against the enemy's schemes. When temptation comes, strengthen me to resist. Help me to put on the full armor of God, that I may stand against the devil's wiles.

Thank You for the authority You've given me in Christ to overcome the enemy. May I walk in that power daily, always aware of Your protection and presence.

In Jesus' name and by the authority of His blood, I pray, Amen.

My own prayer:

_____

_____

_____

_____

_____

Schizophrenia

noun
ˌskit-sə-ˈfrē-nē-ə

1. A severe mental disorder characterized by delusions, hallucinations, disorganized thinking, and impaired functioning
2. A disorder that distorts a person's perception of reality, often leading to difficulty in distinguishing between what is real and what is not

- **2 Timothy 1:7 (NKJV):** For God has not given us a spirit of fear but of power and love and of a sound mind.
- **Romans 12:2:** Do not be conformed to this world, but be transformed by the renewal of your mind, that by testing you may discern what is the will of God, what is good and acceptable and perfect.
- **Philippians 4:6–7:** Do not be anxious about anything, but in everything by prayer and supplication with thanksgiving let your requests be made known to God. And the peace of God, which surpasses all understanding, will guard your hearts and your minds in Christ Jesus.
- **1 John 4:16:** So we have come to know and to believe the love that God has for us. God is love, and whoever abides in love abides in God, and God abides in him.
- **Proverbs 4:7:** The beginning of wisdom is this: Get wisdom, and whatever you get, get insight.
- **1 Corinthians 6:19–20:** Or do you not know that your body is a temple of the Holy Spirit within you, whom you have from God? You are not your own, for you were bought with a price. So glorify God in your body.

Reflections:

_____

_____

_____

_____

_____

Prayer:

Heavenly Father,

I come before You, seeking truth and clarity amid confusion. Lord, as my mind struggles to distinguish between reality and fiction, help me cling to the mustard seed of faith that You are absolute and real. May I no longer serve fear, for You have not given me a spirit of fear, but of power, love, and a sound mind. Forgive me for the times I have conformed to this world rather than submitting to the transformative work of Your Holy Spirit. Renew my mind, Lord, that I may discern Your will-what is good, acceptable, and perfect.

Father, remove from me any lies that I've claimed, which have furthered the deception of a confused and noisy mind. As Jesus spoke with authority and cast Legion out, through faith, I too declare: Depart from me, unclean spirit! Help me to bring everything to You in prayer with thanksgiving, trusting that Your peace, which surpasses all understanding, will guard my heart and mind. May every cell, neuron, and part of my brain know the love that You have for me and operate according to Your divine design.

I believe that You are love, and as I abide in Your love, You abide in me. Grant me wisdom and insight, Lord, to navigate the challenges of schizophrenia. Holy Spirit, reveal any doorways or practices that give way to deception and torment. Remind me that my body is a temple of Your Holy Spirit, and help me to glorify You even in my struggles.

In Jesus' name, and by the authority of His blood, I pray. Amen.

My own prayer:

_____

_____

_____

_____

_____

Seducing

verb
si-ˈdüs-iŋ

1. The act of enticing or leading someone into immoral behavior or sin, especially through temptation or manipulation.
2. Influencing someone to engage in inappropriate or sinful actions.

- **1 Corinthians 6:18:** Flee from sexual immorality. Every other sin a person commits is outside the body, but the sexually immoral person sins against his own body.
- **Genesis 39:12:** She caught him by his garment, saying, "Lie with me." But he left his garment in her hand and fled and got out of the house.
- **Matthew 5:28:** "But I say to you that everyone who looks at a woman with lustful intent has already committed adultery with her in his heart."
- **Revelation 2:20:** But I have this against you, that you tolerate that woman Jezebel, who calls herself a prophetess and is teaching and seducing my servants to practice sexual immorality and to eat food sacrificed to idols.
- **Romans 16:17–19:** I appeal to you, brothers, to watch out for those who cause divisions and create obstacles contrary to the doctrine that you have been taught; avoid them. For such persons do not serve our Lord Christ, but their own appetites, and by smooth talk and flattery they deceive the hearts of the naive. For your obedience is known to all, so that I rejoice over you, but I want you to be wise as to what is good and innocent as to what is evil.

Reflections:

___

___

___

___

___

___

___

Prayer:

Heavenly Father,

I come before You in repentance, seeking Your liberty. As Your Word instructs, help me flee from sexual immorality. Open my eyes to the deception of seducing spirits, and search out every agenda birthed by impure motives or fancies toward myself or others.

O God, as our culture has adopted iconic depictions of seduction, such as Jezebel, grant me the boldness to not tolerate such teachings or influences. Holy Spirit, place in me an appetite to serve You and Your ways alone, fostering obedience to You and Your commands, and granting me Your wisdom.

Lord, guard my heart and mind against lustful intent. Help me to look upon others with purity, remembering that even a lustful gaze is adultery in the heart. Give me the strength, like Joseph, to flee from temptation when it presents itself.

Father, make me wise to what is good and innocent to what is evil. Help me watch out for those who cause divisions and create obstacles contrary to Your doctrine. Let me not be deceived by smooth talk and flattery, but instead be firmly rooted in Your truth.

Let me walk in freedom from operating in seduction, and instead, may my life reflect Your holiness and love.

In Jesus' name I pray, Amen.

My own prayer:

_____

_____

_____

_____

_____

Self-Will

noun
,self-'wil

1. The desire or determination to act according to one's own preferences or decisions, often without regard for others or external guidance
2. The inclination to act independently, sometimes in opposition to divine or moral principles

- **John 3:30:** He must increase, but I must decrease.
- **Philippians 2:3:** Do nothing from selfish ambition or conceit, but in humility count others more significant than yourselves.
- **Proverbs 3:5–6:** Trust in the Lord with all your heart, and do not lean on your own understanding. In all your ways acknowledge him, and he will make straight your paths.
- **Proverbs 16:9:** The heart of man plans his way, but the Lord establishes his steps.
- **John 14:15:** "If you love me, you will keep my commandments."
- **Romans 2:8:** But for those who are self-seeking and do not obey the truth, but obey unrighteousness, there will be wrath and fury.

Reflections:

_____
_____
_____
_____
_____
_____
_____
_____
_____

Prayer:

Heavenly Father,

I come before You in humility, acknowledging that my feet have stumbled due to my own self-will. Lord, I pray that You would increase as I decrease, for I recognize the folly of exalting myself.

Father, as the world promotes self-exaltation and self-will as mainstream culture, remind me to trust in You with all my heart, not leaning on my own understanding. Help me to acknowledge You in all my ways, trusting that You will make my paths straight.

I repent from conceit and rivalry born of self-will, and I submit to Your ways. Holy Spirit, search my heart and purge it of selfish ambitions. Establish my steps, Father, for I know that while my heart may plan its way, it is You who ultimately directs my path.

Lord, I declare my love for You and commit to keeping Your commandments above my own religious mindset or selfish desires. Let me walk out my days displaying Your ways, not my own.

Forgive me for the times I've been self-seeking and disobedient to Your truth. Guard me against the wrath and fury that come from following unrighteousness. Instead, fill me with Your Spirit, that I might live in humble obedience to Your will.

In Jesus' name I pray, Amen.

My own prayer:

_____

_____

_____

_____

_____

Sensation

noun
sen-ˈsā-shən

1. A physical feeling or perception resulting from something that comes into contact with the body
2. A mental or emotional perception or awareness, often associated with heightened awareness or experience

- **Psalm 34:8:** Oh, taste and see that the LORD is good! Blessed is the man who takes refuge in him!
- **1 Corinthians 2:14:** The natural person does not accept the things of the Spirit of God, for they are folly to him, and he is not able to understand them because they are spiritually discerned.
- **Philippians 4:7:** And the peace of God, which surpasses all understanding, will guard your hearts and your minds in Christ Jesus.

Reflections:

_____
_____
_____
_____
_____
_____
_____
_____
_____
_____

Prayer:

Heavenly Father,

I come before You in awe of Your majesty and goodness. Lord, I have tasted and seen that You are good, and I take refuge in You.

As the world around me chases after its own pleasures and sensations, using its natural state as a compass, remind me to operate in unison with Your Holy Spirit. Sharpen my discernment, Lord, keeping me from pursuing sensations or perceptions that lie outside of Your Word.

Father, help me to understand that the natural person cannot accept the things of Your Spirit, for they are spiritually discerned. Grant me the wisdom to seek Your truth above fleeting sensory experiences.

May the peace of God, which surpasses all understanding, guard my heart and mind in Christ Jesus. Let this divine peace be my anchor amidst the tumultuous sea of worldly sensations.

Holy Spirit, guide my senses to perceive Your presence in my daily life. Tune my ears to Your voice, open my eyes to Your works, and let my heart be sensitive to Your leading.

In Jesus' name I pray, Amen

My own prayer:

_____
_____
_____
_____
_____
_____
_____

Sensuality

noun

ˌsen(t)-ˈshə-ˈwa-lə-tē

1. The indulgence in physical pleasures, especially those relating to the senses, often to excess
2. The pursuit of gratification through the senses, which may lead to immoral or excessive behavior

- **Mark 7:21–23:** "For from within, our of the heart of man, come evil thoughts, sexual immorality, theft, murder, adultery, coveting, wickedness, deceit, sensuality, envy, slander, pride, foolishness. All these evil things come from within, and they defile a person."
- **Galatians 5:19, 22–23:** Now the works of the flesh are evident: sexual immorality, impurity, sensuality,. . . But the fruit of the Spirit is love, joy, peace, patience, kindness, goodness, faithfulness, gentleness and self-control; Against such things there is no law.
- **2 Peter 2:2:** And many will follow their sensuality, and because of them the way of truth will be blasphemed.
- **Romans 13:13:** Let us walk properly as in the daytime, not in orgies and drunkenness, not in sexual immorality and sensuality, not in quarreling and jealousy.
- **1 Peter 4:3:** For the time that is past suffices for doing what the Gentiles want to do, living in sensuality, passions, drunkenness, orgies, drinking parties, and lawless idolatry.
- **1 Thessalonians 4:3–5:** For this is the will of God, your sanctification: that you abstain from sexual immorality; that each one of you know how to control his own body in holiness and honor, not in the passion of lust like the Gentiles who do not know God.

Reflections:

_____

_____

_____

_____

_____

Prayer:

Heavenly Father,

I come before You in humility, seeking strength in a world where many follow their sensuality and blaspheme the way of truth. Lord, I renounce the works of the flesh: thievery, coveting, wickedness, deceit, sensuality, envy, slander, pride, and foolishness.

Father, rid me completely of fleshly, sensual desires. I reject orgies, drunkenness, sexual immorality, quarreling, and jealousy. Instead, Holy Spirit, fill me up with Your presence and power!

Grant me the courage to step into sanctification, living a life of holiness that pleases You, Father. Help me to abide by Your commands, placing them above my own sensual inclinations.

Lord, teach me to control my body in holiness and honor, not in the passion of lust like those who do not know You. May I walk properly as in the daytime, leaving behind the deeds of darkness.

I pray for the fruit of Your Spirit to flourish in my life: love, joy, peace, patience, kindness, goodness, faithfulness, gentleness, and self-control. Let these virtues guard me against sensuality and guide me in Your truth.

In Jesus' name I pray, Amen.

My own prayer:

_____

_____

_____

_____

_____

_____

Serpent

noun
ˈsər-pənt

1. A large, elongated, legless reptile
2. In biblical symbolism, often represents Satan or evil, used metaphorically to describe deceit and temptation

- **Isaiah 27:1:** In that day the Lord with his hard and great and strong sword will punish Leviathan the fleeing serpent, Leviathan the twisting serpent, and he will slay the dragon that is in the sea.
- **Revelation 12:9:** And the great dragon was thrown down, that ancient serpent, who is called the devil and Satan, the deceiver of the whole world—he was thrown down to the earth, and his angels were thrown down with him.
- **Revelation 20:2:** And he seized the dragon, that ancient serpent, who is the devil and Satan, and bound him for a thousand years.
- **1 Peter 5:8:** Be sober-minded; be watchful. Your adversary the devil prowls around like a roaring lion, seeking someone to devour.
- **Psalm 91:13:** You will tread on the lion and the adder; the young lion and the serpent you will trample underfoot.

Reflections:

_____
_____
_____
_____
_____
_____

Prayer:

Heavenly Father,

I come before You, seeking protection. Lord, as I feel immobilized in soul and spirit by the serpent, remind me of Your mighty words and promises.

Father, call to my mind the truth that You will punish Leviathan, the fleeing and twisting serpent, with Your great and strong sword. Remind me that the great dragon, that ancient serpent called the devil and Satan, has been thrown down to the earth along with his angels.

Grant me courage, Lord, to hold fast to the knowledge that Satan may yet be bound for a thousand years. Let this bring hope to my soul and spirit, knowing that You have overcome the world. Greater is He who is in me than he who is in the world.

Holy Spirit, build up my discipline to remain sober-minded and watchful. Help me walk in the authority spoken in Your Word, knowing that through You, I will tread on the lion and the adder, and trample the young lion and serpent underfoot.

Father, as the devil prowls like a roaring lion seeking someone to devour, keep me vigilant and strong in faith. Let me stand firm in the knowledge of Your victory over the ancient serpent.

In Jesus' name and by the authority of His blood, I pray, Amen.

My own prayer:

_____

_____

_____

_____

_____

Shame

noun
'shām

1. A painful feeling of humiliation or distress caused by the consciousness of wrong or foolish behavior
2. A sense of dishonor or guilt, often resulting from one's actions or the actions of others

- **Jeremiah 2:36:** How much you go about, changing your way! You shall be put to shame by Egypt as you were put to shame by Assyria.
- **Psalm 31:17:** O Lord, let me not be put to shame, for I call upon you; let the wicked be put to shame; let them go silently to Sheol.
- **Psalm 83:16:** Fill their faces with shame, that they may seek your name, O Lord.
- **Isaiah 61:7:** Instead of your shame there shall be a double portion; instead of dishonor they shall rejoice in their lot; therefore in their land they shall possess a double portion; they shall have everlasting joy.
- **1 John 1:9:** If we confess our sins, he is faithful and just to forgive us our sins and to cleanse us from all unrighteousness.
- **Psalm 34:4–5:** I sought the Lord, and he answered me and delivered me from all my fears. Those who look to him are radiant, and their faces shall never be ashamed.
- **Romans 10:11:** For the Scripture says, "Everyone who believes in him will not be put to shame."

Reflections:

_____

_____

_____

_____

_____

_____

Prayer:

Heavenly Father,

I come before You in humility, acknowledging my weakness and need for Your guidance. O Lord, let me not be put to shame, for I call upon You. Forgive me for the times I have wavered, tossing back and forth between trusting others and trusting You. Remind me of the consequences of misplaced trust and help me to rely solely on You.

Lord, I confess my sins to You, for You are faithful and just to forgive and cleanse me from all unrighteousness. I seek You, knowing that You hear my pleas. Cast off the shame that has hindered me from building Your kingdom, and replace it with Your steadfast love that endures forever.

Father, instead of shame, grant me a double portion of honor. Let me rejoice in the lot You have given me and possess the everlasting joy You promise. Fill me with Your radiance, that my face may never be ashamed.

Holy Spirit, strengthen my faith, for I believe in Your Word that says, "Everyone who believes in Him will not be put to shame." Let me sing of Your steadfast love in the morning and declare Your faithfulness at night.

In Jesus' name I pray, Amen.

My own prayer:

_____
_____
_____
_____

Sit

verb
'sit

1. to rest on the buttocks or haunches
2. to occupy a place as a member of an official body

- **Luke 10:39:** And she had a sister called Mary, who sat at the Lord's feet and listened to his teaching.
- **Proverbs 3:4:** If you lie down, you will not be afraid; when you lie down, your sleep will be sweet.
- **Psalm 46:10:** Be still and know that I m God.
- **Psalm 23:2:** He makes me lie down in green pastures. He leads me beside still waters.
- **Matthew 11:28:** "Come to me, all who labor and are heavy laden, and I will give you rest."

Reflections:

_____
_____
_____
_____
_____
_____
_____
_____
_____
_____
_____

Prayer:

Heavenly Father,

I come before You, weary and desolate. Lord, I long to sit at Your feet like Mary, listening to Your teaching, yet my flesh wrestles with the urge to stay busy, always striving to be ahead. Forgive me, O God, for resisting the stillness of sitting with You, for not basking in the glory of Your presence or feasting on the richness of Your Word.

Holy Spirit, teach me to lie down without fear, that my sleep may be sweet. Grant me the ability to be still, truly knowing that You are the Lord, and there is none like You. Help me see the beauty in Your promise of green pastures, where rest awaits me.

Jesus, when I am weary, may I come to You alone, for Your yoke is easy and Your burden is light. Let me find joy in sitting in Your presence, drinking deeply from the well of Your wisdom.

Father, calm my restless heart and quiet my busy mind. Help me prioritize these moments of sitting with You, knowing that in Your presence, I find strength, peace, and renewal.

In Jesus' name I pray, Amen.

My own prayer:

_____
_____
_____
_____
_____
_____
_____

Slavery

noun
ˈslā-v(ə-)rē

1. The condition of being owned by another person and forced to work without rights or freedoms
2. The state of being under the control or influence of something, often used metaphorically for spiritual bondage

- **Galatians 5:1:** For freedom Christ has set us free; stand firm therefore, and do not submit again to a yoke of slavery.
- **Hebrews 2:15:** And deliver all those who through fear of death were subject to lifelong slavery.
- **Romans 8:15:** For you did not receive the spirit of slavery to fall back into fear, but you have received the Spirit of adoption as sons, by whom we cry, "Abba! Father!"
- **Isaiah 61:1:** The Spirit of the Lord God is upon me, because the Lord has anointed me to bring good news to the poor; he has sent me to bind up the brokenhearted, to proclaim liberty to the captives, and the opening of the prison to those who are bound.
- **Psalm 118:5:** Out of my distress I called on the Lord; the Lord answered me and set me free.
- **John 8:32:** "And you will know the truth, and the truth will set you free."

Reflections:

_____
_____
_____
_____
_____
_____
_____
_____

Prayer:

Heavenly Father,

I come before You burdened by this yoke of slavery. Lord, as I feel buried by my own doing or the oppression of other forces, I cry out for Your deliverance.

I call upon the freedom that Christ has won for me, knowing He is able to set me free. The Lord rebukes the spirit of slavery, and I renounce a slavery mindset, receiving instead the spirit of adoption as Your child.

Holy Spirit, protect me from taking up a yoke not meant for me to bear. Call to my mind the truth of the Lord Jesus Christ, who proclaimed liberty to the captives and freedom to those who are bound.

Thank You, Father, for hearing my cries. Out of my distress, I call on You, trusting that You will answer and set me free. Help me to know Your truth deeply, for Your truth will set me free.

Lord, deliver me from the fear of death and any lifelong slavery it may bring. Let me stand firm in the freedom Christ has won, never again submitting to a yoke of slavery.

In Jesus' name I pray, Amen

My own prayer:

_____
_____
_____
_____
_____
_____
_____

Sober

adjective
ʻsō-bər

1. Marked by seriousness or gravity of thought or behavior
2. Not intoxicated or under the influence of alcohol or other substances; temperate in habits and actions

- **1 Thessalonians 5:6:** So then let us not sleep, as others do, but let us keep awake and be sober.
- **2 Timothy 4:5:** As for you, always be sober-minded, endure suffering, do the work of an evangelist, fulfill your ministry.
- **1 Peter 5:8:** Be sober-minded; be watchful. Your adversary the devil prowls around like a roaring lion, seeking someone to devour.
- **1 Peter 4:7:** The end of all things is at hand; therefore be self-controlled and sober-minded for the sake of your prayers.
- **1 Timothy 3:11:** Their wives likewise must be dignified, not slanderers, but sober-minded, faithful in all things.
- **Titus 2:2, 6, 12:** Older men are to be sober-minded, dignified, self-controlled, sound in faith, in love, and in steadfastness.. . . Likewise, urge the younger men to be self-controlled.. . . Training us to renounce ungodliness and worldly passions, and to live self-controlled, upright, and godly lives in the present age.

Reflections:

_____

_____

_____

_____

_____

_____

Prayer:

Heavenly Father,

I come before You in humility, seeking Your clarity and guidance. Thank You, Lord, that Your Word brings forth truth with power and inspiration to live a sober life.

As culture presents lifestyles filled with indulgences as a means to cope and as socially accepted norms, bring me back to Your sobering words. Let me remain vigilant and sober, unlike others who sleep.

I repent from previously accepted habits contrary to sober living, recalling Your Word to always be sober-minded, endure suffering, do the work of an evangelist, and fulfill my ministry.

Holy Spirit, fill me up. Increase so that my flesh may decrease. As the path becomes narrow, should I become weak and seek indulgences, convict me to remain sober-minded and watchful, knowing my adversary the devil prowls around like a roaring lion, seeking someone to devour.

Grant me self-control and a sober mind for the sake of my prayers. Help me to be dignified, faithful in all things, and to renounce ungodliness and worldly passions. Train me to live a self-controlled, upright, and godly life in this present age.

In Jesus' name I pray, Amen.

My own prayer:

_____

_____

_____

_____

_____

_____

Spirits

noun (plural)
'spir-ət(s)

1. The non-material part of a person, often associated with emotions, will, and consciousness, or the immaterial essence of a being
2. Supernatural beings or forces, often referring to angels, demons, or other non-physical entities

- **Numbers 27:16:** "Let the Lord, the God of the spirits of all flesh, appoint a man over the congregation."
- **1 Corinthians 14:32:** And the spirits of prophets are subject to prophets.
- **Mark 3:11:** And whenever the unclean spirits saw him, they fell down before him and cried out, "You are the Son of God."
- **Leviticus 20:6:** If a person turns to mediums and necromancers, whoring after them, I will set my face against that person and will cut him off from among his people.
- **Mark 6:7:** And he called the twelve and began to send them out two by two, and gave them authority over the unclean spirits.
- **Luke 7:21:** In that hour he healed many people of diseases and plagues and evil spirits, and on many who were blind he bestowed sight.
- **Acts 5:16:** The people also gathered from the towns around Jerusalem, bringing the sick and those afflicted with unclean spirits, and they were all healed.
- **1 John 4:18:** There is no fear in love, but perfect love casts out fear. For fear has to do with punishment, and whoever fears has not been perfected in love.

Reflections:

_____

_____

_____

_____

_____

_____

Prayer:

Heavenly Father,

I come before You in agreement, acknowledging Your unmatched holiness. Thank You, Lord, that You reign above all and are the God of the spirits of all flesh.

My God, I surrender my soul and spirit to You, renouncing any and all previous practices, whether inherited or deliberate, regarding other spirit beings as a means to connect to the spirit world. Father, sharpen my understanding as I seek to know You more deeply.

Protect me from being deceived, hijacked, or used as a vessel for unclean spirits to operate. Holy Spirit build me up so that I may live a life of freedom, an example to all those who are near and far in my comings and goings.

Grant me the trust and honor to assist in prayer or otherwise, guided by the Holy Spirit directly, to those suffering from unclean spirits. Above all else, teach me to operate in LOVE, as perfect love casts out all fear.

Lord, I thank You for the authority You've given Your followers over unclean spirits. Help me to walk in that authority with wisdom and humility. Keep me far from any temptation to turn to mediums or necromancers, knowing that my connection to the spiritual realm is through You alone.

In Jesus' name, Amen.

My own prayer:

_____

_____

_____

_____

_____

Squid

noun
'skwid

1. A marine cephalopod mollusk with a soft body and elongated arms, typically known for its ability to squirt ink for defense

- **1 Corinthians 14:33**: For God is not a God of confusion but of peace. As in all the churches of the saints.
- **James 1:5:** If any of you lacks wisdom, let him ask of God, who gives generously to all without reproach, and it will be given to him.
- **Isaiah 41:10:** Fear not, for I am with you; be not dismayed, for I am your God; I will strengthen you, I will help you, I will uphold you with my righteous right hand.

Reflections:

_____
_____
_____
_____
_____
_____
_____
_____
_____
_____

Prayer:

Heavenly Father,

I come before You, seeking Your guidance and strength to overcome the spirit of confusion that entangles me like the tentacles of a squid. Lord, I know You are not a God of confusion but of peace.

Grant me the wisdom to discern Your truth amidst the murky waters of doubt and uncertainty. As You promise in Your Word, I ask for wisdom, trusting that You give generously to all who ask.

Father, help me to break free from the oppressive grip of confusion. Strengthen me with Your mighty power, that I may walk away from this squid-like spirit that seeks to cloud my mind and heart.

I take authority in Your name, declaring that fear and dismay have no hold over me. For You are my God, and You uphold me with Your righteous right hand.

Clear my thoughts, Lord. Let Your peace reign in my mind and heart. Guide me into Your perfect clarity and understanding.

In Jesus' name I pray, Amen.

My own prayer:

_____

_____

_____

_____

_____

_____

_____

_____

Stand

Verb

'stand

1. To support oneself on the feet in an erect position
2. To take up or maintain a specified position or posture

- **Ephesians 6:13:** Therefore take up the whole armor of God, that you may be able to withstand in the evil day, and having done all, to stand firm.
- **1 Corinthians 16:13**: Be watchful, stand firm in the faith, act like men, be strong.
- **Philippians 4:1:** Therefore, my brothers, whom I love and long for, my joy and crown, stand firm thus in the Lord, my beloved.
- **Galatians 5:1:** For freedom Christ has set us free; stand firm therefore, and do not submit again to a yoke of slavery.
- **2 Thessalonians 2:15:** So then, brothers, stand firm and hold to the traditions that you were taught by us, either by our spoken word or by our letter.
- **Ephesians 6:11:** Put on the whole armor of God, that you may be able to stand against the schemes of the devil.

Reflections:

_____
_____
_____
_____
_____
_____
_____
_____
_____

Prayer:

Heavenly Father,

I come before You in confidence, anchored in Your Word. In these times where good is called evil and evil is considered good, grant me the strength to withstand, putting on Your whole armor.

Lord, help my flesh remain in You—watchful, firm in faith, and strong. Holy Spirit, sharpen my discernment to recognize that true strength to stand comes not from the world, but from You alone.

I thank You for the freedom I have in Christ. Keep me from submitting again to the slavery from which You've liberated me. When false teachings and traditions arise, may I stand firm in Your unchanging truth.

Father, help me to daily dress in Your full armor, that I may take a strong stand against the devil's schemes. Let my life be a testament to Your power and grace.

In moments of weakness, remind me of the freedom for which Christ has set me free. May I stand firm in this truth, not wavering in the face of opposition or temptation.

Lord, make me watchful and alert, ready to stand for Your kingdom in all circumstances. Let my stance be one of love, justice, and righteousness, always reflecting Your character.

In Jesus' name I pray, Amen.

My own prayer:

_____

_____

_____

_____

_____

Steadfast

adjective
'sted-,fast

1. Firm in purpose, resolution, or faith; unwavering
2. Loyal, dependable, and constant, particularly in difficult circumstances

- **Proverbs 20:28:** Steadfast love and faithfulness preserve the king, and by steadfast love his throne is upheld.
- **Psalm 57:7:** My heart is steadfast, O God, my heart is steadfast! I will sing and make melody!
- **Psalm 118:2:** Let Israel say, "His steadfast love endures forever."
- **Psalm 112:7:** He is not afraid of bad news; his heart is firm, trusting in the Lord.
- **Isaiah 26:3:** You keep him in perfect peace whose mind is stayed on you, because he trusts in you.
- **1 Corinthians 15:58:** Therefore, my beloved brothers, be steadfast, immovable, always abounding in the work of the Lord, knowing that in the Lord your labor is not in vain.
- **James 1:12:** Blessed is the man who remains steadfast under trial, for when he has stood the test he will receive the crown of life, which God has promised to those who love him.

Reflections:

_____
_____
_____
_____
_____
_____
_____
_____
_____

Prayer:

Heavenly Father,

I come before You in thanksgiving, declaring that my heart is steadfast, O God! My heart is steadfast! I will sing and make melody to You in praise, for Your steadfast love endures forever!

Lord, Your Word declares that steadfast love and faithfulness preserve the king, and by steadfast love his throne is upheld. Let this be a reminder for me when my faith is tested, when a storm is passing over with no end in sight.

Prepare me, Father, that I may live unafraid of bad news, holding steady to a firm heart, trusting in You above all. Holy Spirit, aid me in keeping my mind set on Jesus! Build up my courage to remain steadfast during the trials of man, withstanding the test.

Grant me perfect peace as I keep my mind stayed on You. Help me to be steadfast and immovable, always abounding in the work of the Lord, knowing that in You, my labor is not in vain.

Lord, bless me as I strive to remain steadfast under trial. May I stand the test and receive the crown of life, which You have promised to those who love You.

In Jesus' name I pray, Amen.

My own prayer:

_____

_____

_____

_____

_____

_____

Stress

noun
'stres

1. A state of mental or emotional strain resulting from demanding circumstances
2. Physical pressure or tension, often caused by external or internal factors

- **Psalm 119:143:** Trouble and anguish have found me out, but your commandments are my delight.
- **1 Peter 5:7:** Casting all your anxieties on him, because he cares for you.
- **John 14:27:** "Peace I leave with you; my peace I give to you. Not as the world gives do I give to you. Let not your hearts be troubled, neither let them be afraid."
- **Psalm 55:22:** Cast your burden on the Lord, and he will sustain you; he will never permit the righteous to be moved.
- **Proverbs 12:25:** Anxiety in a man's heart weighs him down, but a good word makes him glad.
- **Psalm 118:5–6:** Out of my distress I called on the Lord; the Lord answered me and set me free. The Lord is on my side; I will not fear. What can man do to me?

Reflections:

_____
_____
_____
_____
_____
_____
_____
_____
_____
_____

Prayer:

Heavenly Father,

I come before You in humility, overwhelmed by stress. Restore my faith, O God, for trouble and anguish have found me out. Yet, I choose to delight in Your commandments.

I cast my cares upon You, Lord—all the burdens that have crushed my soul and spirit. Despite what I see in the natural, restore my hope in the truth of Your words: "Peace I leave with you; my peace I give to you. Not as the world gives do I give to you."

Out of this distress, I call upon You, Lord. I have faith You will answer me, setting me free. Remain by my side, that I may have no fear. What can man do to me when You are with me?

Holy Spirit, help me to let go and let God! Lift this anxiety that weighs down my heart. Speak Your good word to make me glad. Sustain me, Lord, and don't let me be moved by these circumstances.

I choose to receive Your peace, Jesus. Let not my heart be troubled or afraid. Thank You for caring for me and for being on my side.

In Jesus' name I pray, Amen.

My own prayer:

_____
_____
_____
_____
_____
_____
_____

Stronghold

noun
'strȯŋ-ˌhōld

1. A fortified place, typically used metaphorically for areas of mental or spiritual resistance
2. Strong areas of influence or control, often associated with negative patterns or sinful behavior

- **Ephesians 6:12:** For we do not wrestle against flesh and blood, but against the rulers, against the authorities, against the cosmic powers over this present darkness, against the spiritual forces of evil in the heavenly places.
- **Psalm 27:1:** The Lord is my light and my salvation; whom shall I fear? The Lord is the stronghold of my life; of whom shall I be afraid?
- **2 Corinthians 10:3–5:** For though we walk in the flesh, we are not waging war according to the flesh. For the weapons of our warfare are not of the flesh but have divine power to destroy strongholds. We destroy arguments and every lofty opinion raised against the knowledge of God, and take every thought captive to obey Christ.
- **1 Corinthians 10:13:** No temptation has overtaken you that is not common to man. God is faithful, and he will not let you be tempted beyond your ability, but with the temptation, he will also provide the way of escape, that you may be able to endure it.

Reflections:

_____
_____
_____
_____
_____
_____
_____

Prayer:

Heavenly Father,

I come before You in humility and surrender. Far be it from me to harbor strongholds that hinder the life You've designed for me. Search me, Lord, for any unclean crevices or unforgiving notions that have allowed tenancy for strongholds within my soul and spirit.

Holy Spirit, build up my discernment to know that I do not wrestle against flesh and blood, but against the rulers, authorities, and cosmic powers of this present darkness. Strengthen my faith to declare: The Lord is my light and my salvation; whom shall I fear? The Lord is the stronghold of my life; of whom shall I be afraid?

Grant me the discipline to remain consistent. Though I walk in the flesh, I am not waging war according to the flesh. I wield the weapons of my warfare, which have divine power to destroy strongholds. I commit to destroying arguments and every lofty opinion raised against the knowledge of God, taking every thought captive to obey Christ.

May I live by Your words, giving thanks and praise. I trust that no temptation has overtaken me that is not common to man. You are faithful, God, and will not let me be tempted beyond my ability. With each temptation, You provide a way of escape, that I may endure it.

In Jesus' name and by the authority of His blood, I pray, Amen.

My own prayer:

_____

_____

_____

_____

_____

Suffering

noun
ˈsə-f(ə-)riŋ

1. The experience of pain, distress, or hardship, either physical or emotional
2. Enduring hardship, often seen as a test or trial of faith

- **2 Timothy 2:3:** Share in suffering as a good soldier of Christ Jesus.
- **1 Corinthians 12:26:** If one member suffers, all suffer together; if one member is honored, all rejoice together.
- **Romans 5:3:** Not only that, but we rejoice in our sufferings, knowing that suffering produces endurance.
- **1 Peter 4:1:** Since therefore Christ suffered in the flesh, arm yourselves with the same way of thinking, for whoever has suffered in the flesh has ceased from sin.
- **1 Peter 5:10:** And after you have suffered a little while, the God of all grace, who has called you to his eternal glory in Christ, will himself restore, confirm, strengthen, and establish you.

Reflections:

_____
_____
_____
_____
_____
_____
_____
_____
_____
_____

Prayer:

Heavenly Father,

I come before You in thanksgiving, even amidst life's various sufferings. I declare my gratitude for the salvation found in Jesus Christ, my Redeemer and hope of glory.

Lord, help me to rejoice in my suffering, knowing it produces endurance. As Christ suffered in the flesh, I arm myself with the same mindset, understanding that suffering in the flesh leads me away from sin.

Holy Spirit, fuel me with hope, reminding me that after I have suffered for a little while, You, the God of all grace, will restore, confirm, strengthen, and establish me in Your eternal glory in Christ.

Grant me the discipline to walk alongside my brothers and sisters in Christ who are also suffering. Let me remember that if one member suffers, we all suffer together, and if one is honored, we all rejoice together.

May I share in suffering as a good soldier of Christ Jesus, always keeping my eyes fixed on You.

In Jesus' name I pray, Amen.

My own prayer:

_____
_____
_____
_____
_____
_____
_____

Suicide

noun
ˈsü-ə-ˌsīd

1. The act of intentionally taking one's own life
2. A tragic and extreme action, often driven by deep emotional or mental distress

- **1 Kings 19:4:** But he himself went a day's journey into the wilderness and came and sat down under a broom tree. And he asked that he might die, saying, "It is enough; now, O Lord, take away my life, for I am no better than my fathers."
- **Ecclesiastes 7:17:** Be not overly wicked, neither be a fool. Why should you die before your time?
- **Proverbs 3:5–6:** Trust in the Lord with all your heart, and do not lean on your own understanding. In all your ways acknowledge him, and he will make straight your paths.
- **Psalm 13:2–4:** How long must I take counsel in my soul and have sorrow in my heart all the day? How long shall my enemy be exalted over me? Consider and answer me, O Lord my God; light up my eyes, lest I sleep the sleep of death, lest my enemy say, "I have prevailed over him," lest my foes rejoice because I am shaken.

Reflections:

_____
_____
_____
_____
_____
_____
_____
_____
_____
_____

Prayer:

Heavenly Father,

I come before You feeling hopeless and desperate. This journey feels like an endless wilderness, filled with failures, mistakes, and rejection. I feel alone and overwhelmed.

Lord, I confess that I'm wrestling with thoughts of ending my life. It is enough; now, O Lord. But I know this is not Your plan for me. Deliver me from these destructive ideas, and help me choose life over death.

Holy Spirit, with what little strength I have left, I cry out to You. Breathe new life into me. Help me trust in the Lord with all my heart, not leaning on my own limited understanding. Show me that there's more to life than I can see in this difficult season.

Restore my faith, Lord. How long must I carry this sorrow in my heart? Consider and answer me, O Lord my God. Light up my eyes, lest I fall into the sleep of death. Don't let my inner enemies prevail over me.

Guide me on straight paths, Lord. Help me to acknowledge You in all my ways. Remind me that this pain is temporary, but Your love is eternal.

In Jesus' name I pray, Amen.

My own prayer:

_____
_____
_____
_____
_____
_____
_____

Surrender

verb
sə-ˈren-dər

1. To yield or give up control, often in submission to a higher authority or will
2. To submit oneself fully, particularly in the context of faith and obedience

- **1 Peter 5:6:** Humble yourselves, therefore, under the mighty hand of God so that at the proper time he may exalt you.
- **Luke 9:23:** And he said to all, "If anyone would come after me, let him deny himself and take up his cross daily and follow me."
- **James 4:7:** Submit yourselves therefore to God. Resist the devil, and he will flee from you.
- **James 4:10:** Humble yourselves before the Lord, and he will exalt you.
- **Romans 12:1:** I appeal to you therefore, brothers, by the mercies of God, to present your bodies as a living sacrifice, holy and acceptable to God, which is your spiritual worship.

Reflections:

_____
_____
_____
_____
_____
_____
_____
_____
_____
_____
_____

Prayer:

Heavenly Father,

I come before You in humility, recognizing my struggle with selfish desires. Forgive me for prioritizing my will over Yours, for choosing haste and arrogance over stillness and humility. Deliver me, Lord, from this self-centered mindset.

I surrender to Your ways, humbling myself under Your mighty hand. I trust that at the right time, You will exalt me. As I submit myself to You, God, I know the devil must flee from my mind, body, and spirit.

Jesus, I choose to follow You. Help me deny myself daily and pick up my cross. I present my body as a living sacrifice, holy and acceptable to You, as my spiritual act of worship.

Teach me to resist my own desires and to chase after You instead. May Your will become my priority, and may I always seek Your kingdom first.

In Jesus' name I pray, Amen.

My own prayer:

_____

_____

_____

_____

_____

_____

_____

_____

Temptation

noun
tem(p)-tā-shən

1. The act of tempting or the state of being tempted (enticed), especially to evil
2. Something tempting: a cause or occasion or excitement

- **1 Corinthians 10:13**: No temptation has overtaken you that is not common to man. God is faithful, and he will not let you be tempted beyond your ability, but with the temptation he will also provide the way of escape, that you may be able to endure it.
- **Matthew 6:13 (NASB)**: "And do not lead us into temptation, but deliver us from evil. For yours is the kingdom and the power and the glory, forever. Amen."
- **James 4:7:** Submit yourselves therefore to God. Resist the devil, and he will flee from you.
- **Matthew 26:41:** "Watch and pray that you may not enter into temptation. The spirit indeed is willing, but the flesh is weak."
- **Ephesians 6:11:** Put on the whole armor of God, that you may be able to stand against the schemes of the devil.

Reflections:

_____
_____
_____
_____
_____
_____
_____
_____

Prayer:

Heavenly Father,

I come before You in humility, acknowledging my weakness in the face of temptation. Lord, Your Word assures me that no temptation has overtaken me that is not common to all. I thank You for Your faithfulness, knowing that You will not let me be tempted beyond my ability to resist.

Forgive me, Father, for the times I've lacked trust in Your words and succumbed to temptation. I submit myself to You now, God, resisting the devil and claiming Your promise that he will flee.

Holy Spirit, help me to remain watchful and prayerful, for though my spirit is willing, my flesh is weak. Dress me in Your full armor, O God, that I may stand firm against the schemes of the enemy.

Lead me not into temptation, Father, but deliver me from evil. When temptation comes, grant me the wisdom to recognize and take the way of escape You provide.

For Yours is the kingdom, the power, and the glory forever.

In Jesus' name I pray, Amen.

My own prayer:

_____
_____
_____
_____
_____
_____
_____

Thankful

adjective
'thaŋk-fəl

1. Conscious of benefit received
2. Expressive of thanks

- **1 Thessalonians 5:18**: Give thanks in all circumstances; for this is the will of God in Christ Jesus for you.
- **Ephesians 5:20:** Giving thanks always and for everything to God the Father in the name of our Lord Jesus Christ.
- **Psalm 100:4:** Enter his gates with thanksgiving, and his courts with praise! Give thanks to him; bless his name!
- **Philippians 4:6:** Do not be anxious about anything, but in everything by prayer and supplication with thanksgiving let your requests be made known to God.
- **Colossians 3:15:** And let the peace of Christ rule in your hearts, to which indeed you were called in one body. And be thankful.

Reflections:

_____

_____

_____

_____

_____

_____

_____

_____

Prayer:

Heavenly Father,

I come before You with a heart overflowing with praise and gratitude. Your undeserved grace and mercy for Your children, including me, fills me with joy and wonder. Lord, I thank You for the reminder to be grateful in all circumstances, for this is Your will for me in Christ Jesus. Help me to embrace a spirit of thankfulness, even in challenging times, knowing that You work all things for good. Father, I choose to enter Your gates with thanksgiving and Your courts with praise. I give thanks to You and bless Your holy name, for You are good and Your love endures forever.

Holy Spirit, guide me to bring all things to You in prayer and supplication with thanksgiving. When anxiety creeps in, remind me to turn my worries into prayers, trusting in Your perfect peace.

Lord Jesus, let Your peace rule in my heart. I am thankful for the calling to be part of Your body, united with fellow believers in gratitude and love. Thank You for every blessing, seen and unseen. For life, breath, salvation, and the countless ways You show Your love daily. May my life be a continuous expression of thanksgiving to You.

In Jesus' name I pray, Amen.

    My own prayer:

_____

_____

_____

_____

_____

_____

_____

Transform

verb
tran(t)s-'fȯrm

1. To change in composition or structure
2. To change in character or condition

- **Romans 12:1–2:** I appeal to you therefore, brothers, by the mercies of God, to present your bodies as a living sacrifice, holy and acceptable to God, which is your spiritual worship. Do not be conformed to this world, but be transformed by the renewal of your mind, that by testing you may discern what is the will of God, what is good and acceptable and perfect.
- **Ephesians 4:22:** To put off your old self, which belongs to your former manner of life and is corrupt through deceitful desires.
- **Matthew 4:19:** And he said to them, "Follow me, and I will make you fishers of men."
- **Ephesians 5:8:** For at one time you were darkness, but now you are light in the Lord. Walk as children of light.
- **James 1:2:** Count it all joy, my brothers, when you meet trials of various kinds.
- **Mark 2:22:** "And no one puts new wine into old wineskins. If he does, the wine will burst the skins—and the wine is destroyed, and so are the skins. But new wine is for fresh wineskins."

Reflections:

_____
_____
_____
_____
_____
_____
_____

Prayer:

Heavenly Father,

I come before You in reverence of Your holiness and almighty power. I am in awe of Your transformative love and grace. Lord, I seek to be transformed by You. I present my body as a living sacrifice, holy and acceptable to You, which is my spiritual worship. Renew my mind, Father, that I may not be conformed to this world, but instead discern Your good, acceptable, and perfect will. I choose to put off my old self, leaving behind the corrupt ways of my former life. Help me, Lord, to separate myself from the old wineskin and embrace the new life You offer. Jesus, I answer Your call to follow You. Make me a fisher of men, using my transformed life to draw others to Your light.

Holy Spirit, bring me fully into the light, leaving the darkness behind once and for all. I proclaim that I will walk as a child of light, reflecting Your glory in all I do.

Father, refine my thoughts to align with Your truth. Give me desires that follow You and not deceitful theologies. When trials come, help me to count it all joy, knowing that You are working to perfect my faith. I am filled with hope and expectation for the changes You will bring about in my life. Thank You for Your promise to complete the good work You've begun in me.

In Jesus' name I pray, Amen.

My own prayer:

_____
_____
_____
_____
_____
_____

Trauma

noun
ˈtrȯ-mə

1. A disordered psychic or behavioral state resulting from severe mental or emotional stress or physical injury

- **Psalm 116:9:** I will walk before the Lord in the land of the living.
- **Psalm 34:18:** The Lord is near to the brokenhearted and saves the crushed in spirit.
- **Psalm 56:8:** You have kept count of my tossings; put my tears in your bottle. Are they not in your book?
- **Isaiah 41:10:** Fear not, for I am with you; be not dismayed, for I am your God; I will strengthen you, I will help you, I will uphold you with my righteous right hand.
- **Matthew 11:28–29:** "Come to me, all who labor and are heavy laden, and I will give you rest. Take my yoke upon you, and learn from me, for I am gentle and lowly in heart, and you will find rest for your souls."
- **2 Corinthians 4:16:** So we do not lose heart. Though our outer self is wasting away, our inner self is being renewed day by day.

Reflections:

_____

_____

_____

_____

_____

_____

_____

_____

Prayer:

Heavenly Father,

I come before You with a tender heart, broken, yet seeking Your loving embrace. You are my refuge, the one true God whom I call Father. Lord, I choose to walk before You in the land of the living, even when my steps feel uncertain. I find comfort in knowing that You are near to my broken heart and that You save those crushed in spirit. Father, I acknowledge that only You can truly cradle my soul through this trauma. I repent for the times I've allowed my pain to become my identity instead of seeking Your truth and healing. Thank You for keeping count of my restless nights and collecting every tear in Your bottle. Your attentiveness to my suffering brings me hope.

With trembling hands, I lay the yoke of this trauma at Your feet. Please, Lord, free my soul from the burdens that have accompanied this pain. Release my spirit from the chains of fear and hurt.

I take courage in Your promise that You are with me. When I am weak, You are my strength. When I am dismayed, You uphold me with Your righteous right hand. I come to You, weary and heavy laden, trusting in Your gentle heart to give me rest. Though I may feel broken on the outside, I hold on to the truth that You are renewing my inner self day by day.

Guide me, Father, onto the path of righteousness and redemption. Help me to not lose heart, but to find my hope and identity in You alone.

In Jesus' name I pray, Amen.

    My own prayer:

_____

_____

_____

_____

_____

Treachery

noun
'tre-chə-rē

1. Violation of allegiance or of faith and confidence

- **Isaiah 33:1:** Ah, you destroyer, you yourself have not been destroyed; you traitor whom none has betrayed! When you have ceased to destroy, you will be destroyed; and when you have finished betraying, they will betray you.
- **Jeremiah 3:20:** Surely, as a treacherous wife leaves her husband, so you have been treacherous to me, O house of Israel, declares the LORD.
- **Psalm 119:52:** When I think of your rules from of old, I take comfort, O LORD.
- **2 Corinthians 1:3:** Blessed be the God and Father of our Lord Jesus Christ, the Father of mercies and God of all comfort.
- **Jeremiah 7:5–7:** For if you truly amend your ways and your deeds, if you truly execute justice one with another, if you do not oppress the sojourner, the fatherless, or the widow, or shed innocent blood in this place, and if you do not go after other gods to your own harm, then I will let you dwell in this place, in the land that I gave of old to your fathers forever.

Reflections:

_____
_____
_____
_____
_____
_____
_____
_____
_____

Prayer:

Heavenly Father,

I come before You, seeking counsel, refreshment, and renewal for my soul. In a world where treachery often lurks, I ask for Your guidance and protection. Lord, help me remain trusting in You, even when others may betray me. Grant me the strength to stay vigilant in building Your kingdom, keeping my integrity intact amidst challenges. Soften my heart to maintain a spirit of forgiveness, remembering Your endless mercy toward me. Father, I pray for the gift of discernment to recognize treachery against me, my family, my community, and my nation.

Let me not be naive, but wise as a serpent and innocent as a dove, as Your Word instructs. When I face betrayal, remind me of Your comfort, O Lord. You are the Father of mercies, and in Your ancient rules, I find solace. Help me to truly amend my ways and execute justice, not oppressing others or shedding innocent blood. Guard my heart from going after other gods or seeking comfort in worldly things. Instead, let me dwell securely in the place You have prepared for me, trusting in Your faithfulness even when others prove faithless.

In Jesus' name I pray, Amen.

My own prayer:

_____
_____
_____
_____
_____
_____
_____

Trial

noun
ˈtrī(-ə)l

1. A test of faith, patience, or stamina through subjection to suffering or temptation

- **James 1:12:** Blessed is the man who remains steadfast under trial, for when he has stood the test he will receive the crown of life, which God has promised to those who love him.
- **James 1:2–4:** Count it all joy, my brothers, when you meet trials of various kinds, for you know that the testing of your faith produces steadfastness. And let steadfastness have its full effect, that you may be perfect and complete, lacking in nothing.
- **1 Peter 1:6**: In this you rejoice, though now for a little while, if necessary, you have been grieved by various trials.
- **1 Peter 4:12–13**: Beloved, do not be surprised at the fiery trial when it comes upon you to test you, as though something strange were happening to you. But rejoice insofar as you share Christ's sufferings, that you may also rejoice and be glad when his glory is revealed.
- **John 16:33:** "I have said these things to you, that in me you may have peace. In the world you will have tribulation. But take heart; I have overcome the world."

Reflections:

_____
_____
_____
_____
_____
_____
_____
_____
_____

Prayer:

Heavenly Father,

I come before You in humility, acknowledging Your sovereignty over all things. You are the Lord of my life, and I submit to Your will. Lord, Your Word promises that those who remain steadfast under trials will be blessed. I ask for Your strength and guidance to endure the tests that come my way. Teach me, Father, how to stand firm in my faith when faced with challenges. I repent and renounce any reliance on my own will, pride, or stubbornness as means to deal with life's trials. Instead, I seek Your wisdom and grace to navigate these difficult times.

Holy Spirit, help me to count it all joy when various trials come my way. Grant me the understanding that these tests of faith produce steadfastness and maturity in my walk with You.

Father, when fiery trials surprise me, remind me that I share in Christ's sufferings. Help me to rejoice, knowing that Your glory will be revealed through these experiences. Grant me Your peace, Lord, which surpasses all understanding. In a world full of tribulation, I take heart in the truth that You have overcome the world. Let this assurance be my anchor in stormy times. In all things, help me to trust in Your perfect plan and timing. May these trials refine me and draw me closer to You.

In Jesus' name I pray, Amen.

My own prayer:

_____
_____
_____
_____
_____
_____
_____

Unbelief

noun
ˌən-bə-ˈlēf

1. Incredulity or skepticism especially in matters of religious faith

- **Mark 9:24:** Immediately the father of the child cried out and said, "I believe; help my unbelief!"
- **Matthew 17:20:** He said to them, "Because of your little faith. For truly, I say to you, if you have faith like a grain of mustard seed, you will say to this mountain, 'Move from here to there,' and it will move, and nothing will be impossible for you."
- **Hebrews 3:12:** Take care, brothers, lest there be in any of you an evil, unbelieving heart, leading you to fall away from the living God.
- **Hebrews 3:19:** So we see that they were unable to enter because of unbelief.
- **Romans 4:20:** No unbelief made him waver concerning the promise of God, but he grew strong in his faith as he gave glory to God.

Reflections:

_____
_____
_____
_____
_____
_____
_____
_____
_____
_____

Prayer:

Heavenly Father,

I come before You in humility, acknowledging the power and authority of Your name. Lord, I confess my unbelief and repent of it. Like the father of the demonized child who cried out, "I believe; help my unbelief!", I too ask for Your help with my wavering faith. Grant me, O God, even if it's just a mustard seed of faith, that I may move mountains in Your name.

Holy Spirit, I invite You to search my heart. Remove any evil or unbelieving thoughts that may be leading me away from the living God. I desire to enter into the promises and places You have for me, to build Your kingdom and help deliver others.

Father, I ask that You strengthen my faith as You did for Abraham, who did not waver in unbelief regarding Your promises. Help me to grow strong in faith, giving glory to You in all circumstances. Remind me, Lord, to anchor myself on Your promises. Let me not be shaken by doubt or fear. Instead, may my faith grow and flourish, enabling me to enter the spaces and places where You are calling me to serve.

In Jesus' name I pray, Amen.

My own prayer:

_____
_____
_____
_____
_____
_____
_____

Unclean

adjective
ˌən-ˈklēn

1. Dirty, filthy
2. Morally or spiritually impure

- **Ezekiel 36:29:** And I will deliver you from all your uncleannesses. And I will summon the grain and make it abundant and lay no famine upon you.
- **Acts 8:7:** For unclean spirits, crying out with a loud voice, came out of many who had them, and many who were paralyzed or lame were healed.
- **Matthew 10:1:** And he called to him his twelve disciples and gave them authority over unclean spirits, to cast them out, and to heal every disease and every affliction.

Reflections:

_____
_____
_____
_____
_____
_____
_____
_____
_____
_____
_____
_____

Prayer:

Heavenly Father,

I come before You with a heavy heart, burdened by my own uncleanness. I am ashamed of the impurities that cling to my soul, yet I seek Your encouragement and cleansing power. Lord, as You promised in Ezekiel, deliver me from all my uncleanness. I long for the abundance of Your grace to wash over me, removing the spiritual famine in my life. I acknowledge my need for a Savior, for I cannot cleanse myself. Just as You gave authority to Your disciples to cast out unclean spirits and heal afflictions, I ask that You exercise that same power in my life. Remove any unclean spirits that may be hindering my walk with You. Heal the diseases of my soul that keep me from fully embracing the purpose, path, and destiny You have prepared for me.

Holy Spirit, I invite You to fill the spaces in my heart and mind where uncleanness once resided. Replace my shame with Your peace, my impurity with Your holiness. Renew me from within, refreshing my spirit and restoring my soul.

Father, I trust in Your promise to cleanse and restore. Help me to walk in the newness of life that You offer, leaving behind the old and embracing the new creation You are making me to be.

In Jesus' name I pray, Amen.

My own prayer:

_____

_____

_____

_____

_____

_____

Understanding

noun
ˌən-dər-stan-diŋ

1. A mental grasp
2. The power to make experience intelligible by applying concepts and categories

- **Proverbs 18:2:** A fool takes no pleasure in understanding, but only in expressing his opinion.
- **Proverbs 14:29:** Whoever is slow to anger has great understanding, but he who has a hasty temper exalts folly.
- **Proverbs 3:5:** Trust in the Lord with all your heart, and do not lean on your own understanding.
- **2 Timothy 2:7**: Think over what I say, for the Lord will give you understanding in everything.
- **Isaiah 40:8:** The grass withers, the flower fades, but the word of our God will stand forever.

Reflections:

_____
_____
_____
_____
_____
_____
_____
_____
_____
_____

Prayer:

Heavenly Father,

I come before You seeking Your grace and wisdom. Lord, as I journey through life, I often find myself relying on my past experiences or the outcomes of others, rather than on Your promises and truth.

Father, help me resist the world's obsession with knowing all things. Instead, let me put my complete trust in You. Clothe me in humility, making me comfortable with not knowing all outcomes or confirmations of my days. Before I seek human understanding, remind me to think over what You say, for Your understanding is divine wisdom for my soul. Your truth alone stands the test of time.

Guard me, Lord, from foolishness that seeks to know the days and hours of all things to come. Let me find pleasure in understanding Your ways rather than merely expressing my own opinions. Grant me patience, that I may be slow to anger and grow in great understanding. Keep me from hasty tempers that exalt folly.

May my spirit rest in Your arms all the days of my life, trusting in You with all my heart and not leaning on my own understanding.

In Jesus' name I pray, Amen.

My own prayer:

_____
_____
_____
_____
_____
_____
_____

Unforgiveness

noun
ˌən-fər-ˈgiv-nəs

1. Unwilling or unable to forgive

- **Mark 11:25:** "And whenever you stand praying, forgive, if you have anything against anyone, so that your Father also who is in heaven may forgive you your trespasses."
- **Matthew 18:21–22:** Then Peter came up and said to him, "Lord, how often will my brother sin against me, and I forgive him? As many as seven times?" Jesus said to him, "I do not say to you seven times, but seventy-seven times."
- **1 John 1:9**: If we confess our sins, he is faithful and just to forgive us our sins and to cleanse us from all unrighteousness.
- **Matthew 6:12:** "And forgive us our debts, as we also have forgiven our debtors."
- **Hebrews 12:14:** Strive for peace with everyone, and for the holiness without which no one will see the Lord.
- **Acts 3:19:** Repent therefore, and turn back, that your sins may be blotted out.
- **Luke 17:3–4:** "Pay attention to yourselves! If your brother sins, rebuke him, and if he repents, forgive him. And if he sins against you seven times in the day, and turns to you seven times, saying, 'I repent,' you must forgive him."

Reflections:

_____
_____
_____
_____
_____
_____
_____
_____

Prayer:

Heavenly Father,

I come before You, seeking Your undeserved grace and mercy. I humbly acknowledge my need for Your forgiveness and help. Lord, I confess the hardness in my heart relating to forgiveness. Your Word teaches that to be forgiven, I must forgive. I repent of the unforgiveness I've harbored, recognizing it as sin. Please free my soul from the vengeance that keeps me from a pure heart of forgiveness.

Holy Spirit, grant me true humility and conviction to forgive those whom the world says I am justified to hate. Teach me the currency of heaven, Lord, that I may value forgiveness above my own sense of justice.

Father, I ask for the strength to seek peace above all else. Help me turn away from a heart of vengeance and embrace Your way of love and mercy. Grant me the ability to forgive not just seven times, but seventy-seven times, as Jesus taught.

I confess my sins to You, trusting in Your faithfulness to forgive and cleanse me from all unrighteousness. As I pray, if I'm holding anything against anyone, help me to forgive them, so that You may also forgive my trespasses.

Lord, enable me to walk and talk in a way that displays Your grace and truth, showing true forgiveness even to those I once deemed unforgivable. May I strive for peace with everyone, pursuing the holiness without which no one will see You.

In Jesus' name I pray, Amen.

My own prayer:

_____

_____

_____

Unity

noun
ˈyü-nə-tē

1. The quality of not being multiple
2. Condition of harmony

- **Psalm 138:1:** I give you thanks, O Lord, with my whole heart; before the gods I sing your praise.
- **Ephesians 4:3:** Eager to maintain the unity of the Spirit in the bond of peace.
- **1 Peter 3:8**: Finally, all of you, have unity of mind, sympathy, brotherly love, a tender heart, and a humble mind.
- **Ephesians 4:13:** Until we all attain to the unity of the faith and of the knowledge of the Son of God, to mature manhood, to the measure of the stature of the fullness of Christ.
- **1 Corinthians 1:10**: I appeal to you, brothers, by the name of our Lord Jesus Christ, that all of you agree, and that there be no divisions among you, but that you be united in the same mind and the same judgment.

Reflections:

_____
_____
_____
_____
_____
_____
_____
_____
_____

Prayer:

Heavenly Father,

I come before You in humility, seeking Your wisdom. With my whole heart, I give You thanks and sing Your praise, for You are worthy of all honor. Lord, I am eager to maintain the unity of the Spirit in the bond of peace. Grant me the strength and discernment to foster harmony among my brothers and sisters in Christ. Help me to have unity of mind, sympathy, brotherly love, a tender heart, and a humble spirit in all my interactions.

I pray for Your favor as I strive to attain the unity of faith and grow in the knowledge of Your Son, Jesus Christ. Guide me toward spiritual maturity, molding me into the fullness of Christ's character.

Father, I appeal to You in the name of our Lord Jesus Christ; help me to be an instrument of agreement and reconciliation, working to heal divisions and promote unity within the body of believers. Grant me the wisdom to be united with others in mind and judgment, always seeking Your will above my own.

May Your Spirit of unity prevail in my life and in the church, for Your glory and the advancement of Your kingdom.

In Jesus' name I pray, Amen.

My own prayer:

_____
_____
_____
_____
_____
_____

Unworthy

adjective
,ən-'wər-thē

1. Lacking in excellence or value
2. Not meritorious

- **1 Corinthians 15:9**: For I am the least of the apostles, unworthy to be called an apostle, because I persecuted the church of God.
- **Romans 3:23:** For all have sinned and fall short of the glory of God.
- **Ephesians 2:8–10:** For by grace you have been saved through faith, and this is not your own doing; it is the gift of God, not a result of works, so that no one may boast. For we are his workmanship, created in Christ Jesus for good works, which God prepared beforehand, that we should walk in them.
- **Ephesians 1:5:** He predestined us for adoption to himself as sons through Jesus Christ, according to the purpose of his will.
- **Ephesians 1:11:** In him we have obtained an inheritance, having been predestined according to the purpose of him who works all things according to the counsel of his will.
- **Genesis 1:26:** Then God said, "Let us make man in our image, after our likeness."

Reflections:

_____

_____

_____

_____

_____

_____

_____

_____

Prayer:

Heavenly Father,

I come before You with a heart full of desperation and despair, acknowledging my unworthiness. Like Paul, I am the least of Your servants, unworthy to be called Your child, for I have sinned and fallen short of Your glory. Yet, in my brokenness, I remember Your promise of grace. Lord, I cling to the truth that by Your grace I have been saved through faith, not by my own doing, but as Your gift. I am Your workmanship, created in Christ Jesus for good works, which You prepared beforehand.

Despite my unworthiness, You predestined me for adoption as Your child through Jesus Christ. In Him, I have obtained an inheritance according to Your purpose. Father, remind me that You created me in Your image, and that Your love for me is not based on my merit but on Your boundless mercy. Wash away my unworthiness, Lord. Draw me nearer to You and increase my faith. In my desperation, I seek Your mercy and transforming power. Help me to walk in the good works You have prepared for me, not to earn Your love, but to express my gratitude for Your undeserved grace.

In Jesus' name I pray, Amen.

My own prayer:

_____
_____
_____
_____
_____
_____
_____
_____

Vanity

noun
'va-nə-tē

1. Inflated pride in oneself or one's appearance

Proverbs 31:30: Charm is deceitful, and beauty is vain, but a woman who fears the Lord is to be praised.
Ecclesiastes 1:2: Vanity of vanities, says the Preacher, vanity of vanities! All is vanity.
Psalm 119:37: Turn my eyes from looking at worthless things; and give me life in your ways.
Ecclesiastes 5:10: He who loves money will not be satisfied with money, nor he who loves wealth with his income; this also is vanity.
Philippians 2:3: Do nothing from selfish ambition or conceit, but in humility count others more significant than yourselves.
1 Timothy 4:8: For while bodily training is of some value, godliness is of value in every way, as it holds promise for the present life and also for the life to come.

Reflections

___

Prayer:

Heavenly Father,

I come before You in humility, seeking Your mercy. I acknowledge, Lord, that Your Word says, "Charm is deceitful, and beauty is vain, but a woman who fears the Lord is to be praised." I ask that You instill in me a deep reverence for You, rather than fear of man or the trials of this world. Lord, I confess that I have often been caught up in vanity and the pursuit of outward beauty. Help me to keep my eyes focused on You, not on the worthless things of this world. Grant me the wisdom to see beyond physical appearances and to value what truly matters in Your sight.

I repent, Father, for making an idol of appearance and vanity. Forgive me for the times I've placed more importance on how I look than on cultivating a godly character. Please guide me, Lord, to pursue godliness in all my affairs and conduct. Help me to reflect Your love and grace in my actions and attitudes, rather than seeking the approval of others through my appearance.

In Jesus' name I pray, Amen.

My own prayer:

_____
_____
_____
_____
_____
_____
_____
_____
_____

Vengeance

noun

ˈven-jən(t)s

1. Punishment inflicted in retaliation for an injury or offense

- **Deuteronomy 32:35:** Vengeance is mine, and recompense, for the time when their foot shall slip; for the day of their calamity is at hand, and their doom comes swiftly.
- **Leviticus 19:18:** You shall not take vengeance or bear a grudge against the sons of your own people, but you shall love your neighbor as yourself: I am the Lord.
- **Hebrews 10:30:** For we know him who said, "Vengeance is mine; I will repay." And again, "The Lord will judge his people."
- **Romans 12:9:** Let love be genuine. Abhor what is evil; hold fast to what is good.
- **Romans 5:11:** More than that, we also rejoice in God through our Lord Jesus Christ, through whom we have now received reconciliation.
- **Ephesians 4:31–32:** Let all bitterness and wrath and anger and clamor and slander be put away from you, along with all malice. Be kind to one another, tenderhearted, forgiving one another, as God in Christ forgave you.
- **Matthew 5:9:** Blessed are the peacemakers, for they shall be called sons of God.

Reflections:

_____

_____

_____

_____

_____

_____

_____

Prayer:

Heavenly Father,

I come before You in humility, acknowledging Your supreme authority. In a world quick to seek revenge, remind me, O Lord, of Your words: Vengeance belongs to You alone. Forgive me for the times I've sought to hunt down my enemies with vengeance. I repent from such toxic behaviors, mindsets, and carnal desires. Cleanse my heart of bitterness, wrath, and anger.

Father, let my love be genuine. Help me to abhor what is evil and hold fast to what is good, according to Your Word. Grant me the strength to love my enemies, trusting in Your ways above my emotions.

Holy Spirit, empower me to put aside all malice and embrace kindness, tenderheartedness, and forgiveness. May I reflect Your love, even to those who wrong me, remembering that You will judge justly in Your time.

Lord, when I'm wronged, help me to release my hurt into Your hands, knowing that You will repay and bring justice. Transform my heart to seek reconciliation rather than retaliation.

In Jesus' name I pray, Amen.

My own prayer:

_____
_____
_____
_____
_____
_____
_____

Victim

noun
ˈvik-təm

1. One that is acted on and usually adversely affected by a force or agent

- **Psalm 9:9:** The Lord is a stronghold for the oppressed, a stronghold in times of trouble.
- **Psalm 103:6:** The Lord works righteousness and justice for all who are oppressed.
- **Genesis 9:6:** Whoever sheds the blood of man, by man shall his blood be shed, for God made man in his own image.
- **Galatians 5:1:** For freedom Christ has set us free; stand firm therefore, and do not submit again to a yoke of slavery.
- **John 8:36:** So if the Son sets you free, you will be free indeed.

Reflections:

_____
_____
_____
_____
_____
_____
_____
_____
_____
_____
_____

Prayer:

Heavenly Father,

I come before You, acknowledging that I am Your child, created in Your image. In my moments of weakness and pain, I remember that You are my stronghold, my refuge in times of trouble. Lord, I have felt oppressed and victimized, but I trust in Your promise to work righteousness and justice for all who are oppressed. Help me to see myself not as a victim, but as an overcomer through Your strength. I am grateful that Christ has set me free. Grant me the courage to stand firm in this freedom and not submit again to any yoke of slavery, whether it be fear, resentment, or unforgiveness.

Father, I claim the truth that if the Son has set me free, I am free indeed. Help me to walk in this freedom, to forgive those who have wronged me, and to find healing in Your love. Lord, fill me with hope for the future. Let Your light shine through the darkness of my past experiences. Help me to use my story to bring comfort and encouragement to others who are hurting. I am not defined by what has happened to me, but by who You say I am. Thank You for Your love that restores and Your grace that empowers.

In Jesus' name I pray, Amen.

My own prayer:

_____
_____
_____
_____
_____
_____
_____
_____

Victory

noun
ˈvik-t(ə-)rē

1. The overcoming of an enemy or antagonist
2. Achievement of mastery or success in a struggle or endeavor against odds or difficulties

- **1 Corinthians 15:57**: But thanks be to God, who gives us the victory through our Lord Jesus Christ.
- **1 John 5:4**: For everyone who has been born of God overcomes the world. And this is the victory that has overcome the world—our faith.
- **Deuteronomy 20:4:** For the LORD your God is he who goes with you to fight for you against your enemies, to give you the victory.
- **John 16:33:** I have said these things to you, that in me you may have peace. In the world you will have tribulation. But take heart; I have overcome the world.
- **Psalm 108:13:** With God we shall do valiantly; it is he who will tread down our foes.

Reflections:

_____
_____
_____
_____
_____
_____
_____
_____
_____

Prayer:

Heavenly Father,

I come before You with a heart full of gratitude and excitement! Thank You for being the God of victory who gives us triumph through our Lord Jesus Christ. I rejoice in the knowledge that as Your child, born of God, I am an overcomer. My faith in You is the victory that conquers every challenge this world throws at me.

Lord, I am filled with courage knowing that You go before me in every battle. You fight for me against my enemies, securing my victory even before the struggle begins. Though I may face tribulations, I take heart in Jesus' words that He has overcome the world. In Him, I find peace and the strength to persevere.

With You by my side, I shall do valiantly! I trust in Your power to tread down every foe and obstacle in my path.

Thank You for making me more than a conqueror through Christ. I step forward in confidence, ready to claim the victories You have prepared for me.

In Jesus' mighty name I pray, Amen.

My own prayer:

_____

_____

_____

_____

_____

_____

_____

Waiting

verb
'wā-tiŋ

1. to remain stationary in readiness or expectation
2. to hold back expectantly

- **Psalm 27:14:** Wait for the Lord; be strong, and let your heart take courage; wait for the Lord!
- **Hebrews 10:13:** Waiting from that time until his enemies should be made a footstool for his feet.
- **Luke 8:40:** Now when Jesus returned, the crowd welcomed him, for they were all waiting for him.
- **Proverbs 8:34:** Blessed is the one who listens to me, watching daily at my gates, waiting beside my doors.
- **Titus 2:13:** Waiting for our blessed hope, the appearing of the glory of our great God and Savior Jesus Christ.
- **Jude 1:21:** Keep yourselves in the love of God, waiting for the mercy of our Lord Jesus Christ that leads to eternal life.
- **Micah 7:7:** But as for me, I will look to the Lord; I will wait for the God of my salvation; my God will hear me.
- **Psalm 130:5:** I wait for the Lord; my soul waits, and in his word I hope.

Reflections:

_____
_____
_____
_____
_____
_____
_____

Prayer:

Heavenly Father,

In Your infinite wisdom, You call me to wait. I come before You with a heart full of hope and faith in Jesus Christ. Lord, grant me the strength to wait patiently for Your perfect timing. As I watch daily at Your gates, may I be blessed by Your presence and guidance.

Jesus, my Savior, I eagerly await Your glorious return. Help me to keep myself in Your love as I wait for Your mercy that leads to eternal life.

Father, like the psalmist, I look to You and wait for my salvation. In times of uncertainty, may my soul find rest in Your promises. Grant me courage to persevere, knowing that You hear my prayers. May my waiting be active, filled with trust and expectation of Your goodness.

In Jesus' name I pray, Amen.

My own prayer:

_____
_____
_____
_____
_____
_____
_____
_____
_____
_____

Wall

noun
'wȯl

1. A high thick masonry structure forming a long rampart or an enclosure chiefly for defense
2. An extreme or desperate position or a state of defeat, failure, or ruin

- **Psalm 89:40:** You have breached all his walls; you have laid his stongholds in ruins.
- **Psalm 51:18:** Do good to Zion in your good pleasure; build up the walls of Jerusalem.
- **Proverbs 25:28:** A man without self-control is like a city broken into and left without walls.
- **Deuteronomy 3:5:** All were cities fortified with high walls, gates, and bars, besides very many unwalled villages.

Reflections:

_____
_____
_____
_____
_____
_____
_____
_____
_____
_____
_____
_____
_____

Prayer:

Heavenly Father,

I come before You with a humble heart, recognizing my need for Your protection and guidance. Lord, as You built the walls of Jerusalem, I ask that You build spiritual walls around me. Grant me, O God, the wisdom to fortify my life with Your Word and Your presence. Like a city with high walls and strong gates, may I stand firm in my faith, guarded against the attacks of the enemy.

Father, I pray for self-control, that I may not be like a city broken into and left without walls. Strengthen my resolve to live according to Your will, maintaining the boundaries You have set for my protection. Lord, in Your good pleasure, do good to Your people. Build up the walls of our communities, our churches, and our nations. May these walls not divide but unite us in Your love and purpose. I thank You for Your faithfulness throughout generations. Even when I falter, You remain my strong tower and refuge. Help me to trust in Your unfailing protection.

In Jesus' name I pray, Amen.

My own prayer:

_____

_____

_____

_____

_____

_____

_____

_____

_____

Warfare

noun

ˈwȯr-ˌfer

1. Struggle between competing entities

- **2 Corinthians 10:4**: For the weapons of our warfare are not of the flesh but have divine power to destroy strongholds.
- **1 Timothy 1:18**: This charge I entrust to you, Timothy, my child, in accordance with the prophecies previously made about you, that by them you may wage the good warfare.
- **Psalm 144:1:** Blessed be the Lord, my rock, who trains my hands for war, and my fingers for battle.
- **Ephesians 6:13—8:** Therefore take up the whole armor of God, that you may be able to withstand in the evil day, and having done all, to stand firm. Stand therefore, having fastened on the belt of truth, and having put on the breastplate of righteousness, and, as shoes for your feet, having put on the readiness given by the gospel of peace. In all circumstances take up the shield of faith, with which you can extinguish all the flaming darts of the evil one; and take the helmet of salvation, and the sword of the Spirit, which is the word of God, praying at all times in the Spirit, with all prayer and supplication. To that end, keep alert with all perseverance, making supplication for all the saints.
- **1 Peter 5:8**: Be sober-minded; be watchful. Your adversary the devil prowls around like a roaring lion, seeking someone to devour.
- **Luke 10:19:** "Behold, I have given you authority to tread on serpents and scorpions, and over all the power of the enemy, and nothing shall hurt you."
- **Zechariah 4:6:** Then he said to me, "This is the word of the Lord to Zerubbabel: Not by might, nor by power, but by my Spirit, says the Lord of hosts."

Reflections:

_____

_____

_____

_____

Prayer:

Almighty God, our Heavenly Commander,

I stand before You, ready for battle in the spiritual realm. Lord, I thank You for equipping me with divine weapons that have the power to destroy strongholds. Father, train my hands for war and my fingers for battle. I take up the whole armor of God–the belt of truth, the breastplate of righteousness, the shoes of the gospel of peace, the shield of faith, the helmet of salvation, and the sword of the Spirit.

Grant me courage, O Lord, to wage the good warfare. I am sober-minded and watchful, knowing my adversary prowls like a roaring lion. Yet I fear not, for You have given me authority over all the power of the enemy.

Remind me, Father, that this battle is not won by might or power, but by Your Spirit. I pray boldly, knowing that in Christ, I am more than a conqueror.

In Jesus' name and by the authority of His blood, I pray, Amen.

My own prayer:

_____
_____
_____
_____
_____
_____
_____
_____
_____

Watchman

noun
ˈwäch-ˌmen

1. a person who keeps watch : guard

- **Ezekiel 33**: The word of the Lord came to me: "Son of man, speak to your people and say to them, 'If I bring the sword upon a land, and the people of the land take a man from among them and make him their watchman, and if he sees the sword coming upon the land and blows the trumpet and warns the people, then if anyone who hears the sound of the trumpet does not take warning, and the sword comes and takes him away, his blood shall be upon his own head. He heard the sound of the trumpet and did not take warning; his blood shall be upon himself. But if he had taken warning, he would have saved his life.
But if the watchman sees the sword coming and does not blow the trumpet, so that the people are not warned, and the sword comes and takes any one of them, that person is taken away in his iniquity, but his blood I will require at the watchman's hand.' So you, son of man, I have made a watchman for the house of Israel. Whenever you hear a word from my mouth, you shall give them warning from me.
If I say to the wicked, 'O wicked one, you shall surely die,' and you do not speak to warn the wicked to turn from his way, that wicked person shall die in his iniquity, but his blood I will require at your hand. But if you warn the wicked to turn from his way, and he does not turn from his way, that person shall die in his iniquity, but you will have delivered your soul.
"And you, son of man, say to the house of Israel, Thus have you said: 'Surely our transgressions and our sins are upon us, and we rot away because of them. How then can we live?' Say to them, As I live, declares the Lord God, I have no pleasure in the death of the wicked, but that the wicked turn from his way and live; turn back, turn back from your evil ways, for why will you die, O house of Israel?
"And you, son of man, say to your people, The righteousness of the righteous shall not deliver him when he transgresses, and as for the wickedness of the wicked, he shall not fall by it when he turns from his wickedness, nor shall the righteous be able to live by his righteousness when he sins. Though I say to the righteous that he shall surely live, yet if he trusts in his righteousness and does injustice, none of his righteous deeds shall be remembered, but in his injustice that he has done he shall die.
Again, though I say to the wicked, 'You shall surely die,' yet if he turns from his sin and does what is just and right, if the wicked restores the pledge, gives back what he has taken by

robbery, and walks in the statutes of life, not doing injustice, he shall surely live; he shall not die. None of the sins that he has committed shall be remembered against him. He has done what is just and right; he shall surely live.

"Yet your people say, 'The way of the Lord is not just,' when it is their own way that is not just. When the righteous turns from his righteousness and does injustice, he shall die for it. And when the wicked turns from his wickedness and does what is just and right, he shall live by it. Yet you say, 'The way of the Lord is not just.' O house of Israel, I will judge each of you according to his ways."

In the twelfth year of our exile, in the tenth month, on the fifth day of the month, a fugitive from Jerusalem came to me and said, "The city has been struck down." Now the hand of the Lord had been upon me the evening before the fugitive came, and he had opened my mouth by the time the man came to me in the morning, so my mouth was opened, and I was no longer mute.

The word of the Lord came to me: "Son of man, the inhabitants of these waste places in the land of Israel are saying, 'Abraham was only one man, yet he got possession of the land; but we are many, and the land is surely given to us to possess.' Therefore say to them, Thus says the Lord God: You eat flesh with the blood and lift up your eyes to your idols and shed blood. Shall you then possess the land? You rely on the sword, you commit abominations, and each of you defiles his neighbor's wife. Shall you then possess the land?

Say this to them, Thus says the Lord God: As I live, surely those who are in the waste places shall fall by the sword, and whoever is in the open field I will give to the beasts to be devoured, and those who are in the strongholds and in caves shall die by pestilence. And I will make the land a desolation and a waste, and its proud might shall come to an end, and the mountains of Israel shall be so desolate that none will pass through. Then they will know that I am the Lord, when I have made the land a desolation and a waste because of all their abominations that they have committed.

"As for you, son of man, your people who talk together about you by the walls and at the doors of the houses, say to one another, each to his brother, 'Come and hear what the word is that comes from the Lord.' And they come to you as people come, and they sit before you as my people, and they hear what you say, but they will not do it; for with lustful talk in their mouths they act; their heart is set on their gain. And behold, you are to them like one who sings lustful songs with a beautiful voice and plays well on an instrument. For they hear what you say, but they will not do it. When this comes—and come it will!—then they will know that a prophet has been among them."

- **Isaiah 62:6:** On your walls, O Jerusalem, I have set watchmen; all the day and all the night they shall never be silent. You who put the Lord in remembrance, take no rest.
- **Isaiah 52:8:** The voice of your watchmen—they lift up their voice; together they sing for joy; for eye to eye they see the return of the Lord to Zion.

- **Ezekiel 3:17:** Son of man, I have made you a watchman for the house of Israel. Whenever you hear a word from my mouth, you shall give them warning from me.
- **Jeremiah 51:12:** Set up a standard against the walls of Babylon; make the watch strong; set up watchmen; prepare the ambushes; for the Lord has both planned and done what he spoke concerning the inhabitants of Babylon.

Reflections:

Prayer:

Heavenly Father,

I come before You with a humble heart, grateful for the calling of watchman. Lord, You have placed me as a guardian on the walls, entrusting me with a sacred duty. Grant me, O God, the vigilance to stand firm day and night, never silent in my watch. Sharpen my spiritual senses that I may discern Your voice clearly and swiftly relay Your words to Your people.

Father, fill me with Your Holy Spirit, that I may be alert and unwavering in my post. Give me courage to sound the trumpet of warning when danger approaches, and wisdom to recognize the signs of Your return. Lord Jesus, as You are the ultimate watchman, teach me to watch and pray as You did. May my prayers be fervent and persistent, breaking strongholds and releasing captives. I thank You for the privilege of serving as watchman. Help me to remain faithful in this calling, always ready to lift my voice in joyful praise as I witness Your work in Zion.

In Your holy name I pray, Amen.

My own prayer:

_____
_____
_____
_____
_____
_____
_____
_____
_____

Whoredom

noun
ˈhȯr-ˌdəm

1. The practice of having sexual intercourse as or with a sex worker
2. practices or pursuits that are unworthy, debasing, unseemly, or false

- **1 Corinthians 6:18–20**: Flee from sexual immorality. Every other sin a person commits is outside the body, but the sexually immoral person sins against his own body. Or do you not know that your body is a temple of the Holy Spirit within you, whom you have from God? You are not your own, for you were bought with a price. So glorify God in your body.
- **Galatians 5:19–21:** Now the works of the flesh are evident: sexual immorality, impurity, sensuality, idolatry, sorcery, enmity, strife, jealousy, fits of anger, rivalries, dissensions, divisions, envy, drunkenness, orgies, and things like these. I warn you, as I warned you before, that those who do such things will not inherit the kingdom of God.
- **Proverbs 4:23:** Keep your heart with all vigilance, for from it flow the springs of life.
- **Romans 12:2:** Do not be conformed to this world, but be transformed by the renewal of your mind, that by testing you may discern what is the will of God, what is good and acceptable and perfect.
- **1 Corinthians 9:27**: But I discipline my body and keep it under control, lest after preaching to others I myself should be disqualified.

Reflections:

_____
_____
_____
_____
_____
_____
_____

Prayer:

Heavenly Father,

I come before You with a humble heart, acknowledging my weakness and need for Your guidance. Lord, Your Word teaches me to flee from sexual immorality and to honor my body as the temple of Your Holy Spirit. I pray for strength to resist temptation and to keep my heart pure. Help me, O God, to be vigilant in guarding my thoughts and actions, knowing that from my heart flow the springs of life.

Forgive me, O God, for conforming to the world's standards instead of Your holy design. Wash me clean by the blood of Jesus, and restore my heart to purity and righteousness. Father, I ask for Your transforming power to renew my mind. May I not be conformed to the patterns of this world, but instead discern and follow Your perfect will. Grant me the discipline to control my body and desires, Lord. I recognize that I was bought with a price—the precious blood of Jesus. Help me to glorify You in all I do and say. Guide me to live a life that reflects Your holiness and love. May I walk in purity and honor, always mindful of my calling as Your child.

In Jesus' name I pray, Amen.

My own prayer:

_____

_____

_____

_____

_____

_____

_____

Wicked

adjective
ˈwi-kəd

1. Morally very bad or evil
2. Causing or likely to cause harm, distress, or trouble

- **Job 36:13:** The godless in heart cherish anger; they do not cry for help when he binds them.
- **Psalm 28:3:** Do not drag me off with the wicked, with the workers of evil, who speak peace with their neighbors while evil is in their hearts.
- **Psalm 7:9:** Oh, let the evil of the wicked come to an end, and may you establish the righteous—you who test the minds and hearts, O righteous God!
- **Jeremiah 7:24:** But they did not obey or incline their ear, but walked in their own counsels and the stubbornness of their evil hearts, and went backward and not forward.
- **Psalm 7:10:** My shield is with God, who saves the upright in heart.
- **Proverbs 21:3:** To do righteousness and justice is more acceptable to the Lord than sacrifice.

Reflections:

_____
_____
_____
_____
_____
_____
_____
_____
_____
_____

Prayer:

Almighty God, Righteous Judge of all the earth,

In the authority granted to me by Your Son Jesus Christ, I come before Your throne. I stand firm against the schemes of the wicked and declare Your justice over this world. Lord, You test the minds and hearts of all. I pray that the evil of the wicked would come to an end. Expose their hidden motives and thwart their deceitful plans. Let not their false words of peace deceive when evil lurks in their hearts.

Father, I reject the stubbornness of evil hearts that turn away from You. Break the chains of anger that bind the godless. May they cry out to You for help and turn from their wicked ways. I declare Your righteousness over my life and land. You are my shield, O God, and I trust in Your salvation. Strengthen me to do what is right and just, for this is more pleasing to You than empty religious acts. Establish the righteous, Lord. May I walk in Your counsels and move forward in Your purposes. Let Your light shine in the darkness, exposing and defeating all wickedness.

In the mighty name of Jesus Christ I pray, Amen.

My own prayer:

_____
_____
_____
_____
_____
_____
_____
_____
_____

Wisdom

noun
ˈwi-zdəm

1. ability to discern inner qualities and relationships
2. good sense

- **James 1:5:** If any of you lacks wisdom, let him ask of God, who gives generously to all without reproach, and it will be given to him.
- **Proverbs 1:7:** The fear of the Lord is the beginning of knowledge; fools despise wisdom and instruction.
- **Proverbs 2:6:** For the Lord gives wisdom; from his mouth come knowledge and understanding.
- **1 Corinthians 1:30**: And because of him you are in Christ Jesus, who became to us wisdom from God, righteousness and sanctification and redemption.
- **James 3:17:** But the wisdom from above is first pure, then peaceable, gentle, open to reason, full of mercy and good fruits, impartial and sincere.
- **Proverbs 3:5:** Trust in the Lord with all your heart, and do not lean on your own understanding.
- **Ephesians 5:15:** Look carefully then how you walk, not as unwise but as wise.
- **Proverbs 15:15:** All the days of the afflicted are evil, but the cheerful of heart has a continual feast.

Reflections:

_____
_____
_____
_____
_____
_____

Prayer:

Heavenly Father,

In humility, I come before You, recognizing my need for wisdom. Your Word tells me that if I lack wisdom, I should ask You, for You give generously to all. Lord, I acknowledge that the fear of You is the beginning of knowledge. Help me to revere You and seek Your guidance in all I do.

I thank You that all true wisdom comes from You. May I always turn to Your Word for knowledge and understanding, rather than relying on my own limited perspective. I'm grateful that in Christ Jesus, I have access to Your divine wisdom. Help me to walk in this wisdom daily, being pure, peaceable, gentle, and full of mercy. Father, teach me to trust in You with all my heart and not to lean on my own understanding. Guide my steps that I may walk carefully, not as unwise but as wise. Even in times of affliction, grant me a cheerful heart that feasts continually on Your goodness and wisdom.

In Jesus' name I pray, Amen.

My own prayer:

_____
_____
_____
_____
_____
_____
_____
_____
_____

Word

noun
'wərd

1. a speech sound or series of speech sounds that symbolizes and communicates a meaning usually without being divisible into smaller units capable of independent use A brief remark or statement something that is said

- **Matthew 12:37:** "For by your words you will be justified, and by your words you will be condemned."
- **Luke 24:8:** And they remembered his words.
- **Psalm 12:6:** The words of the Lord are pure words, like silver refined in a furnace on the ground, purified seven times.

Reflections:

_____
_____
_____
_____
_____
_____
_____
_____
_____
_____
_____

Prayer:

Dear Heavenly Father,

I come before You with a humble heart, recognizing the power of my words. Lord, Your Word teaches me that my speech can bring life or death, justification or condemnation.

Help me, O God, to use my words wisely. May I speak truth, encouragement, and love. Let my speech reflect Your grace and kindness.

Father, I remember the words of Jesus and ask that You help me to treasure them in my heart. May His teachings guide my conversations and shape my interactions with others.

Lord, Your words are pure and perfect, refined like silver. Teach me to value and respect the power of language. Help me to think before I speak, considering the impact of my words on those around me.

Grant me wisdom to know when to speak and when to remain silent. May my words bring healing, hope, and reconciliation to a world in need of Your love.

In Jesus' name I pray, Amen.

My own prayer:

_____
_____
_____
_____
_____
_____
_____

Worry

verb
ˈwər-ē

1. To afflict with mental distress or agitation
2. To subject to persistent or nagging attention or effort

- **Proverbs 12:25:** Anxiety in a man's heart weighs him down, but a good word makes him glad.
- **1 Peter 5:7**: Casting all your anxieties on him, because he cares for you.
- **Philippians 4:6–7:** Do not be anxious about anything, but in everything by prayer and supplication with thanksgiving let your requests be made known to God. And the peace of God, which surpasses all understanding, will guard your hearts and your minds in Christ Jesus.
- **John 14:27:** "Peace I leave with you; my peace I give to you. Not as the world gives do I give to you. Let not your hearts be troubled, neither let them be afraid."
- **Psalm 55:22:** Cast your burden on the Lord, and he will sustain you; he will never permit the righteous to be moved.
- **John 14:1:** "Let not your hearts be troubled. Believe in God; believe also in me."
- **Luke 1:37:** For nothing will be impossible with God.

Reflections:

_____
_____
_____
_____
_____
_____
_____
_____

Prayer:

Dear Heavenly Father,

I come before You with a heart weighed down by worry, remembering Your promise that, "a good word makes him glad." Lord, I humbly seek Your uplifting words to lighten my spirit.

As Your servant Peter instructed, may I also cast all my anxieties upon You, for I know You care for me deeply. Help me to truly release these burdens into Your capable hands.

Father, guide me to follow Paul's wisdom. Teach me to approach You with prayer and supplication, always with a heart of thanksgiving, making my requests known to You. I ask for Your peace that surpasses all understanding to guard my heart and mind in Christ Jesus.

Lord Jesus, I thank You for the peace You promised. Help me discern the difference between Your divine peace and the fleeting comfort the world offers. Let not my heart be troubled or afraid but rather filled with Your enduring peace.

Forgive me, Father, for the times I've carried the weight of worry upon myself. As David wrote, I cast my burdens onto You, trusting that You will sustain me. I receive Your peace with gratitude and faith.

Strengthen my belief in You, as You encouraged, so that my heart may find rest in Your promises. And remind me, Lord, as the angel declared to Mary, that nothing is impossible with You. In this truth, I find courage to face my worries.

In the precious name of Jesus I pray, Amen.

My own prayer:

_____

_____

_____

_____

Worship

noun
ˈwər-ˌship

1. to honor or show reverence for as a divine being or supernatural power A form of religious practice with its rites and ceremonies
2. to regard with great or extravagant respect, honor, or devotion

- **Matthew 4:10:** Then Jesus said to him, "Be gone, Satan! For it is written, 'You shall worship the Lord your God and him only shall you serve.'"
- **John 4:23:** "But the hour is coming, and is now here, when the true worshipers will worship the Father in spirit and truth, for the Father is seeking such people to worship him."
- **John 9:31:** We know that God does not listen to sinners, but if anyone is a worshiper of God and does his will, God listens to him.
- **Acts 18:7:** And he left there and went to the house of a man named Titius Justus, a worshiper of God. His house was next door to the synagogue.

Reflections:

_____
_____
_____
_____
_____
_____
_____
_____
_____
_____

Prayer:

Dear Heavenly Father,

I come before You with a humble heart, filled with joy and gratitude. You alone are worthy of all praise and worship. I thank You for Your love and grace that surrounds me each day. Lord, help me to worship You in spirit and in truth. May my life be a living sacrifice, pleasing to You. Open my eyes to see Your goodness and my ears to hear Your gentle whispers.

Jesus, You taught us to worship God alone. I pray that my words, actions, and thoughts would honor You in everything I do. Let my worship be sincere and my service to You be faithful.

Father, I long to be a true worshiper, one who seeks Your face and delights in Your presence. Guide me in Your ways and help me to do Your will. Thank You for the privilege of worship. May my life bring glory to Your name, now and always.

In Jesus' name, Amen.

My own prayer:

_____
_____
_____
_____
_____
_____
_____
_____
_____

Acknowledgements

This book is a testament to the power of faith, community, and family. It would not have been possible without the following individuals who have been instrumental in its creation and my journey.

First and foremost, I give thanks to the Lord Jesus Christ for the divine revelation and guidance to share what was once confined to my prayer closet with my brothers and sisters in Christ.

I am deeply grateful to the intercessory prayer warriors who diligently covered this project in prayer. Their dedication created an atmosphere of God's presence that flowed through every page. My heartfelt thanks go to Dalora Cortez, Danielle Heart, Kim Tolero, and Pastor Rocio Gonzalez

To my Barnabas, Aarons, and Hurs of various seasons–those who shouldered many of the very topics I cried out to the Lord about in my prayer closet–I extend my profound appreciation. Rachael Roberts, Trina Angeles, Adrienne Herrera, Sheril Phillips, the Monday night group, and the Secret Sisters, Firestarter group and Legendary Church of Antioch: your support has been invaluable.

A heartfelt thank you to my incredible mentors, Shurvone Wright (@la_bosspreneur) and Roberta Thorndike (@joyful_one_editing), for your dedication and guidance in bringing this product to life. Your support and leadership have made all the difference.

Last, but certainly not least, I want to acknowledge my husband, children, and grandchildren. Without sharing in their lives, I would not have had the rich human experiences captured in many of these topics.

It is with sincere love and joy that I bless each one of you for the impact you've had and for the space and time we've shared in doing life together. Your contributions to this work and to my life are immeasurable.

About the Author

Reyna Inguanzo is, first and foremost, a devoted servant of Jesus Christ. Her unwavering faith, rooted in a childhood memory of her mother's fervent prayer during a powerful earthquake, laid the foundation for a life anchored in trust, prayer, and God's enduring presence.

A woman of many cherished roles, Reyna is a loving wife of over 30 years, a proud abuela (grandmother), a devoted daughter and sister, and a treasured friend to many. Residing in Northern California, she draws on her professional background in procurement, finance, and sales in her role as a Solutions Representative, while also serving her community as a dedicated Notary.

Reyna's creative spirit shines through in her writing and culinary passions. Whether she's penning words of inspiration or crafting lavish meals and homemade breads for loved ones, she lives each day as a reflection of God's grace.

Her journey is a testament to the power of prayer, resilience, and purpose. That same heart for spiritual empowerment led Reyna to write *Warfare Battlecards* a powerful resource birthed from her personal battles and victories in prayer. Designed to equip believers for spiritual warfare, the cards are filled with Scripture-based declarations that encourage others to stand firm in faith and fight from a place of victory.

With heartfelt compassion and unwavering determination, Reyna continues to walk boldly in faith—encouraging others to do the same.

Learn more at reynainspires.com or follow her on social media @reynainspires.